Yoga inVision 21

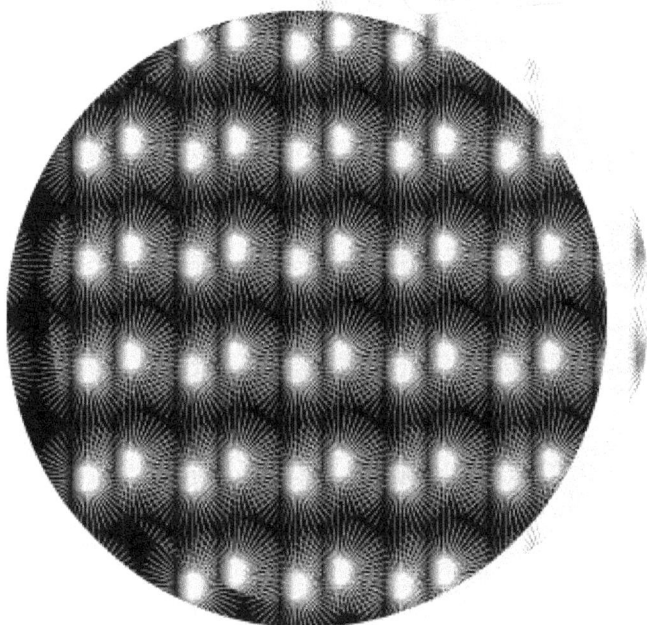

Michael Beloved

Illustrations: Author
Correspondence:
Michael Beloved
7211 41ST CT E
Sarasota FL 34243
USA
Email: axisnexus@gmail.com
                michaelbelovedbooks@gmail.com

Paperback ISBN: **9781942887591**
eBook ISBN: **9781942887607**
LCCN: **2025902609**

Mi-Beloved

Table of Contents

INTRODUCTION

This is the twenty-first of the Yoga inVision series. It relates experiences and practices done in 2021 - 2024. These give beginners ideas of the physical, psychological, and spiritual experiences one may have when doing *asana* postures, *pranayama* breath infusion and *pratyahar* sensual energy withdrawal. Beyond that is higher yoga, which Patañjali named the *samyama* procedures. He defined *samyama* as a combination of *dharana* deliberate focus, d*hyana* spontaneous focus and *samadhi* continuous spontaneous focus. During practice, these progress one into the other. If one is expert at *pratyahar* sensual energy withdrawal, one may graduate to *dharana* which is deliberate focus of the attention to a higher concentration force or person. As soon as one masters *dharana* one may slip into *dhyana* which is an effortless focus on a higher concentration force or person. Once you practice *dhyana*, *samadhi* happens as the continuous effortless focus on a higher concentration force or person.

Many persons on a spiritual path feel that they can construct a process as they advance. This idea denotes failure. After all, if the supernatural and spiritual environment, is not already there, no one can create it now. It is either there or it is not. For instance, if one intends to moves to a different country, then of course one will fail if the country intended does not exist. It has to be there prior. Similarly, what you aim for as spiritual life, must be there already, or one will find that the aspiration is incorrect. This is why I speak of a concentration force or person. I could have said concentration person or divine person, or God. I did not because I do not know how anyone's spiritual path will develop.

One may leave an island in the safest boat and still the vessel may sink. One should keep one's mind open and be willing to work with fate. In spiritual development, there is providence too. What one desires to have one may not achieve. What one wishes to see may never appear.

These Yoga inVision journals show how sporadic my course of yoga was. This is after years of practice. It gives some idea of what to expect. Once you get through the lower yoga practice, you will see advancement in a more stable way but it may be incremental, accruing little by little, with bright flashes here and there.

Part 1

Yogi Bhajan Divine Eye Practice (December 22, 2021)

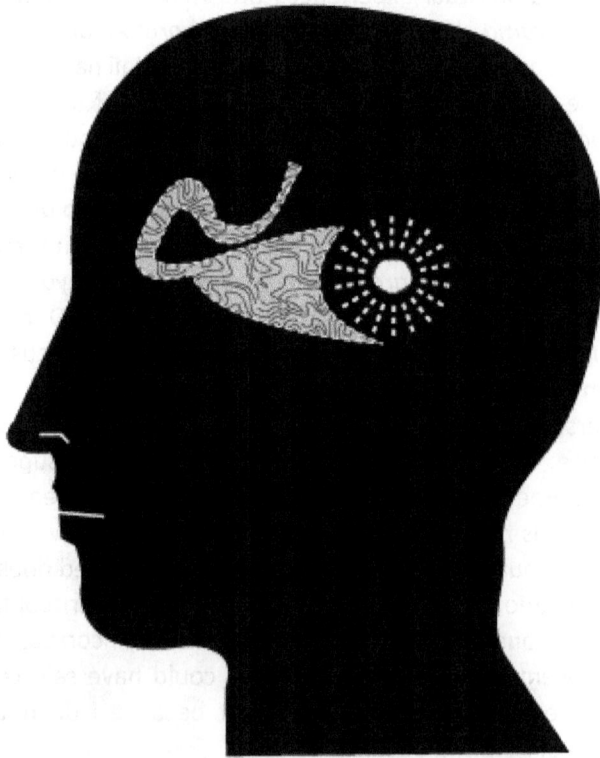

Yogi Bhajan Attention Energy Curl
in Quest for Divine Eye

Subjective Light *(atma jyoti)* (January 4, 2022)

Atma jyoti or self-illumination is a subjective glare of spiritual light which emanates from the coreSelf. Many students of yoga aggressively pursue this light or would like it to declare itself. How does a source of illumination see itself?

If something is other than, that something is objective to the viewer. But if something is the same, that something is subjective to the viewer which means that it must use subjective means to determine itself.

In meditation, one should learn how to use subjective perception to realize the light of the self. Consider three objects, a bird, sunlight, and fruit. In that case of three objects only the bird has visual perception. It does not illuminate anything not even itself. Still, it can use illumination of the light source which is the sun. Here we have three factors involved in a scene, a light source, a visual perception means and a fruit.

Let us consider another circumstance where we have only a glowing bird and a fruit. In this case however, this bird is like the sun. It emanates light but it also has a perception means which is visual. It also has eyes. This bird illuminates and sees the fruit which it illuminates.

Now let us consider another scene, where we have only the bird. There is no sun and no fruit. The bird is present with eyes and with illumination power such that the illumination shines within the bird and into the environment around the bird. In this case however the eyes of the bird are useless because there are no objects exterior to the bird. How can the bird realize itself? Can its illimitation energy reveal itself?

Something similar faces the yogi in meditation, whereby the physical eyes and the eyes of the subtle body prove to be insufficient for revealing the light of the self *(atma jyoti)*.

Because of long use of the physical and subtle eyes, the yogi is habituated to objective-viewing of objects which are external to the psyche. There is no practice of subjective viewing of the coreSelf. Hence the method for subjective assessment is unknown. In fact, if there is no objective viewing the self is left with no sensual perception. It assumes that nothing is present because it lacks the means of subjectively contacting itself.

Yogeshwarananda from within my psyche, did a meditation to show how to access the light of the self by using subjective perception. This involves the use of naad sound resonance.

Yogeshwarananda's method is to relax away from the quest for finding objective light in the psyche. Instead, one should look without looking and feel without feeling, the energy which emanates from the core. While peering down, up, or ahead for a short distance, short enough that the rays of interest do not go beyond the membrane of the psyche, one should hold to the energy and wait.

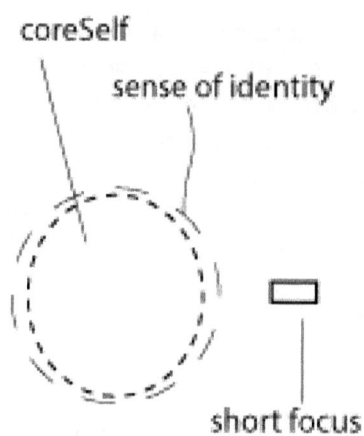

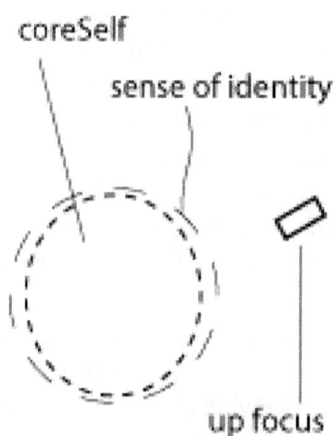

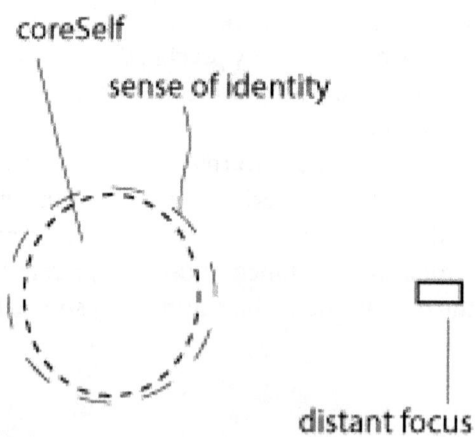

If one finds that one loses this mild focus, one should resituate in naad resonance and again look without looking while peering down, up or ahead for a short distance. As soon as one feels a glow of light usually slightly to the right or left of center, one should hold it timidly. It may elude one's grasp. Or it may respond to be in one's grasp. Then it may hold the focus and feel as if one is in total darkness but seeing gold nuggets which are like small pebbles.

This will disappear and one will find the self to be out of it, to be near naad, or to be in the occupied mind viewing images or ideas. This practice must be repeated. Eventually it will be a definite step by step practice which causes the yogi to revert attention to the light of the self. This gives relief from the self's craving for spiritual light.

Gut Bacteria and Constipation

After some thirty years of studying my stomach/intestines/colon system, as it related to the slow or rapid movement of food and food waste, I concluded that besides the type of diet and the aging of the organs, there is the factor of gut bacteria. If the diet is correct, if the aging is at its best because of assistive lifestyle, then if the gut bacteria is incorrect, there may be slower movement of food and food waste which will result in constipation.

Many factors are involved. A yogi should study the operation of the stomach, intestines, colon, and rectum. He should determine what can be done to ease the system. I made an internet search about this matter and was surprised to find that my conclusion about gut bacteria facilitating or preventing food movement from throat to anus, is correct.

I can say with certainty that lactobacilli facilitate food movement in my body. Its removal or shortage causes the system to become sluggish. It appears that the lactobacilli provide lubrication through the winding intestinal passage and the colon tubing. That removes the need for strenuous muscular pushes during evacuation. Such pushes are unbeneficial and may cause hemorrhoids, hypertension, and internal irritation.

I knew a person who used a spicy, peppery, diet. He had hemorrhoids due to having to strain the related muscles during evacuation. A simply cure for this is a change of diet to one which increased the number of lactobacilli. But there are other lifestyle changes which may be considered.

Elusive Satisfaction Need

There is an elusive, evasive satisfaction need faculty in the psyche, which disrupts subjective perception and deprives the coreSelf of taking advantage of subjective reality. This need pivots and corrals the self into pursuing objective perception. It encourages the self to think that subjective reality is not worth pursuing.

The fallacy of this is that the core itself is a subjective principle. No matter what it fancies, for itself unto itself, it is subjective. For it to evaluate itself, and understand itself, for it to be objective to itself, it must use subjective perception.

Because this need goads the self from behind, from the blind spot of the core, its arrest is a difficult accomplishment. It hides in a bland spot behind the core. It pilots the core to avoid subjective reality, and to pursue only objective factors. This leads the core more and more to appreciate whatever is objective to the five senses, and to depreciate any hint even of anything subjective.

To begin to reform this method in the psyche, where the core only pursues what is objective to its perception, a yogi should focus on naad sound resonance. He/She should spend months, years even, doing naad immersion meditation. Then after a time, after this meditation is rooted in the psyche and becomes an involuntary and persistent focus and immersion, the core should locate naad light which is subjective. This is like a light seeing a light but using the light which emanates from itself to perceive itself.

When the self grasps this light of the self or a portion of it, the satisfaction need will come forward because it instinctively will make an attempt to pull the core from its grasp on subjective light. When it attempts to do so, the core should gently slide forward the satisfaction need so that it imbibes the subjective light and feels fulfilled using it. This will happen in the chamber of the psyche.

In that room of the psyche, the core will be present with naad spontaneous sound and naad spontaneous light being present, but with a small childlike presence which is the satisfaction need. That need energy will imbibe the subjective light and will be sustained by it. When all is said and done in meditation practice, when the effort is made for some years or lives, then objective evaluations of the all-surrounding reality, and the coreSelf, will be abandoned for the subjective perception of the core.

Ananda Maya / Bliss Format Existence

Ananda maya is a legendary state of consciousness where the coreSelf is itself a piece of spiritual bliss floating in a cosmic expanse with other innumerable spiritual bliss selves *(atma ananda / atmananda)*. Different yogis label different states as *ananda maya*. Here I will describe a seemingly bodiless state where the coreSelf is by itself with no adjuncts, not even with the sense of identity *(ahankar)*, such that by itself the core exists with innumerable coreSelves in a cosmic space which has no other energy besides spiritual substance or *chit akash*.

This seems to be a bodiless state because no immediate border or membrane is perceived. There are no limbs used, nor surfaces touched. There are no eyes but there is vision which is omniVision where innumerable selves of similar constitution are perceived nearby in that sea of bliss consciousness. The color of the environment is like that of the dark blue sky. Selves like sparks sparkle in it.

This environment is bliss in all directions, through and through. The coreSelf is uncovered, unshrouded, timeless, radiant, and self-existent. This is a *satchidananda* state with the self existing, being aware of itself as bliss essence only, in an environment which is the same.

Light Radiance Absorption

Naad sound resonance listening and keen absorption is the first step in deliberate deep meditation. This is because there is a reliance need of the coreSelf where it requires support. As it is with everything which is not absolute, the core must have a reliance. Otherwise during meditation, it tends to drift in search of a shelter, or relationship.

Naad sound provides support for absorption. It should be used intensely for some time, for weeks, months, or years, until the yogi is anchored in it even involuntarily, where even when the core is not compelling itself to listen to naad, it finds that it listens to naad spontaneously.

Enough of this naad absorption will lead to perception of spiritual light. This is the perception of the radiance which the self emanates. It radiates spiritual light but due to the subjective nature of the radiation, the core rarely perceives this light. Constant listening to naad, will make it possible to subjectively see the light which emanates from the core.

After repeatedly becoming aware of this light by switching from seeing other aspects in the psyche, the self will find that it can make itself perceive the selfLight. When this happens time and time again, the self should imbibe this light, to drink it, to absorb it. This will give a satisfaction which is craved by the coreSelf. This will allow the self to be relieved from anxiety and hankering for response and reaction.

Base Chakra Stimulation

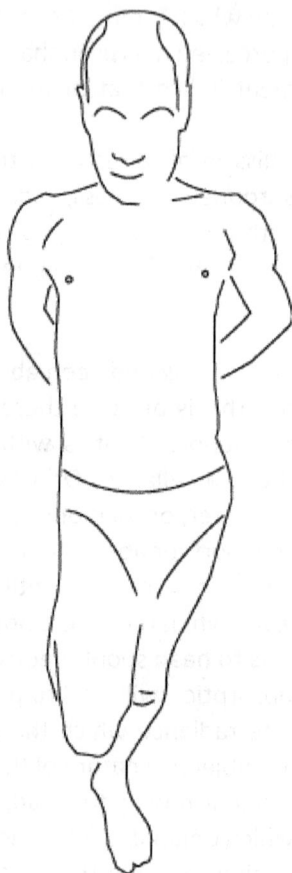

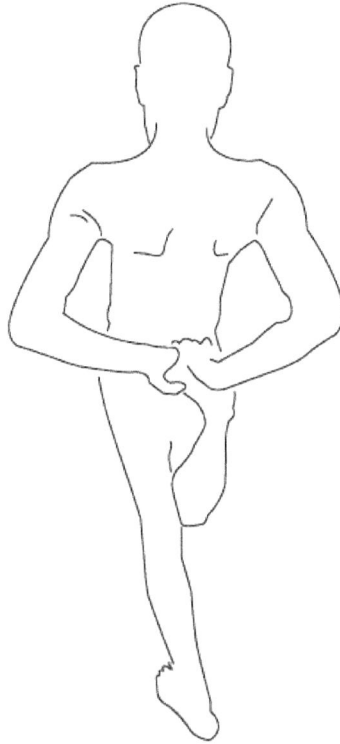

On the date of February 8, 2022, on the astral side of existence, this posture was shown by Yogeshwarananda. This causes the yogi to focus on and upgrade the base chakra in the subtle body. A yogi should stay in this posture for at least five minutes. It demands intense inner concentration and balance of the weight of the physical body against the earth centering force of gravity.

This is an advanced posture. One should master naad sound resonance absorption before doing this posture. It is considered to be an advanced practice in the first steps to higher yoga.

There is no need to do this in a beginner's practice because the focus is on the base chakra, *muladhara*. A beginner cannot focus there. Eyes are closed to intensify the focus while doing this.

Astral Hereafter City

On February 14, 2022, I became aware of an astral city where my deceased mother lives. Somehow by some power, she compelled my astral body to visit there. This astral place was a combination copy of Linden, Guyana and Denver, Colorado USA. In the astral existence, depending on what is possible, a person can create places or be in a created place where his/her geographic wishes are met to a greater degree.

In that place, my astral body climbed stairs with no heart stress, no shortness of breath, even though at this time, the physical body I use, is seventy years of age The astral body acted as a youthful physical form.

This was a mountainous astral region which was filled with hills and valleys. Some houses were built on the sides of steep mountains. There were roads but only in the valleys and meadows. Otherwise, there were stairs. To get from one house to the next, one used stairs. A relative of my mother suddenly appeared. Without speech, she directed me to follow her.

She moved quickly. She was one turn ahead of me such that as soon as I climbed some steps and then saw her, she turned again and I did not see her until, I made the next turn, at which time she disappeared around another turn.

Then I was in a building where the children of my body existed. These however were at the age just as they were when my mother passed away some thirty years ago.

I followed the relative and arrived in a room where my mother sat. She interrogated me to get my opinion of the place. She suggested that I relocate there as soon as possible. Her view was that this was the ideal place to live as an enduring existence.

When I followed the relative to the room where my mother resided, I noticed a jeep moving down a road. There was no sound of an engine but the vehicle moved as if it had an engine.

This experience is a premonition about the death of my body. Sometimes a yogi is invited to a place where he could live after he is departed. It is important that he accept or deflect the invitation.

Yogi Garment

On February 20, 2022, while doing meditation, I was approached by an astral yogi. He is part of a group of astral yogis who practice the *kriya* method taught by Babaji. Many people feel that what was taught by Yogananda is the complete method. That is not a fact. The method happens to be many skills according to the needs of the particular yogi.

The yogi who approached me said this, "For recognition, you should wear the shawl. Otherwise, many will not approach you. That shawl given by Babaji has a particular vibration, which they use to detect your presence. Consider that if they cannot recognize you, it may stall their progress because they will not approach for instructions."

coreSelf's Interest

I listed the attention energy of the coreSelf as being its single expression. This is its interest which focuses as attention energy though the sense of identity. This however is not the purest expression of the core. That self is conditioned when it makes contact with the sense of identity. At that time, it converts into an aggressive attention force which may be converted into willpower or into a quest energy, which doggedly pursues mental and sensual phenomena, which is conjured by the intellect and the kundalini psychic lifeForce.

The inversion of the aggressive attention force is known as *pratyahar* sensual energy withdrawal. It is the fifth stage of the eight-staged yoga process expounded by Patanjali.

When the coreSelf is alone, being segregated from its adjuncts especially from the sense of identity, that is a rare condition which happens by chance, infrequently, during some meditations. At that time, the core experiences its single expression as a state of indifference, nothingness, or deep fulfilling satisfaction, *santosha*.

When the coreSelf experiences itself as light, as an active quivering river of light, there is a satisfaction which is continuous, which is all fulfilling where the self knows that as self bliss, *atmananda*. This light emanates in and through the coreSelf.

core is unaware of
sense of identity

core is aware of itself
and sense of identity

sense of identity is
pronounced

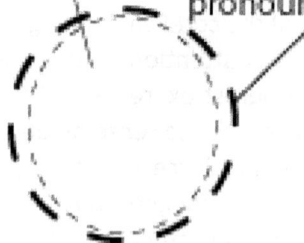

Atmayoga / coreSelf Focus

Atmayoga is coreSelf discovery and focus. It is a vast undertaking, which is riddled with patience, subtlety, and mystery. It is when in the course of inSelf Yoga™, one leaves aside the quest to partition and understands the adjuncts, which doggedly adhere to the core of the psyche.

Initially a yogi becomes obsessed with curbing the senses. Taking hints from books like *Bhagavad Gita* and the *Yoga Sutras*, discussing the matter with an advanced ascetic, the yogi gets hints that the psyche is not a person, but is rather a complexity of a core power, and adjuncts in an enclosed complexity which passes as a person, a *purusha*.

The yogi then patiently withdraws the attention which courses from the psyche. This is the preliminary *pratyahar* sensual energy practice. When after mastering that practice, the yogi gets the psyche to cease its cravings for external objects, he/she begins to realize, that within the psyche, there are several factors. Sorting these, partitioning and isolate them, so that their interaction ceases during meditation, becomes the objective of the yogi.

The yogi must discover what the self is, what the adjuncts which are fused to the self are, and how each is related to the other. He/She must know which adjunct is unconcerned about the core, and which cooperates with another adjunct or the core.

In that practice, the yogi/yogini will eventually bring the adjuncts under relative control, so that they cease their operations during the meditation session. This allows for the segregation of the core from the other aspects in the psyche.

Naad is helpful in this practice. *Pranayama* breath infusion accelerates this practice. A yogi will hear naad. While doing so, he/she may imbibe the light of the self, its radiance.

Light of the Self Connect

This practice is best done after a session of breath infusion, whereby the physical body, and the subtle one, are energized with compressed fresh breath energy. This impaction of breath energy causes the subtle system to shift to a higher plane of consciousness, the result of which is interiorization in a higher astral environment.

After doing breath infusion, preferably *bhastrika/kapalabhati*, the yogi should immediately sit to meditate. The condition of the inners of the subtle body are checked during the breath infusion, and immediately after the breath infusion. Noting the condition of the mind, the head space of the subtle body, the yogi/yogini should note if the head space is cleared of thoughts, images, and ideas, which are concocted by the intellect. Particularly, the imagination function of the intellect should not show. Memories should not arise. The intellect itself should be as if it is non-existent.

Noticing this, the yogi/yogini should hear naad. It may be heard to the right, left, up, down, in, or out. Wherever it is heard, the yogi should link to it using a mild linking energy which is not abrupt nor jerky. He/She should hold the connection with naad. Then he/she should look forward within an inch and no more. This is psychic distance. When I did this practice, I looked forward only one quarter of an inch.

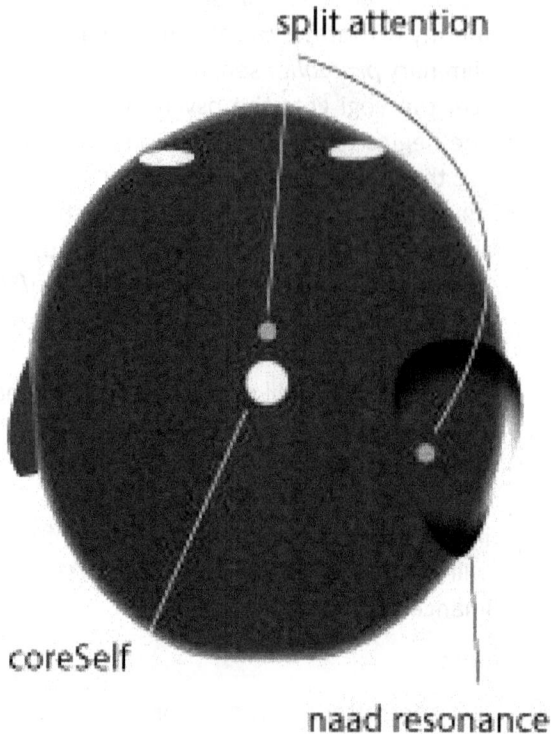

split attention

coreSelf

naad resonance

There one should see a mild shine of light in light within a radius of about one half of an inch. This will cause one to be aware that the vision energy is absent. Even though it is absent, still one will see a shine area. Then one will notice that there are shards of light, mini-shards, like slivers of broken glass or fragments of icicles.

One should hold that focus on that light, with a mild grasp. Then one will realize that this holding is done by an interest energy which is an inquiring seeking attention. This reaches, like an arm, to grasp something.

If during the experience, one loses the grasp and finds the coreSelf to be somewhere else, one should resume, the connection with naad sound. Then again one should resynchronize with selfLight. One should do this repeatedly during the meditation. Then for days, weeks, months, or years, one should repeat in this practice.

When a small portion of the indivisible self see the light of the self, this happens when the interest of the self, its one and only deliberate expression, converts into a tiny eye which, in the light of the self, sees a portion of the light of the self.

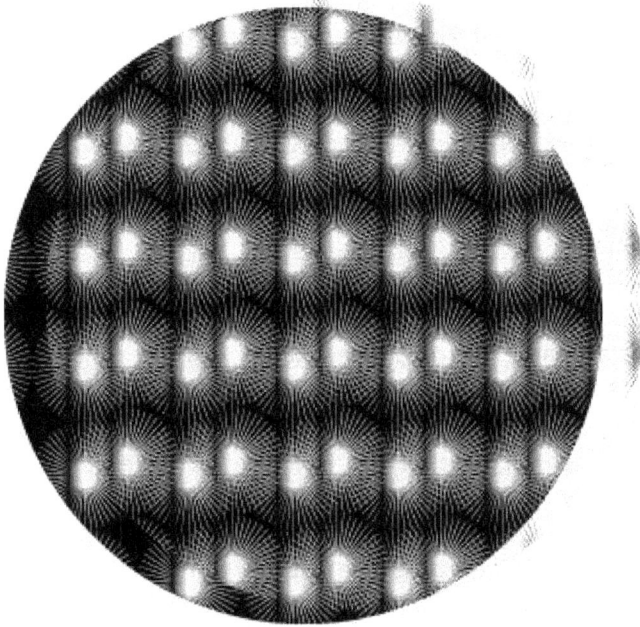

When this happens, the yogi should hold the perception by mildly maintaining a grasp on hearing naad resonance and levying all other attention to perceiving the light of the self. This is a subtle experience. This is *atmajyoti*, satisfaction in completion.

Mental Anguish Hereafter

For the next body, one should expect a rehashing and continuation of what happened in the current life time. This is what I explained to Chairman Mao, whom I am in touch with on the astral side of life.

He wants to have only positive aspects in the next life, so that his tarnished history in his past body, as the ruler of China, would not be repeated. He asked me to read a biography which was written by Dr. Zhisui Li, titled, *"The Private Life of Chairman Mao."*

I told the chairman that his behavior from the previous life will shoot into the next birth he would take, where he would again emerge as a political leader somewhere somehow. Then he would build a security apparatus, and repeat the same positive and negative tendencies. He asked if there was any way that could be avoided. I said that the only way would be to come under the influence of a saintly person during that life and keep that influence near him as a checking force. But even then, the tendency to control others, and to secure one's footing as head of state, would prevail.

On April 6, 2022, suddenly I realized that Mao sat near to me leaning on my shoulder the way a dear brother would. This happened on the subtle side, as I sat upright on a bed. He was perplexed about how he would solve the consequential energies which follow him from his life as Mao Tse Tung. A deceased person may be haunted, not so much by others whom he offended, but by the residual energy in his mind, which is lodged there from antisocial acts, committed in a previous physical body.

Voices in My Head

It frequently happens that there are voices in my head. These are from people who reside in my psyche. Some are there for a short time, like for half hour. Others are there for some time, like for years.

Instead of remaining there quietly. These persons have opinions about everything which I would or would not do. From time to time, in bursts, they speak their views with a pressure for me to act, or at least for me to release control of the psyche, so that it can act on their behalf.

Usually only one of these persons speak an opinion in the mind, with the expectation that I would repeat what was said in my mind or act to comply with what was stated. The problem with this is that the consequences of their actions are not taken into account. Hence if I acted as they desire, I would have the liability, and carry the consequences, which could be positive or negative.

A clarification is necessary. That is regarding why those persons live in my psyche. Can I evict them? What right do they have to operate the physical body? Why can they make suggestions of what the body should say, see, or do?

Naad Reliance (April 11, 2022)

Some yoga philosophy, and religious presentations, propose a self which is absolute but I have so far failed to find any evidence that every self is that. I have not found also a non-self which is absolute or which will become absolute through austerities and/or meditation.

The evidence I present is that the coreSelf is real. It is a constant selfReality but it is a portion of the dependentAbsolute. This dependentAbsolute something has a perpetual reliance need for a supportive environment. It is always reliant. Its quest of inquiry is a reliance need which it constantly seeks to fulfill.

For higher meditation, the research for this is completed in naad sound resonance practice. There are three stages but these take years, if not lives to practice. Most students are not interested in such a long process. They expect a flash event which gives proficiency in rapid time after a few days or weeks.

When there is no rapid result, they molest a teacher about the failure. Their feeling is that they deserve instant success.

There are basically three stages of naad meditation. Anyone may take years or lives to master. If someone can master this rapidly, it means that person came with a past life history of successful intense practice. It is not because the person was assisted miraculously in this one life.

The three stages are.

- Reach naad resonance in meditation after being on a lower level with the mind indulging itself. This is similar to leaving a war zone where the sound of the weapons cease, where there is no danger of being killed or wounded.
- Being in naad resonance in meditation at the very beginning of the session with no display from a lower mental level. This is like being in a heavenly place, where there is no misbehavior in the mind, and no effort is required to keep the mind from negative indulgence.
- Being in spiritual light, selfLight, and having slight contact with naad all the same.

These three states are reliant on a long successful practice of the four higher stages of the eight-staged *ashtanga* yoga which is explained in the *Yoga Sutras of Patanjali*. This is the application of meditation *(samyama)* to inner sound and light.

Successful Yoga Practice Hereafter Not Likely

I was in an encounter with Yogeshwarananda on April 13, 2022. Due to this incidence, I drew the conclusion that it is hardly likely that any ascetic would complete the practice in the astral situation which is near to this physical place. This however is more reason why a yogi should batten down and tighten the practice, using every bit of spare time to consolidate the yoga disciplines.

I did an afternoon session of breath infusion. After some twenty minutes, I challenged the sleep *vritti* energy which was accumulated since the last session of practice. This was located inside the body by the sacral bones.

Usually as I do this, Yogeshwarananda appears. On this occasion, during this session he was prompt. He was there. He took his seat at the northern entrance to the place. It is a secured place for yogis and yoginis who practice under his supervision. Most of the students are departed souls.

As soon as he sat down, he asked about Sir Paul Castagna, who was left there in a supervisory role, while Yogeshwarananda was away. Just as I was about to say that I did not see Sir Paul for some days now, Sir Paul appeared. He said this to Yogeshwarananda.

"They left. One by one, each left. They were pulled away by affectionate energies from physical acquaintances."

It appears that Sir Paul was in a hidden place behind a building at the place. There he practiced. He put himself there, to remain isolated from the ones who left to associate with physical people who were acquaintances.

The pull from acquaintances is powerful enough to thwart the plans of a yogi. This means that after one is departed from the present body, it is hardly likely, that one will avoid rebirth. The pull of emotions between one, and any person who is physically based, is difficult to resist.

Astral Planet and Moon

I had an astral encounter of the strange type. I became conscious on another planet which was similar to the earth, except that the people there had some earthly needs, which they could not fulfill, except by bits and pieces of their desires. Suddenly I was aware that everyone there expected an astronomical event which was frightening but which occurs frequently.

The incidence was that the moon of that planet orbited that earth slowly as if it traveled about five miles per hour around that planet. Except that the elliptical orbit caused that moon to come very close to the planet where one saw the moon approaching on a curve whereby it grazed the planet and causes some land to grate off and fall back to the earth.

Everyone was partially afraid that the moon would crash into the planet and something ghastly would happen. When the moon grazed the planet, one set of people tried to move away, to avoid being killed. Another set moved in another direction to save themselves. Then the moon passed but there was this fear that within a short time, it would again appear, when it would make its next orbit. The moon was bright and silverish. It was similar to our moon in color and with pot marks everywhere as if it was bombarded by meteors in some past age.

There were some other strange features of that place. Like for instance there were no houses as we use on earth. There was no fire for cooking. I saw a woman whom I knew from the earth, but she did not recognize me. I said nothing to her. I acted with indifference. In the astral existence one should not force anyone to be recognized, or to remember his/her existence elsewhere.

I felt the need to eat something. When I did so, there was a flash that this was the need of some other people there whom I resided with. One lady signaled mentally for me to cross a floor. There was a pot with food. She said that I should take meals from that pot.

When I moved to the place of the pot, it was on a stove but there was no fire. I had a flash then that this was a permanent condition, where there is no fire and there is a pot with cooked food. I ate nothing, nor did anyone else. There was this need to eat. Yet there was no food consumption, even though food was prepared.

There was no money there. There was no buying nor selling. Nothing. The only feature of the place was its slow moving, terrifying moon, people shifting from place to place to avoid being crushed by it, and a conjoint conscious contact, mind to mind, about the uncertainty of living there.

Everyone was stressed over the moon. Everyone was fearful of being crushed. There was nowhere to go. There was no jet travel, no rockets, and no scientific instruments. That is a place of anxiety, ongoing, unrelenting. No one there knows of life elsewhere. Everyone only knows the situation there as the life to live, with continuous fearfulness of being crushed by the moon.

Suppression, then Expansion of Desire

This applies to any desire even the most insignificant one. I became aware of myself in an astral dimension which is near to this physical earth. This astral location was similar to a physical place where I lived during the teen years of my body.

I met a woman who was the mother of a friend. Early on in this physical life, when I was friendly with and lived near a friend, I saw his mother infrequently. The exchanges between us were cordial and normal, just as it is expected of a friend of someone, and that person's mother. In this astral encounter, which happened over fifty years after, the woman met me at the entrance of a liquor establishment, and indicated that we should go upstairs where music played and people drank alcohol.

Her mood was one of wanting to indulge in liquor and hear music so that she could abolish inhibitions and banish her moral values regarding sexual attraction between a woman and the friend of her son. In her psyche, the promise of the liquor was that it would remove the liabilities for such disapproved behavior.

As I followed her up a stairway, I saw that the cause of this encounter was her desire from long ago. Instantly reliving the situation of my teen years when I knew the lady, I saw that she once regarded me as a possible spouse, but due to the convention, she could not fulfill that. However, the desire remained sealed in her psyche until now, when it exploded and dominated her astral body.

At the time prior, during my teen years, I did not see the sexual attraction potential. It was present then, but it was suppressed sufficiently to be absent from my conscious mind. Later that night, after I left that astral place, I met another woman who knew me at the time and who also knew my friend's mother.

This other woman explained that she arranged for my friend's mother to meet me because the lady inquired, and expressed a pressing need to have access to me. When I pressed for more explanation, the other woman said this.

"She was eager to see you. She said I should share your astral frequency so that she could contact you.

"She pressured me. She said this, 'I love this man. Please put me in touch with his identity.'"

Middle Kundalini Spread

According to how it is energized, there are many kundalini configurations in the subtle body. These occur by plane of consciousness it assumes or is synchronized into.

If one does breath infusion using *kapalabhati/bhastrika pranayama,* one should expect to discover various kundalini spreads, zones, alignments and more. Students should note the formations which arise, as to the intensity, diagramming, bliss, or neutral feelings, and even as if no formation occurs, during breath infusion practice.

It is best to have an open mind, and not to imagine this or that, so that the mind can properly experience whatever happens, with no distortion nor misconception. The yogi should not use the imagination faculty to creatively conjure anything.

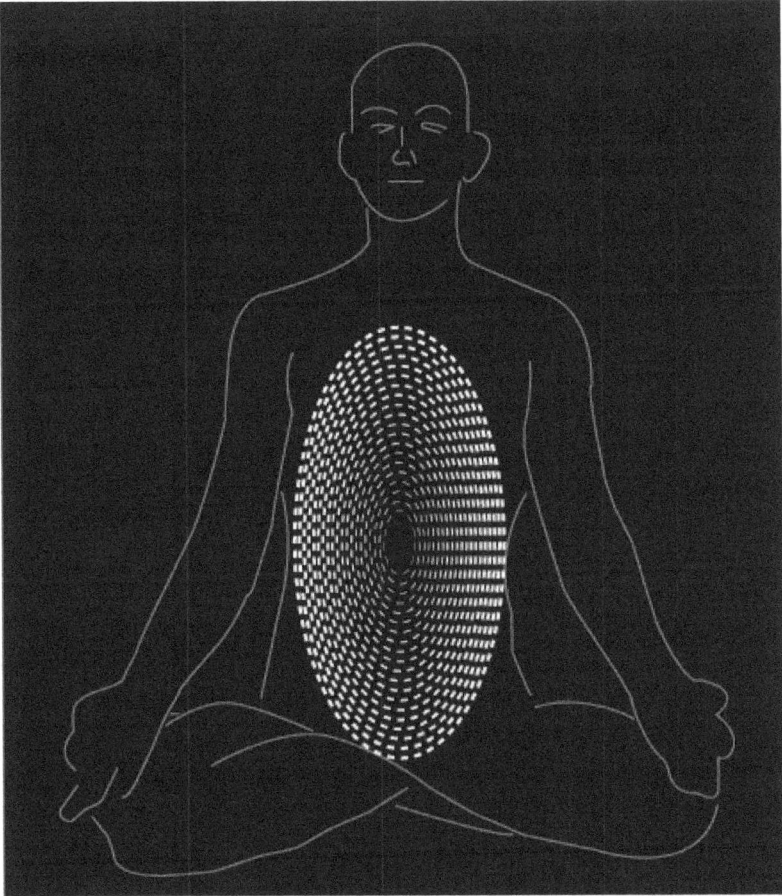

On April 19, 2022, I had a middle oval shape kundalini spread through the abdomen of the subtle body. It began as a small oval shape which was about one inch across the narrow diameter and two inches for the height. This spread quickly though the abdomen and radiated one oval spoke after the other, rendering a bliss feeling which was not intensive, which was mild and desirable. I was in a posture sitting on a floor, grabbing the flesh over the knee cap with the thighs, legs and feet extended.

Habits Transfer to Astral Hereafter

On April 24, 2022, I encountered a woman whom I used to know during the teen years of my body. This happened on an astral plane, where when one is there, it seems that one lived there only, and that the activities are a continuation of what one did before. There is little or no recall of any other life from any other time.

Somehow due to mystic perception, I knew that I was in that alternate place. It was a slip in time, because of having a previous social connection with this woman, when her physical body lived. She is deceased. It flashed in my mind, that she did not assume a new embryo. She was deceased some years ago which meant that she was on the astral planes for some time. In that astral place she advises people and acts as she did before.

The lady discussed events which happened long ago, some fifty years prior, just as if those events were current. I realized that even though there was a time slip, she had no idea about it. Suddenly she made a criticism and provided a recommendation to solve the problem.

She proposed that she should purchase a pair of nylon black socks for me. I said nothing in reply. I realized that this was because my astral body had grey socks which to her mind, was inappropriate for the occasion we would attend. It was a function at which one should be well-dressed. Men should wear polyester slacks with matching nylon socks, shining shoes and other attire.

Just as she suggested this, there was a checking force in her psyche which alerted her that for me it was inappropriate to recommend that. I was a yogi who was focused on everything but physical existence and its requirements, especially the customs and ideas, which do not serve the purpose of being aware of psychic events.

The lady then apologized for wanting me to wear the black socks. She said this, "Never mind the suggestion. When I was alive as a physical body, I strictly adhered to the customs of society. Now I know that such attire and customs, does not assist one in spiritual awareness. You may do what you do in the way that you do. It is the best way."

coreSelf as Radiance

After making absorption in naad sound resonance, the natural state of mind during meditation sessions, a yogi can go further into transcendence, and integration, as the coreSelf (atma), by becoming absorbed into atmajyoti, the light that is the coreSelf.

It is radiance itself. It is liquid spiritual light. It is one part of selfLight perceiving another part of the very self, but subjectively. No eyes are used, only vision ability, or vision interest, which remains confined to the very core.

The shift to do this occurs when naad resonance is mastered, and the coreSelf comes to understand, that the satisfaction it seeks is easily and readily achieved, if it turns to itself, and feels itself subjectively. Then it knows, that the question for fulfillment comes to an end, by seeing the radiance that it is, as a light seeing its rays without using eyes subjectively.

Musician's Ghost

Early in the morning on April 28, 2022, three persons came to me on the astral side. These were Sir Paul Castagna, Bhaktivedanta Swami, and Jimi Hendrix. Each is deceased.

Sir Paul discussed his fame situation, where after his body became unusable, someone was supposed to manage his paintings. He wondered about it. He asked me to check the previous day.

I did that but I reported to him that it appears that the website which was established to display his work was somewhat stagnant. I also checked with TerriAnn Yogini, an artist colleague of Sir Paul, and a dear friend of both of us. She said that the person managing the site recently stated that next summer things will happen.

It is interesting how when one becomes deceased and loses the footing on physical history, one becomes concerned about how people remember and assess one in the physical world. From the astral side, the hereafter, one pries to know if anyone remembered one, and if such memories are favorable.

This is a strong tendency. A yogi should adjust himself so that he does not become a victim of this fame addiction.

After talking to Sir Paul, I perceived that Bhaktivedanta Swami was nearby. He was in another dimension which was adjacent to the place where I spoke to Sir Paul. Bhaktivedanta was near to someone else, whose subtle body was like a shadow. Then, that person manifested. It was Jimi Hendrix the famous guitarist, who passed from his body at the apex of his career.

Bhaktivedanta wanted Hendrix to speak up but Hendrik said nothing, as if he was embarrassed to be there with the swami. Seeing the situation of Hendrix' silence, Bhaktivedanta said this,

"Show him the *pranayama*. That would be the process for him. Chanting Hare Krishna did not work for the others. How will it work for him? He apologized for putting himself as Krishna in the Vishvarupa. That is fine. Now he should practice yoga to make advancement. But what I taught did not work for many like him. I can no longer promise that it will do anything."

After Bhaktivedanta said that, Hendrix lost the shyness and spoke. It was not speech like physical talking. It was mental communication. What he expressed was this, "I feel miserable. I am a ghost. I am not getting happiness. What can be done about this?"

After that, Hendrix expressed a desire to learn breath infusion *(pranayama)*. I told him he could come when I practice. Otherwise, he could learn from Sir Paul.

A person like Jimi Hendrix becomes a ghost because of massive karmic returns from the popularity he had while using a physical body. Nature becomes displeased with anyone who becomes more famous then necessary, especially those who cannot properly manage the acclaim. One does many things as a celebrity. The repercussions from that may be unfavorable towards the self.

Here is the album cover where Jimi Hendrix got himself portrayed instead of Lord Krishna. There were many lawsuits towards Hendrix, and his album/products/producers, concerning the use of the original image.

Nourishment States of Consciousness

There are nourishment states of consciousness which arise spontaneously in meditation. Some types are rarely mentioned in meditation books. Mostly light in meditation, or bliss consciousness in it, are given as markers for advancement. Even in my numerous writings I hardly mentioned the nourishment states.

This is due to the fact that when one encounters such states one underrates them. Or one may be absorbed in them without an observational perception. This means that one will meditate, benefit from such states, and be unaware of the benefits gained

These nourishment states are important for nourishing the subtle body on a higher plane, so that it can become saturated with energy from higher levels. However, an elementary but important use of such states, is imbibing the energy to nourish the coreSelf or the subtle body.

This feels similar to when a person is starved of water, and then reaches a refreshing spring. He/She becomes satisfied. The feelings of inadequacy due to thirst are removed. A fullness is felt. It may be compared to a starving infant who is suddenly placed near its mother's milk-full breast. The infant's anxieties and insecurities are immediately removed. Calmness and satisfaction instantly spread.

A yogi should be on the lookout for being in nourishment states of consciousness, where no light is seen or no sound is heard, but there is fullness all around which should be suckled into the self. When this is done there will be a feeling of fulfillment.

Music and Mantras

On May 17, 2022, I was in a conversation with a Swami who is deceased. This person began a Vaishnava religious sect in the Western countries. He was staying astrally at Yogeshwarananda's astral place. He went there to avoid contact with his deceased disciples, who hound him in the astral world, because of the failure of his process to give them a divine life, after death of their physical forms.

He said this to me, "I am staying here because it is the only place where I can avoid those people, my former disciples. How was I to know that the process would not work to give the results intended? I was told by my guru that it would work. That is what I said to others. It is not my fault except that I could not check it. Until my body actually perished, I could not die and realize the failure.

"Here no one will come to me. They feel that this guru is an impersonalist *mayavadi*, just as I explained to them. After death, if you owe someone anything, when that person is deceased, that offended person pursues you, and demands compensation, or tries to inflict some harm to you."

Two days before this happened, while I did a session of *bhastrika pranayama* breath infusion, I met this Swami in a different place. By interspacing his subtle body into mine and mimicking whatever I did, he learned the practice. After that session, he followed me to a place where I meditated. During the meditation, he interrupted because in his mind there was music playing.

He wanted to ask me about it. At that time because of the request energy, I became aware of the music which played in his mind. It was a song composed by George Harrison, a British musician who is now deceased. The song was *'While my Guitar Gently Weeps'*.

I said to the Swami, "Why do you sing that song? For this meditation no music or image should occur in the mind."

He replied, "That is the problem where this song continues to play in the mind. I heard it when I associated with George Harrison. I am amazed how my mind recorded that song and plays it. I did some research about this. My conclusion is that the idea of using a mantra is fine, but if it is combined with music, it is likely that the melody will overpower the mind. The mantra's effect will be diminished.

"George was involved to produce the music for our main deity greeting *artik* mantras. I am in his association regularly in an astral place, The thing is that sometimes I find myself with him and others as they play popular music.

Once when he played his song, *'While my Guitar Gently Weeps,'* I found that I was attracted to the song. I could not stop following the music for it. I then decided to test myself to see how music affects the psyche. I listened to his group in the astral world. They sang some songs he produced for my institution. I realized that my mind was more involved with the music than it was with the Sanskrit words. The mind enjoyed the rhythm of the music with about 95% of attention. The remaining 5% was for the mantras. Please give a method for ceasing this in the mind."

I replied to him, "Use *om namo shivaya*. Use that in the mind when you are in it with all doors closed. If you do that it will usher you to naad sound resonance. Cling to naad. If, however, you are in a situation where you do not hear naad, and if the sound of the song continues, after you desire not to listen to it, emphatically chant *om namo shivaya* in the mind. Resist the undesirable sound. Do this repeatedly until naad becomes available. Then cling to naad."

Special Note:

One song which George Harrison produced, is on the album which has the *Govindam Adi Purusham* mantras. This can be heard on the Radha Krsna Temple LP album.

Popular Song Mantra

On May 23, 2022, I was with Bhaktivedanta Swami. In his head, a song composed by the deceased George Harrison played. The Swami wanted to stop the song but it kept playing in his head nevertheless.

Soon after this George Harrison appeared. He wanted to bring his harem of women to the place where we were in the astral existence, but he found that he could not transport them. This place, a special location of Yogeshwarananda, is for persons who are serious about completing yoga practice, after being deceased. Because Bhaktivedanta had access to the place, Harrison came there but it did not allow Harrison to bring anyone else.

Harrison, because he was hard pressed in his mind, to bring his harem of women wherever he went, was not happy that he could not shift them to the place. He left and returned to where the harem was located in another dimension.

Soon after he returned by himself. By that time, I did a session of *bhastrika pranayama* breath infusion. The swami did whatever I showed. When Harrison returned, the swami instructed Harrison to do exactly what the swami did. Harrison could not perceive my subtle body but the swami could.

One other person present was Sir Paul Castagna, who is also deceased. He expressed dismay over the fact that his art work, which was somewhere in the physical existence, was not being displayed. He was unhappy about that.

This is worth noting. One may be afflicted hereafter by desires to have a certain impact in the physical world. Then, one would have to influence others to act on one's behalf. These persons may be too occupied with other events to be of use to oneself.

Questionable Finances

On June 1, 2022, I was in a conversation with Bhaktivedanta Swami, who is deceased. This was on the astral side. He reviewed the Vaishnava philosophy of the sect he represented, and which he introduced to the Western society. He asked for my opinion which I did not give because he was aware of my view on the topic. I had objected to it some years ago in 1980, when two of his senior disciples challenged me, and stated that he authorized that they could commit certain acts, which were contrary to his regulative principles.

They cited his encouragement and benefit, when hallucinogenic drugs were sold for a profit, and the money was given to the swami for Krishna conscious activities. Since the swami accepted this type of finance, those disciples felt that it was a valid method of devotional service.

As time would have it however, their society faced legal difficulties, and tragic incidences, even murders, because of being involved with the acquirement, and distribution of drugs.

Now however the Swami is of a different opinion. On the astral side, he showed me why indulgence in harmful activities could not bring good results to his society. What this amounted to, is that he now argues that if someone indulges in a vice, which runs contrary to the prohibitions in their scriptures, as for example the use of narcotics, then their deity, Krishna, would not handle the incidences and their effects. This means that the devotees who participated will be ruined accordingly.

What was not clear, was how the negative energies of the actions would be distributed as immediate or future consequences. If the consequences are remote, these will not be assessed for their worth. Hence devotees will make mistakes, and may be confident of the acts of acquiring money by criminal means. That in turn, may boost confidence in the deviant methods which in turn, will increase the negative returns which in the future will afflict all persons involved.

It is best therefore, not to be involved in a lifestyle which runs contrary to righteous conduct, because the idea that the benefits can be offered to Krishna is invalid. Of course, the deity or icon will be silent. That itself is a warning. Those who acquire money by criminal means, and who use that money to build, and outfit temples, and to manufacture devotional literature, may think, or be assured, that the funds can be sanitized by offering it to Krishna, by purchasing expensive items for temples, and their related paraphernalia, by sponsoring the luxurious lifestyle of their swamis and officials. But these acts do not sanitize the money as some devotees feel. Krishna does not accept their service in that way, but Krishna is not here physically to inform them about his view. Hence, they are prone to operating in a counterproductive way.

Bhaktivedanta said that he got the wrong idea from his authorities in the Vaishnava community in India. Now he desires to change the opinion, but he is not on the physical side to do so.

Risks of Astral Samadhi

On June 2, 2022, a yogi who was in an astral samadhi state awakened. He was radiant with smiles but had no sensual perception except for subtle sound. This person was in samadhi for over two hundred years, since he lost his last physical body and assumed a subjective consciousness state.

In such a state, it is like one is in a state of nothingness where one has no idea of one's whereabout. One has no sense of individuality. I was at a seat which was used by Babaji, but which he told me to assume for the purpose of helping yogis, who could reach that place. Babaji is not longer staying there. Hence if anyone goes there, if that person qualified, he/she will see me sitting there, and can inquire about spiritual practice, and related matters.

When this yogi saw me, he was happy but he recognized that I was not Babaji. He looked at a scarf which Babaji put across my shoulder before, as an insignia through which yogis who needed advice, would trust me.

For about nine or so months, I did *bhastrika* near the place where this yogi was in an astral trance state. During that time, this yogi existed in a place which had a dark grey, dark brown energy. He was sunk into that energy in which his subtle body had no definite format.

Since this yogi could use his hearing sense, I questioned him mentally about the practice he did, concerning what happened once he entered the samadhi so long ago. He did not answer because he could not recall anything about his former practice. He entered a samadhi with no objectivity, which for all practical purposes, is a stupor samadhi.

If one practices meditation hereafter, that is good, but there is a risk that one may enter a stupor samadhi, and with that there is no telling when or where one would manifest, once the trance expires.

All control is lost when one enters a stupor samadhi. It should not be assumed that if one enters samadhi, one will be enlightened, or will be liberated. That may or may not be the case.

Subtle Body / Resentment Reservoir

For those who are serious about taking no other physical body, their hopes for doing this are near to nil. Despite this, many people have the desire for liberation and will strive in any way possible to achieve it. The greatest of these aspirants are those who realize that even though it is unlikely that liberation will occur, still one should strive using the best methods admissible.

The physical body seems to be a problem but actually it is the least of the difficulties because it will be finished in less than one hundred and fifty years. The evidence is that no human body lasts beyond that. At this time, there is no proof that there is a human body which exists for more than one hundred and fifty years. Of course, there are stories. There are myths about people living longer, but at this time in history, there is no human existing for that long.

Since the physical system will only survive for less than two hundred years, its problems will soon be over. It is struct down as being out of the picture. This means that what is left is the subtle body or the psychic parts of the person who was a physical body. Whatever will survive the physical body must be its psychic aspects. That is the subtle body.

We are already familiar with that form as much as we are familiar with dream awareness. We can safely assume that once dead, someone will continue to exist as a dream form, a subtle body. Will there be pain in that form? Will there be social hassles as we have in this physical existence?

The answer is yes. That is the answer because while being a physical body, when the physical system sleeps, one experiences hassles in dreams. Actually, we experience unfavorable incidences in the subtle body, even when the physical body is awake.

On the night of June 5, 2022, I had several dream encounters with numerous persons. It was a busy night on the astral side of life, with one troublesome association after another. Each of these concerned the venting of resentments which someone held towards me.

The subtle body collects and hoards resentments, hard feelings, and records of stored credits. In the dream experiences, these persons set up circumstances in which I was in position only to confirm to their desires, even when such ideas were contrary to what I preferred.

The meaning of this is that no matter what, a yogi cannot rely on the subtle body to be free from negative aspects. He/She must industriously scrub the psyche so as to clear the subtle body of anything which would cause it to be subjected to harassments.

Even if the yogi has no resentment energy stored in the psyche, even if there are absolutely no hard feelings, even if he/she can neutralize any idea about anyone being obligated to him, still there will be that type of energy in the psyche of others. If they held resentment towards the yogi, if they serviced him, that cannot be dissolved except by interaction with him. That is a danger.

The subtle body should be tightly monitored. After being evicted from the physical form, the problems of existence will continue in the subtle world. One will be subjected to harassments if one encounters anyone to whom one had an obligation.

Swami Rejects Personal Servant

A swami who established a religious institution globally, met me in the astral world recently. He took residence at Yogeshwarananda's astral place, because he needed to escape from harassment, from many of his deceased disciples, who discovered that his method of liberation was invalid.

This swami's astral body recently began the *kapalabhati/bhastrika* breath infusion practice. While talking to him when he was to my right, another person who was his servant for some years, stood to my left. The swami wanted this person, his former servant, to go away. He thought to me like this,

"He should go away. They know I cannot help. What I promised did not work. Providence did not honor it, or it did so superficially, and as a belief system. Please ask him to go away."

After he said this, his former servant thought mentally to tell me, that he had no where to go. Since he was with the swami for many years, serving him and his mission, he had no other reference for reliance.

Hearing this, the Swami thought to me mentally in secret like this.

"There is another issue. There is something personal which I must tell you. I no longer want a personal servant. It leads to moral problems like homosexuality, sexual erections during massages, sexual affectionate feelings which arise due to touching and nudity. I need to protect myself from this. I should avoid male persons to whom such feelings would arise. This happened with him as he was my masseur for many years.

"You know that the Mughal emperors had concubines and eunuchs. Sometimes there would be sexual affairs with the concubines or eunuchs. The royal lifestyle is risky. Please send him away."

To this I replied,

"He cannot be expelled. I will do something to keep him at a distance from you, but I cannot send him away. He has permission from Yogeshwarananda just as you do. On that authority he can stay. But he will not approach you at this place. He will always keep at a distance from you. Have no fear."

Special Note:

A swami is supposed to have a personal servant who serves his meals, tidies his quarters, provides his attire, monitors his visitors, and accompanies him on trips. Ideally this person should be a celibate adolescent. The principle is that a senior renunciant or sannyasi, should be convenienced with a junior renunciant who has no carnal knowledge, a person whom is without sexual experience in the present life.

In some situations, on a daily basis, this personal assistant will give the Swami massages. He may cook the Swami's meals. He may monitor appointments between anyone and the swami. He may present the views of the swami.

If, however either the Swami or the assistant has carnal knowledge or is experienced sexually in the present body, there is the likelihood that there may be sexual arousal, during some services rendered by the assistant. For instance, during bathing when there is nudity or during dressing when there is the same. It may happen during massaging.

Originally in bygone times, a swami was a person who was a lifelong celibate. He had no sexual experience in the present body. His personal servant was a boy or young man who did not have sexual experience. This means that the idea of sexual intercourse was not present in his psyche as an active memory in that life time.

The risk is there in any case, but it is definitely present if the swami and/or the servant had sexual experience or masturbated in the current body.

Swami and Women Disciples

On June 7, 2022, I was in an astral place with a Swami who is now deceased. In his last body he established a devotional sect globally. He read some of my literature and wanted to discuss the issue of a swami having female disciples.

First of all, in the ancient definition of a swami, it is not possible for that person to have female disciples. This is due to the fact, that the original rules for swami meant that such an ascetic did not get involved in social affairs. He did not participate in activities with women. He was a celibate renunciant who did not have carnal experience any time in his current body.

This original definition is no longer in place. At this time, anyone who adheres to a certain dogma, and dedicates his life to propagating a certain religious doctrine, can be declared as a swami. This means that he can be socially engaged, and can have female followers.

The astral swami made these remarks.

"It is near impossible for a swami to avoid female association, and the sharing of sexual energies with women whom he influences. His exposure to a congregation where women are present, will inevitably lead to astral encounters and psychic communication.

"The main threat is thinking exchanges between the swami and females. That happens during day or night. Secondly there may be astral encounters. In those situations, there may be private meetings which may result in visual attractions, touching and even sexual intercourse.

"To avoid this, a swami may be in an enclosure of male disciples during waking times. On the astral side, while sleeping, he may be surrounded by male disciples as well. Thus, there may be no opportunities for females to approach him. But as it is in the astral existence, it is likely that even during the non-sleeping periods there will be sexual energy transmission in the psyche. Then by a law of nature, that swami will find himself in a sexual tryst with a female."

Portals in any Direction

The idea that there is only one way to see into higher dimensions, especially to see into the *chit akash* sky of consciousness, is not a valid statement. Some *kriya* yoga sects give the third eye as the location where one may access the *chit akash* and any other wonderful realm or dimension. In the Bhagavad Gita, the center of the eyebrows is mentioned.

स्पर्शान्कृत्वा बहिर्बाह्यांश्

चक्षुश्चैवान्तरे भ्रुवोः ।

प्राणापानौ समौ कृत्वा

नासाभ्यन्तरचारिणौ ॥५.२७॥

sparśānkrtvā bahirbāhyāṁś
cakṣuścaivāntare bhruvoḥ
prāṇāpānau samau krtvā
nāsābhyantaracāriṇau (5.27)

sparśān — sensual contact; kṛtvā — having done; bahir = bahiḥ — external; bāhyāṁś = bāhyān — excluded; cakṣuścaivāntare = cakṣuḥ — visual focus + ca — and + (eva) — indeed + antare — in between; bhruvoḥ — of the two eyebrows; prāṇāpānau — both inhalation and exhalation; samau — in balance; kṛtvā — having made; nāsābhyantaracāriṇau = nāsa — nose + abhyantara — within + cāriṇau — moving

Excluding the external sensual contacts, and fixing the visual focus between the eyebrows, putting the inhalation and exhalation in balance, moving through the nose. (Bhagavad Gita 5.27)

However, Krishna made no statement stating that this was the only portal. I suggest keeping in mind that this is the conventional recommendation to be used during meditative focus. One should be aware of the fact that many other locations may become evident.

Kundalini Burst Downward

The convention is that kundalini should rise from the base of the spine, from *muladhar*, and should ascend *sushumna nadi* central spinal passage. This information from India, controls the practice, to such an extent that it limits what a student can achieve, because of having this iron-clad objective.

In the year of 1970, while I was in the Philippines, I found a book written by an Indian where he stated that he was alarmed by the conventional information about kundalini, because it did not explain anything about front kundalini.

Before reading this, I did not even consider that there was a front kundalini. Actually, that ignorance was due to following the conventional information, as well as being careless in observing the nerve tracts, and bio-electric energy, of the physical body. When the bio-electric energy flows through it, the physical system is declared to be alive. As soon as that power no longer moves through the body, it is declared as dead.

An observation about the passages and transits of the bio-electric power is an observation of kundalini. This means that one does not have to be a yogi, to know something about kundalini. Anyone using a living physical body, is familiar with the bio-electric energy, but most persons are unaware that it is a version of kundalini, which is felt as nerve feelings, being transmitted through the body in various places.

Pranayama breath infusion of *kapalabhati/bhastrika* is the sure way to energize and startle kundalini, so that it flares, and then moves here or there in the subtle body. However, the idea that it must begin at the base chakra and move up through the central spinal passage is incorrect. It may or may not do so.

There is front kundalini which may begin either at *muladhar* chakra, or from the sex organ chakra in the front of the body, or from the lower abdomen pubic area, from the navel area, from above the navel, or from any other centered, or non-central place, in the front of the body.

Surprisingly, kundalini can sparkle from anywhere in the body. It may sparkle from the armpit(s), inner chest, surface of the chest or any other place. Even though the belief is that kundalini will rise when it is aroused, it may go down, across, to the left or right. It does not have to rise. A yogi should not be surprised if it does, and should not necessarily try to force it to go in any conventional direction.

When I did an early morning practice on June 11, 2022, an astral student was present. Due to his increased psychic ability, he followed every practice I did using *asana* postures and breath infusion. He noticed that kundalini flared in the shoulder and then rushed downward through the arm. Just after this, kundalini flared in the center behind the ribs. That spread downward through the chest of the body. It made no attempt to go upwards. This is a valid rise of kundalini, just as an upward movement of the flared kundalini is regarded as a bliss burst.

For that matter, during meditation at any moment, there may be a spontaneous involuntary access which is not the third eye. The intellect can give access. The special location itself can bore through from the spiritual side to this side into the mind space of the yogi.

When this happens usually the chit akash is seen as a blinding light, not like sunlight but like intense moon light with or without a cooling bliss aspect. It can last for a single second or more.

Plane of Non-Perception

I searched for someone who is deceased. Recently I did not see that person. I checked to see where that person was located. I have an obligation to assist this person in figuring the perplexities of life.

After checking various astral levels, I was transferred to a plane of non-perception. There is more than one of these realms. I was in the one where it is pitch dark. Notably no light is visible there. One has vision there except that it is spatial vision through awareness only. There is a strong sense that one should access from there to find light. Even though this need is there, there is no light. One notices that it is pitch black darkness like on a dark moon night with no stars are overhead. No light appears anywhere in any direction.

There is nothing with odor, nothing with flavor, nothing with color, nothing with surface and nothing with sound. One sees and feels darkness. A coreSelf is there in the darkness with a suspicion that in every direction there are innumerable cores radiating darkness in darkness.

This is similar to being emerged in the brahman spiritual plane of existence, except that in the brahman energy, one is surrounded by golden light shining, blasting in every direction. One is a speck of that energy radiating that light, with innumerable other cores doing the same.

It would be unusual if the deceased person I searched for, was transferred to that plane of non-perception. This person was not a yogi but that would not stop a transfer. In any case, if someone is in that plane of awareness, it is near impossible to sort the person, much less determine definitely if the person is located there. When one is in that plane of consciousness, communication with someone else does not occur.

Breath Nutrition / Pranayama

In a conversation on June 18, 2022, with a swami who established a devotional institution from India in the Western countries, he made an appraisal of *pranayama* breath infusion. This person is deceased. The discussion was on the astral side during a session of breath infusion practice, using the *kapalabhati/bhastrika pranayama* procedure.

He said this.

"There is little understanding in India about the practice and effects of *pranayama*. People assume that it means to cease breathing. They think that if someone can hold the breath without inhalation for an extended period, that is the accomplishment.

"I, myself, felt that way about it, until I practiced *bhastrika*. Then I realized that it was breath nutrition, not breath starvation. It is more fresh air into the physical body and positive *prana* into the subtle form. The result is the elevation of the subtle body to higher planes of consciousness and higher environments.

"It is not a matter of arresting and preventing breath intake but rather increasing breath intake substantially."

Edge of Infinity

Neem Karoli Baba, an ascetic on the astral planes, got wind that a swami and myself discussed the possibility of finding a portal to the spiritual world. This swami is deceased but in his last body he established a devotional sect which promised that its fulltime devotees would, at the moment of death, enter the spiritual world. Since he and none of his deceased followers attained the result, he considered some alternative methods.

After reviewing the methods given in many scriptures of his sect, he is of the opinion that perhaps the ancient ascetics who attained the spiritual world, did so by doing mystic yoga, in addition to some methods which became prominent later, but which by themselves do not give the results.

As we discussed this, suddenly, Neem Karoli appeared to our right. He floated in the astral environment. Suddenly we were on an infinite plane which stretched in the distance as if it went forward forever. Neem pointed and said this,

- Go to the edge. Call from there. He will come! He will come!
- When! When! Who knows? Who knows?
- It could be forever. They left from there from the edge.
- Go and sit there. Wait there!
- Wait there forever! Forever!
- It will turn after a time. *Pratyahar* is complete then. Not otherwise.

After saying that, he left. We sat after going forward for a time. There was no edge. It was like the infinity horizon, as if once you got to the edge, it continued again forever. Understanding that, we sat. We sat. The plan was to come here in each meditation to sit and wait to be called. There was some light from everywhere streaming, but ahead it extended forever.

We will wait. We understood that. He will come but we will wait. What would he say? We have no idea. We will wait! We will wait!

Chest Inside Kundalini Orbs

There are two kundalini orbs which when surcharged in breath infusion, radiates light energy. The color is that of ice. The bliss of it is mild and spreading from the center left and center right. The orbs are shaped like round door knobs. This is not based on spinal kundalini. These orbs are independently shining but they are not activated when there is insufficient fresh subtle energy surcharged into the chest on either side.

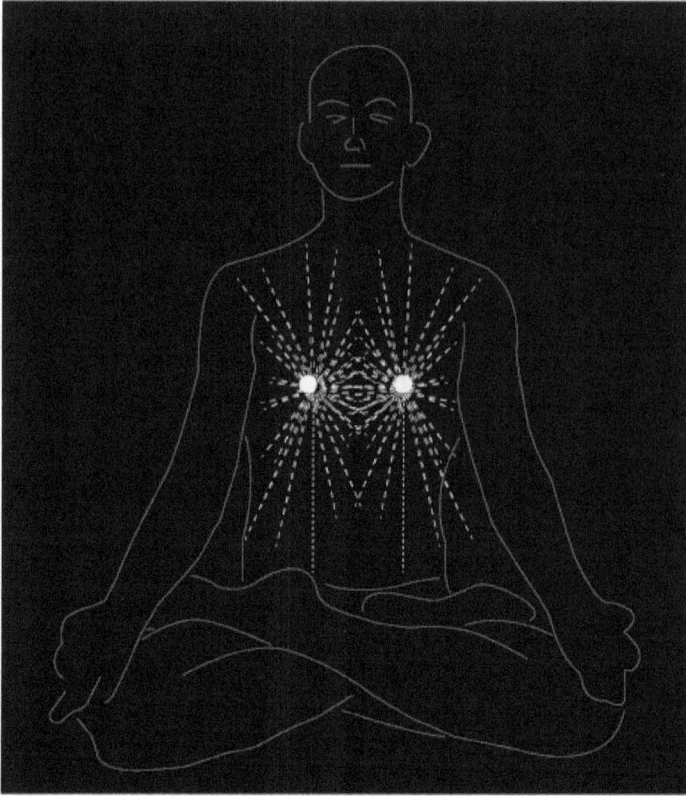

Memory and the Death Process

A student yogi approached on the astral planes with a question about the *death-to-rebirth* process, as to how it is, when someone takes a new body through human parents, that person does not recall the past life.

There is a doubt about reincarnation. If it is true, how is it that most people have no recall, and the few that do, have only partial experience, and cannot accurately describe every scene from the previous existence.

In reference to the new life as an embryo, the transit from the old body into the astral existence, and then to being a child of somebody, is a natural one which is formatted by the physical and psychic nature. This means that one must study how nature operates, and do one's best to make the transit as convenient as possible.

The incidence of lack of recall in the new life, can be studied by observing what happens to someone who is born as an infant. Such children show no or very little cohesive recall. Why is that? It would be much easier for people to accept reincarnation as a fact, if there was recall. However, we must understand that in so many facets of existence, nature is unconcerned to make the situations service our needs.

During the life of a body, even then, even in the young adult stage, one experiences memory lapses. This is when the physical body is at its healthiest stage. Hence during the infant stages and during the elderly years, it is unreasonable to think that nature would allow for full recall on demand.

The evidence is that an infant body is derived from the parents with no memory from a past life. Even if the subtle body has memory from a past life, still the infant body does not come with that information installed into its brain. It seems that nature manufactures the infant form with no capacity to hold previous memories.

In the process of assuming the infant form, the personSelf, as a subtle body, loses grasp on the memories which are stored in the subtle body. It shifts to having the blank memory capacity of the embryo it will assume.

In an old or damaged physical body, someone should prepare for the process of rebirth, by considering that some memory will be unavailable as the physical body ages. This would be memory which required a physical brain for its storage.

Some memories are stored in two locations. Some others are in one or the other location but not in both. A memory may be stored in the subtle body and in the physical brain. Some other memory may be only in the physical system. Yet, another memory may be in the subtle body only.

Access to memory is reliant on various factors. One should not assume that one will recall every memory. It depends on the access of the information. When a person first departs from the physical body, he/she lives as a ghost but not in the negative meaning of the word. Ghost means a subtle body which is difficult to perceive by those who have physical forms. If it is perceived, it may be regarded as spooky and frightening. The fact is however, that it is neither spooky nor frightening because it is just the subtle body of the person. It is the same subtle body which was used by that person when that someone had a physical form. It is the same body which was used in dreams, when that person was on the physical side.

Because humans are usually anchored to the physical side of life, their awareness of a dead person's subtle body, or ghost, may cause feelings of fear and trepidation. One can get over this in time, if one switches one's reference to the subtle side, abandoning the physical existence as the primary place.

During dreams one can have some idea about the condition of memory after death. This is because in the hereafter, one will be left with only the memories which are in the subtle body. None of the memories in the physical system will be available unless those memories were duplicated to the subtle body when those events took place. In addition, when from the hereafter one takes a new infant form, one will have little or no access to the subtle body memories during the early years of that new body.

Part 2

Divine Eye Development

Divine eye development is a demanding and longwinded achievement for a yogi. It happens when the sense doors are closed for a time, and the coreSelf lost interest in using them to procure physical and psychic objects. The closing of the sense doors is the *pratyahar* fifth stage of yoga in its highest level of achievement, where in the mind, there is no ideation or no urgency for outward adventures.

The coreSelf is turned away from its tendency to experience the mental and emotional environment around it. Patanjali aptly stated it as the termination of the *chittavritti* displays in the psyche.

During meditation, the divine eye can be operative, and the yogi may have no idea that it is. However, after meditating for some time, a sensitivity develops, where the yogi can know that even though there is no clear perception of subtle and supernatural events, still the divine eye operates, but on a lower frequency.

Sometimes there will be spot clarity where one sees through a portal into the *chit akash* sky of consciousness and taps into its bliss feature. These momentary experiences are important and should be appreciated by the yogi. Later as the practice develops, the yogi will have more lasting access into the sky of consciousness. Instead of a split-second opening, it will be for several moments, say for ten or fifteen moments. Such lengthened experiences indicate that the practice is developing. More meditation should be done.

Death Event

The urgency of this life is its upcoming and unavoidable end which we term as death. From the moment of birth, this body, this self, is threatened day and night with death. There is no single moment where death is absent. It prevails under the aegis of time, which is the inscrutable timer of this physical world.

On the night of June 24, 2022, I was in a discussion with someone whose physical body has a terminal disease. He estimated that soon he must relinquish the body. Actually, every living body on this planet of any species, will soon die. Ten minutes? Ten hours? Ten days? Ten years?

An assassin is not concerned with the condition of the victim, regarding if he is young or old, useful, or non-productive. The assassin is focused only on death. That assassin is the time factor which will kill the body in due course.

Since death is the problem, why is it that hardly a human faces it. Why would a human not develop a lifestyle which reinforces the psychic aspects of the self, where that self is focused on the psychic world around us, thus giving less credence to the physical aspects?

My friend who is threatened by death and who has no way out, who is boxed in by a terminal disease in an old body, said this:

"If I knew about the subtle body's importance, I would have practiced breath infusion earlier. I would have focused in and through the subtle body more frequently. I am now like a pilot who sat in the cockpit and rotated the steering but who never started the engines and never taxied the run way. I never lifted off.

"I could have practiced more frequently. How does one expect to pilot an aircraft if one never practiced? Sitting in the cockpit is not the same as lifting off and getting the feel of flying."

Throat Kundalini Spread

As one does *kapalabhati/bhastrika pranayama*, there will be kundalini rises from and in various places in the subtle body. One should be receptive to these experiences, and not think that kundalini has to rise in the publicized way, from *muladhara* base chakra through the spine into the brain.

The way kundalini is formulated and aroused is not limited to the way it occurs during rises through the spine. One should also recognize other involuntary rises of kundalini elsewhere in the body. For example, when kundalini rises when there is urine held in the bladder, and suddenly during urination, one feels electric sensations in the arm pits, arms, forearms, and bladder. Or for instance, when there are sexual pleasure experiences where kundalini is startled in the sexual apparatus, and strikes out from there to other parts like into the thighs, or up through the front, or center, of the body, into the throat and head.

All kundalini rises should be observed. By that examination, one will get some idea about the location of *nadis* in the subtle body, and electrical circuits which are routed here and there.

During a session of breath infusion on June 24, 2022, I had a rare and unusual kundalini arousal, strike, and distribution, with a snow-white bliss spread of energy in the throat, and higher central chest area. This was with ripples of energy. Even doing breath infusion for many years using this body, I do not recall having this experience prior. My conclusion is that this is a rare event.

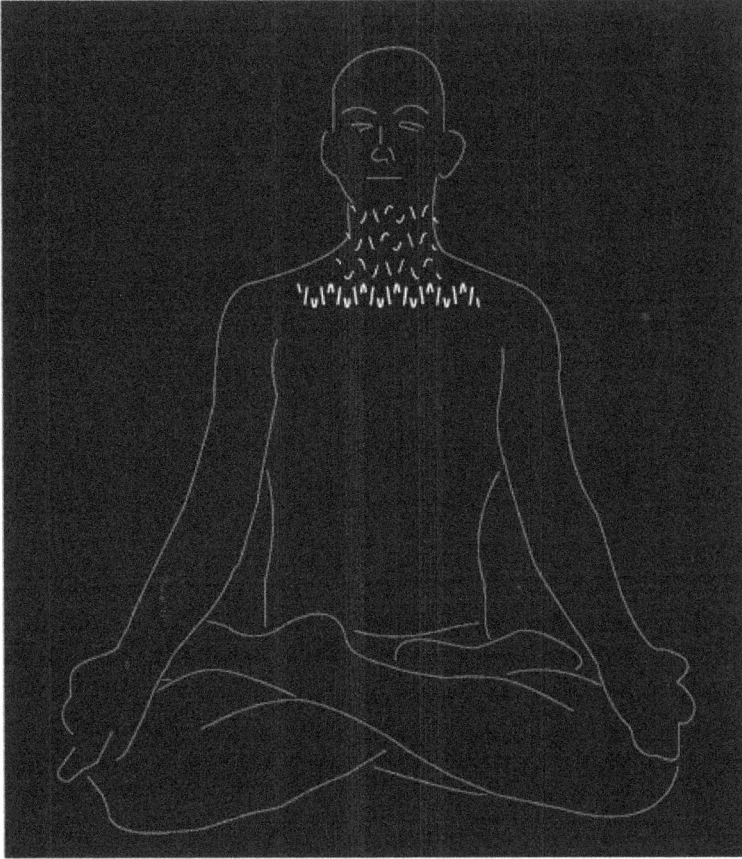

Influence of Feces

Yogeshwarananda instructed that I explain the hidden influence of feces. He said that if feces are not promptly evacuated, its retention produces a sluggish mood which negatively affects the moods and actions of the body. That energy is subtle, so subtle, that it may not be noticed even by a yogi who practices regularly. It will shift a yogi's priorities where he becomes lackadaisical and loses focus on the spiritual practice and on social duties which he should promptly comply.

Patanjali warned about the sleep *vritti* as an obstruction for yoga practice. When waste lingers in the body, specifically in the colon and/or rectum, it produces a dulling force which influences the person to neglect certain duties, which if completed would accelerate practice.

The physical body has a maximum lifespan. A yogi should construct his lifestyle in consideration that nothing should be done which will reduce the duration of the body. One should act in a way which will not increase the illness capacity of the body, such that there should be no action which would reduce the body's healthy condition. Retaining feces instead of promptly evacuating it, will reduce the health, and increase the sick potential of the body.

It has a dulling stupefying influence on the subtle form. That is unwanted. That may cause the yogi to reside on a lower astral plane hereafter. Not a day should pass, where a yogi does not check to be sure that there is prompt evacuation. This is a vital part of yoga practice.

Yogi Bhajan's Astral Palace

On June 26, 2022, I was at a place which is Yogi Bhajan's astral palace. A friend who is in the process of being deprived of his physical body, was looking to find Yogi Bhajan's ashram. He could not find it because Yogi Bhajan's astral place is inaccessible.

When I got there, I saw Yogiji and a yogini lady who was his servant-assistant at that place. At least that is how the place is formatted for visitors. I left an astral manuscript there about kundalini yoga. It was an explanation which Yogi Bhajan asked me to prepare. I gave the document to the yogini. She took it to the inner area of the palace. This place is on the astral side of New Mexico in the USA.

This happened within an astral hour, where I prepared the manuscript and submitted it. It was returned to me by the yogini with editorial and illustrative changes made by Yogiji.

About an hour after this, I did the morning breath infusion session. The student who was looking for Yogi Bhajan, did the session with me. Yogi came there but that student was unaware of him because Yogiji was in a dimension which the student could not access.

Checking the student's practice, Yogi made some criticism. After a while, Yogi said that students should be sure to brush through *sushumna nadi* central spinal channel thoroughly. His remark was that even if other kundalini rises happen, still in each session *sushumna nadi* should be brushed aggressively.

Rebirth Anxiety Prevalent

From the birth of an embryo to the death of its adult version, then from being hurled into the subtle existence without a physical body, to staying in the astral existence until one is fused into the feelings of the parent-to-be, there is constant attraction to reproductive locations. It is ongoing, unrelenting, and continuous. It is no respecter of persons or places.

Where is the place for the event?

When is the time for the circumstance?

The subtle body is obsessed with, and compelled for, the tendency for rebirth. It is felt as an impulsive attraction to any place which appears as a possible birth environment.

The attraction is to go there, sit there, and wait there to be in a central position. Of course, the nature of the place is that one cannot stay there, no more than a canoe can always ride the crest of a wave.

Astral Sun

There is a *savitur gayatri* mantra which states that the sun gives energy to three planetary realms, *bhuh, bhuvah* and *svah*. The hint there is that the sun controls life in the lower, median, and higher systems of which the earth is in the median range.

Here is the mantra, word for word meanings and translation:

ॐ भूर्भुवः स्वः
तत्सवितुर्वरेण्यं ।
भर्गो देवस्य धीमहि
धियो यो नः प्रचोदयात् ॥

om bhūr bhuvaḥ svaḥ
tat savitur vareṇyaṁ।
bhargo devasya dhīmahi
dhiyo yo naḥ pracodayāt। ।

om - be attentive to sacred information, bhūr = bhūh = physical existence, bhuvaḥ - astral existence, svaḥ - super-astral existence, tat - that, savitur = savituh - sun deity, vareṇyaṁ - that which is the best, bhargo = bhargah - what is self luminous, devasya - of the supernatural persons or influences, dhīmahi - we meditate on, dhiyo = dhiyah = the perceptive insight, yo = yah = who, naḥ - us, pracodayāt - for inspiring

Be attentive to this sacred information!

There are the physical, astral, and super-astral existences. These are energized by the self-luminous sun-deity Savituh, who is the best of the supernatural influences. We meditate on him for inspiring perceptive insight.

It is understood that the bhuh realm is the lowest. The bhuvah is median. The svah is the highest. This is not in terms of physical geography. This is in terms of mystic distance. If anyone anywhere on earth went up physically, up and up through the sky and outerspace, he/she would not locate the svah higher region. The direction and distance are mystic not physical.

I was in an astral realm on June 30, 2022. I had influenza on that day and took a day nap as a result. During that time, on the astral side of existence, I found myself being pulled to a place in the Caribbean. As soon as I got there, I was at a beach where two persons I knew over fifty years ago were located. One was a friend I knew, whom I have not seen in fifty years.

He took me to a lady who was his mother at that time. This lady passed on several years prior. The sun was bright at that place but it was not in the sky, only its radiance was there. It shined just as it does on a cloudless day on a tropical island.

The lady spoke to me. As soon as she did another woman appeared. The interesting thing is that the lady used a youthful subtle body, while the second woman used a subtle form, which was similar to one she had, when her last physical body was about eighty years of age.

Both women were pleased to speak with me. They showered me with affection. I could not identity the woman who used the older body, but a mental hint was given to me, which suggested that she was the mother of the first woman. Soon after this, the friend who pulled me to the island left on an urgent matter, to return to his physical body. I spoke with the women for some time. They discussed their astral situations, and mentioned some incidence which occurred while I knew them physically so many years ago.

After the conversation, the older lady left. Then, the younger of the two said she wanted to travel with me, to where my physical body was located. She wanted to have a marker of where I could be located if need be. She accompanied me back to my physical body. I awakened as that body. She stayed on the astral side of that place for some hours before departing.

Before leaving she explained that after reading the *sex you!* book, she was no longer interested in being a physical being. She was satisfied being only a psychic presence. She felt that she could live on the island as a subtle being from then onward.

After this, it was time for me to do the afternoon session of breath infusion. I grabbed a yoga mat and walked outdoors. As soon as I stepped out the building, I noticed the sun shining overhead. Right then I felt an inspiration in my mind from the sunDeity. He this.

"I am the same sun which was on the astral side, except that there I radiate through a different level of consciousness. I maintain those places."

Hearing in the Devotional Cult *(Bhakti)*

On the day of July 2 2022, I was in a discussion with a deceased swami on the astral side. This conversation summarized a topic which we considered for the past six months. This person is deceased. He established a devotional movement, and is currently reconsidering his philosophy and beliefs, because some of his followers did not get the promised results, when they became deceased.

The topic of discussion was hearing music but he realized that it applied to any sensual intake including tasting foods. Here is a listing of the aspects which this pertains to.

- smelling pleasing odors like incense
- tasting gourmet foods which are pleasing to the tongue
- seeing pleasing colors like painted deities, curtains, buildings, and clothing
- touching smooth and soft surfaces like garlands and fabric
- hearing pleasing sounds, like bhajan, kirtan and choirs

Any of these activities when done in the name of devotion may cause degradation of the ascetic, if particular disciplines and restrains are not in place, while consuming the sense object, which is a target for the greedy sense which pursues it.

There was music being played loudly from a house which was nearby. The swami heard this and recognized that his mind was attracted to it. He wanted to go nearer to the building to hear it more clearly, and to sing it in the mind as it was heard.

He said that even though he chanted (sang) devotional hymns for many years, still his mind, like a prostitute, was eager to enjoy radio songs. He condemned himself because he said that he promised his disciples, while he his last body, that by hearing his music and songs, their minds would cease chasing popular songs, which had no devotional content, and which were unauthorized. Now his mind was attracted, even though he was the religious leader who gave those guarantees.

His conclusion was that the addiction of the senses to their objects continues unabated, even if the ascetic restricts the mind to devotional compositions. Each sense transcends the devotional intention and sticks to its sensual need, such that while hearing a devotional song, for instance, the mind will enjoy and consume the music content, the rhythm, and will ignore the devotional message.

It happens with food where the tasting sense consumes the blend of flavors and does not graft over into the intention to make it focus on the sanctity of the offered meals.

History Jump to Astral Side

History as one participates in it, could be slipped to the astral side of existence, such that one can fulfill whatever desires one has or whatever needs one developed while using the physical body, and not have to come back to the physical level, not have to take an embryo for the fulfillment of many desires.

Some desires can be performed on the astral side during the life of the physical body, and when that physical system is no longer serviceable, and is deceased. It so happens that there is some correlation between this physical plane of activity and the astral world. If one is keen to recall dreams, and to note psychic communication, one can develop the tendency to be satisfied with what is available, and what can be acted out, on the astral side. One does not need to be physical to fulfill many desires.

The few desires which one has, which require only a physical environment, can be researched in meditation. Methods for eliminating those energies can be practiced, so that the desires do not force one to take an embryo, after one is deprived of the current physical body.

I was in an astral encounter with a friend on July 10. 2022. This person was absent from my life for the past thirty years. Somehow, he wanted to speak with me, and to continue our relationship and interaction after such a long time. As soon as I was aware of him in that astral place, he left aside some persons whom he was with. He asked me to do some carpentry work.

When I complied and began doing the project, he mentioned a lady whom we knew at the time. He wanted to know if I could arrange for him to speak with that person. I explained that I would make an effort to contact that person on the physical side. In his mind there was memory of yet, another lady whom we both knew. He wondered if I was interested in this other person. I told him mentally, that I would speak to this other person if she could be reached. This all took place without speech. On that astral plane, communication occurs rapidly before the mental ideas can be transformed into speech.

The significance of this experience is that one does not have to take another body to fulfill some desires. The major portion of unfulfilled desires can be worked out astrally, such that one does not have to use the risky and dangerous physical body to act out various roles, and do various things. For instance, the carpentry project which my friend wanted me to complete, could be done either on the physical or astral side. One does not need to have a physical pressure in it. It can be ushered on the astral side, and be fulfilled there with no necessity for physical rebirth to manifest it.

Sex and Devotion

On July 11, 2022, I was in an astral communication with two people who are officials of a devotional sect. One, a male, who is one of the current sexual partners of the other, who is a female, left as soon as they arrived. The other, the female, wanted to discuss the matter of how, in her case, sexual attraction was not conquered by the devotional method of chanting holy names, attending worship ceremonies, eating sanctified meals and some other processes which are part of the method used by their religious institution.

At first, I thought that I should not publish the conversation. I felt that some readers would be critical. Some others would be alarmed. The lady however insisted that I publish her opinion. Here is what she said.

"My view now as compared to years ago when I first joined the sect, is that its process did not cure me of sex desire. I also noticed that it did not do so for many of the followers who were my friends. This is speaking about male and female members.

"It was frequent, that some senior people, myself included, made sexual trysts physically in secret, but mostly it occurred in the astral world with the subtle body breaking away, and meeting with some other senior member for sexual love.

"According to the leader of the sect, he promised that those who sincerely followed the method, would not be afflicted with this sex desire, but it did not apply in my case, that I was freed from it and for that matter, especially on the psychic plane, my subtle body pursued every sexual opportunity, where it felt attracted to someone else.

"My body is elderly now. But even with that condition, the subtle body is just as eager and ardent, at pursuing sexual opportunities for sexual behaviors. The devotional process did not remove sex desire. For that matter when we mixed to complete one or the other of the devotional process, that association merely accelerated our desires to have sex with each other. Even when we resisted the urge in the physical body, or could not complete the act, because of not having physical privacy, the subtle body ardently hunted for the opportunity, and completed it on an astral plane or did so mentally."

Astral Lessons in Absence

If the teacher is not present, provided the teacher leaves the relevant techniques in the astral place where the instructions are usually given, it is possible for someone to receive *pranayama* breath infusion and meditation practice instructions in the astral world.

If for instance in the physical world, a student should meet a teacher at some location for lessons, and if that student does not attend for one reason or the other, the teacher cannot teach the student merely by doing the practice at that place in the student's absence.

This does not hold true on the astral side of existence. There, the teacher, if a student does not attend at a specified time, may do the practice in the student's absence, at that time at the specific location. When the student arrives some time after, even if the teacher is not there or is in attendance but cannot show the practice, the student can learn from the energy of practice which the teacher left when he/she practiced earlier at that place.

This applies to students using physical bodies, as well as those who lost the physical forms, and who only have psychic bodies. Students who have a physical body, can gain access to many techniques if they become versed in subtle awareness.

Detachment from Social Affairs

There is a question which arises in terms of when to cease one's interest in social affairs. Should that be done abruptly or gradually? When should it begin, where one greatly reduces the interest one has, or one is compelled to have, in the social affairs of relatives and friends?

Social pressure comes from every side. It powerfully disrupts yoga practice. The worse of it comes from relatives and friends. Relatives are people whom one is related to physically. Friends may be yogis or non-yogis. The main humbug surprisingly is not relatives, but yogi friends. This is due to the fact that when someone is related to a yogi, it is expected that this person may pressure the yogi to keep him in the social loop of relationships, and services shared in a family, and with in-laws, or people who are closely related to family.

But there are also fellow yogis who feel that a yogi should assist in their social responsibilities by being interested, and by keeping track of their social affairs. This is injurious to a yogi because it exposes the yogi to more social trauma. It is one thing to be a physician, and to open a clinic for treating diseases. It is another issue for the physician to get so close to a patient, that he develops the disease he treats in the patient.

How about if the patient request that the physician should meet at the patient's residence? What would happen there? How involved should the physician be with the patient's relatives and friends?

Guru Release Hereafter

It may be necessary when one is deprived of the physical body, to gain release from following a path which proved to be useless.

I was with a deceased Swami who founded a devotional sect. Then there was another person who is deceased, and who was an important leader in the sect. The first person, the founder, did breath infusion on the astral side as I did it on the physical plane. Then his disciple who was an authority in the sect, after the founding Swami was departed, came there astrally.

He wanted to do the *bhastrika pranayama* practice but the founding Swami, his guru, did not encourage him. Feeling the discouragement, the second Swami said this to me,

"Why did you not show this to me when I was alive. You never explained this. Now you teach it to my guru but he is disinclined for me to learn this."

I replied, "How can you be taught a process which was banned in your sect? And besides if the Swami wanted you to learn it, he would have requested that you be shown, or he could show you the portions of it which he practiced."

The second Swami was offended by this. He said this, "I should be able to learn it directly from you. We were friends during some of the period of my last body. Teach it to me, I do not need his approval. And to booth, his process did not result in the spiritual changes which he described."

I explained this,

"Unless you are released from him, you cannot learn another process. Your relationship with him is such that you are still linked to him in a manner which makes it impossible for you to learn another process. He must release you from his hold on you. Then you may practice something else."

After hearing this, the second Swami was despondent. The first one, the founder Swami, ignored him. The founder considered if there was a way to release the second Swami.

If one becomes fanatical, it will be difficult to shift one's submission energy to someone else. And unless that is completed, one cannot truly accept another teacher.

Meditation Preparation

For meditation there needs to be preparation on a daily basis so that the body is at its best health and is properly rested. Meditation when the body is unhealthy or when it is exhausted, has value, but it does not yield the optimum result. There should not be a habit of haphazard meditation at odd times, here and there. A yogi/yogini should standardize the schedule. In event that there is a mishap or a twist in time, the meditation can occur at an odd time, in a rush, with haphazard focus.

After doing meditation formally since 1970, after studying yoga theory, after writing books about the practice, I declare that a certain time should be dedicated to preparation for meditation. Then a certain time should be used for meditation. This should be done at a minimum, twice per day with the first session after the night's rest. And the second session sometime before the following night's rest.

Of these sessions, the one after the night's rest is the most important. If meditation is the priority, most of what is done otherwise, should not be allowed to interfere with it. In fact, beginning with the effort to take rest, the yogi/yogini should set the mind and body in a way which facilitates meditation.

When one rises to meditate, it should be after full rest, otherwise there will be drowsy states, irritability, mental chaos, and other negative emotional and mental conditions when one makes the attempt to meditate.

For the main session, one's mind should be free of stress. This does not mean forcing the mind into a stress-less condition. It is a state of lifestyle, which causes minimum stress, and which allows for the release of stress from day to day. The modern idea of using meditation as a quiet time to quell stress is not the process of meditation which I describe. That is another system of psychological calming.

This system is different, in that there is elimination of stress sources in the activities of the yogi's lifestyle, so that there is little stress in the first place. This little stress is relieved by completing duties promptly from day to day.

When preparing for meditation, getting the self in order to meditate, the yogi/yogini should check the mind and emotions for stress issues. These should be resolved then and there if that is possible. They should be resolved before the session, not in the session, not as part of the practice.

Any stress issues which remain in the psyche during meditation, will affect the mental state, even if such issues are suppressed. Therefore, a yogi/yogini should eliminate the issues, by completing the duties which cause the stress.

There is a tendency, and it is unwanted, where a yogi/yogini attempts to meditate daily and does so under stress, with some of the stress suppressed for the time being. That way of regarding meditation, is unwanted. Such a method will never cause consolidation of practice, and will never graduate the yogi to an advanced stage.

Swami and the Abortion

On August 25, 2022, on the astral side, I had an encounter with a deceased yogi who in his past life taught kundalini yoga. He was with a woman who aborted his child. When the lady got pregnant, this yogi instructed her to get an abortion in India. This she did, but it happened under the hand of a village woman, who had no modern medical knowledge.

The result was that the pregnant lady became terribly sick, and was transported to a more modern country, where she was treated to save her body from death. This lady stayed in the service of the yogi for many years after the incident, until she became so intolerant of him, that she left his organization, married someone, and created a new life for herself.

Now, many years after, this disturbing situation between them came alive again, where the lady still felt undone and cheated. In her presence, the yogi asked me if I could take her under my care. The main issue he said, was that there was a resentment energy towards him in her psyche. She made efforts to remove it but was unable to. The yogi also had uneasy feelings about the abortion. Apparently, the would-be child has still not acquired an embryo, and follows the yogi wherever he goes, even on the astral side of life.

After we discussed some methods of dealing with this, the conversation shifted to a woman whom I spoke to just once in 1973. The yogi said that this woman, who owned a boutique bazaar in Boulder Colorado, had a crush on him. He too was attracted to her. He wanted to know if I remembered the woman, and if I could visualize her face. Considering that I met the woman once, and it was some forty-nine (49) years ago, how is it that the yogi thought that I could remember her facial appearance.

As I combed through my memory, I saw some scenes from the day I met the woman. Her face I did not recall, because I did not emphasize it. There was no firm imprint of her features in memory.

The yogi wanted me to look at the woman's face, and decide if the woman was attractive or not, if she was worth a sexual appreciation. As far as I recall, this incidence with the woman, was that I lived at the yogi's ashram in Denver, Colorado in 1973. I had a Volkswagen beetle car. From India, a man named Sagaar arrived. He was a friend of the yogi and was such an expert cook that it was said in India, that he could turn rotten food in the most delicious meal.

Sagaar had to go to a boutique in Bolder. There were only two cars at the ashram at the time; one was mine. I was requested to take him. We got to Boulder soon after. We went into the shop where a lady managed the boutique business. She greeted Sagar. The lady turned to me to ask where I lived in India. I told her I was from Guyana. She observed me as if to say, "What is your importance?"

While talking to Sagaar, she made a remark speaking loud enough for me to hear. She said, "We are in the business of curios. The yogi is in the business of religion. What is the difference?"

I drifted through the shop looking at the curios which were displayed for sale. Soon after Sagar and I left that place.

It is interesting that even though this happened so long ago, nearly fifty years, it still has mental potency, and affects my life. The same goes for the deceased yogi who is afflicted with his attraction to the lady, as well as to his act of influencing a woman whose pregnancy for him was aborted. Death does not free someone from offensive acts. Those who think that in dying their troubles will be over, are flawed in that idea.

Reverse Abandonment in Relations

The traditional approach to abandonment in human relationships, has to do with dependents abandoning their guardians. For example, when children become adults, and move away from the influence of parents. Instead of staying with parents and complying with the rules of conduct established, some children leave. They throw away the lifestyle which the parents formatted.

But there is a reverse abandonment, where guardians abandon their dependents. That would be like if parents moved from a place where the family was domiciled, where the parents leave the young adult children in the home. The parents move from the home, giving up the security and lifestyle which the very same parents constructed and maintained.

This extends further where the parents resist being influenced by their young adult children, such that the parents lose interest, and tend to avoid the conveniences and security, which staying in the social structure, would afford them.

There is a danger, however. Just as when young adult children leave aside their parents, the children lose financial and residential security, so when parents walk away from their adult children, they, the parents, lose benefits and must live with inconvenience.

Children who leave aside the luxurious, and formatted lifestyle, of their parents, must deal with the flow of resentment energy, which replaces the original feelings of happiness, they used to experience, when they complied with the parents. Similarly, parents who renounce or abandon the conveniences of fitting into the social format of the family, are also resented by their adult children who feel a loss, and uncertainty, when their parent leave them aside.

In the Vedic culture, it was recommended that after children reach maturity, some parents, especially males ones, should go to an unknown place where they cannot be traced or related by their children. There, the parents should turn the focus on the future to be achieved after death of the elderly body. This was known as *vanaprastha* or residence in a forest *(vana)*.

One Vidura advised his half-brother Dhritarashtra to go to an isolated forest, to internalize the mind, in preparation for passing from the body. Vidura was particular to tell Dhritarashtra to go where no one recognized him.

However, one must deal with the resentment energy which may find one, if one does this in the elderly years.

Naad / Hearing Sense Located

There are many uses for naad in meditation practice. And yet, it is not easy to determine what to do with naad, regarding how to use it, to reach deeper levels of consciousness, and access portals to other dimensions. Even persons who have no interest in other dimensions can use naad to advance their meditative objectives, but the methods for doing so are mostly unknown. This is due to the fact that when a yogi hears naad, there is a holding power in it. This causes him/her not to be interested in doing anything, besides hearing naad.

For those who are interested, naad can be used to help to access intellect and/or third eye portal vision into other dimensions, even to the *chit akash* sky of consciousness. I will describe a method for identifying and leaving aside, or using, one or more of the self's urges.

In the coreSelf there is an attention protrusion which can be withdrawn from all interest or applied to some interest. This singular sense is the interest of the core. When it becomes tense, it is experienced as the applied attention of the self. The *pratyahar* or withdrawal of this interest energy, means that when it is withdrawn into the core, it enters with its five expressions, and becomes invisible. These five sense urges, with the singular interest energy, goes into a relaxed condition in the core.

As a total of six senses or expressions, these are listed;
- interest
- hearing
- touching
- seeing
- tasting
- smelling

The first, the interest sense is mandatory and remains inside any other of the five remaining senses which are used. Most of this usage is involuntary. The linking of the interest sense to any other one is connected so rapidly as to be instantaneous.

However as one meditates more and more, and develops the required sensitivity over time, the rapidity is comprehended. One can track the linking and unlinking with ease.

When hearing naad, one should first be sure that one gives full attention to this hearing. This would mean that there is the interest energy in the self in combination with the hearing interest, so that there is a focus awareness whereby there is only the following aspects combined.

- coreSelf
- interest of coreSelf
- naad sound

One becomes aware of those three aspects, and any other interest which is in the mind space, but one ceases any attention which goes to other interest. The residual interest which went to other concerns is curtailed and withdrawn. It is placed in the interest of the core as the core focuses on the naad sound.

This will cause one to be aware of one other aspect which is the hearing sense. There will be four aspects only which are:

- coreSelf
- interest of coreSelf
- naad
- hearing sense which pursues and aggressively contains naad

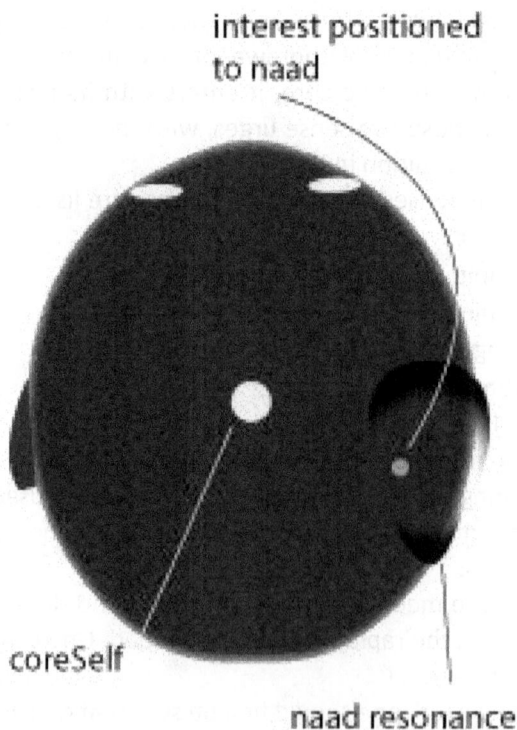

interest positioned
to naad

coreSelf

naad resonance

This state of consciousness should be maintained for a time. There should be no interest in, nor pursuit of anything else.

After a time, after this state stabilizes, one remains in that condition easily and spontaneously. The yogi should hold that state while considering that there are five senses besides the interest, but with the interest being mandatory. However, the yogi should observe if the interest has any other concern, or if it secretly is involved with another sense besides the hearing collector. If it is discovered that it has another sense in consideration, the yogi should continue to adhere only to the hearing sense as it contains, and focuses on naad.

However, if the yogi found that the interest sense has no other concern and is only concerned with the hearing sense and naad, he/she should consider the smelling sense. He/She will know that this sense has no value in this application. He should then consider the tasting sense. This sense will seem to be irrelevant in this type of meditation. He should then consider the seeing sense which is relevant but he should not apply it. He should only note that even though it is not in use, it could be useful.

The yogi should consider the touching sense, but he should realize that this sense was being used secretly with the hearing sense, which listened intently to naad. At this point in the meditation, he should engage the seeing sense so that it focuses forward. This will happen if he switches on that sense. Usually, the seeing sense is closed. It is an interference in most meditations. In this practice he will open that sense forward. This should be done while keeping the naad focus through the listening and touching senses.

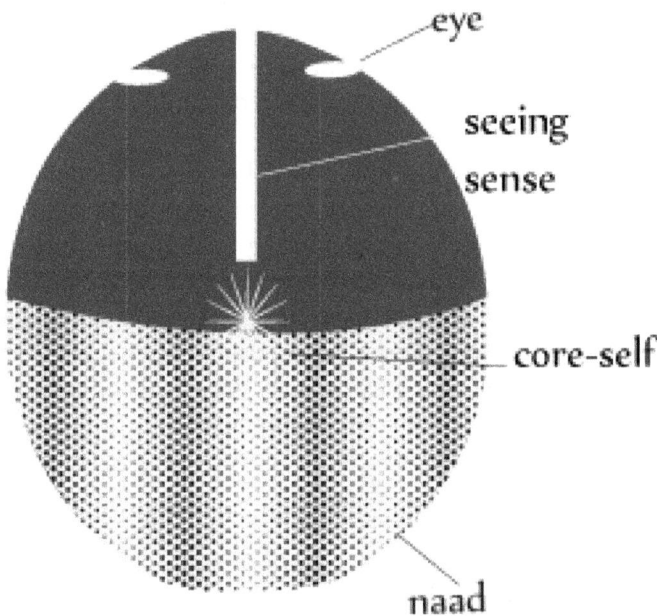

eye

seeing sense

core-self

naad

Somehow by steadiness he should keep this focus and wait for a portal to open.

Omen of Death

Death means losing one's social status. On the basis of the fear of bodily pains just prior to death, many people are afraid of dying. Once the death event is concluded, there will be no physical pain to endure. The physical pain which is present immediately prior to death, does not carry over into the death experience. All feelings in a physical body cease at its death.

Hence the fear of death, due to fear of physical pain prior to death, is questionable. However, I got a few portents of death within the past four weeks. These were psychic events where I was contacted by three friends who are deceased.

If after fifty-five years of age, one has many dreams with friends or relatives who are deceased, one can take that as indications of one's death. It is even more eventful if one is beyond seventy years.

I had a contact with a friend whom I served with in the US Air Force. This person used the name, Fred. I saw his physical body some years ago in northern Minnesota. This was before 1979. Prior to that we associated in the Philippines. Then we met in Denver, Colorado. About a week ago, I got an email from a mutual friend of ours who informed me that Fred was deceased. This friend wanted a copy of an out-of-print book of mine.

Again, I got an astral meeting with another friend who served in the US Air Force with Fred and myself in the Philippines. This person was Freeman, who was from Decatur, Georgia. After leaving the Air Force, I did some travelling with Freeman. As fate would have it, we lost track of each other. However, Freeman wanted to ask me for a recommendation for residence at Yogeshwarananda's ashram.

I inquired of it, and found that unless he could abandon narcotic and other drug use, it was not permissible for him to be at Yogeshwarananda's place. In the meantime, he could stay close to the place. He could use an astral tent. After a time if he gave up the habit, he would live on the premises.

Freeman did inquire of something. He asked.

"Why is it that by smoking marijuana, using cocaine, using liquor even, one does not transfer fully to the astral side? Why does the tendency to want a physical body continue. These substances shift the mind and feelings to the psychic side, but when their effects disappear, once again one seeks the physical side, abandoning the astral level."

I replied in this way.

"The shift which is due to substance use, is based on an action of the substance. If it was based on a direct psychological action, then there would be the likelihood of a shift of interest to the astral side. When a substance is the conveyor, the system of consciousness will shift back to the physical interest as soon as the substance loses effectiveness."

Last week, I got a visit from a friend of my deceased father. He wanted to locate my father, to see where my father was located on the astral or physical sides of existence. I directed this person, or rather his ghost, to go to that place of a relative, who was now the parent of my father. He went there and was surprised that my father already developed as a child of someone else.

The friend of my father asked if I could help to procure a body. He said this.

"Do you know of any potential parents for me. Better yet, if I could be born so that I could associate with your father again. We would be professional seamen again."

I told him this,

"Currently, it is hardly likely that this desire of yours would be fulfilled."

Then he was downcast. He said this.

"Young women are no longer interested in having infants. I noticed that even in the Caribbean and Guyana. It used to be that pregnancies were developed rapidly, but not anymore. Everywhere I go, I am rejected. Potential mothers turn away. What is the solution for this."

I replied.

"Solution!

"Only God can fix that. That is more than a human event. Supernatural power is required for that."

Unrecognized Divine Eye

It is likely that one may have usage of the divine eye and be totally unaware that it happened. This is due to some faults in practice.

- false expectations
- wrong method
- lack of recognition
- failure to comply with Patanjali's second sutra about termination of the mento-emotional energy *(chittavrittis)*
- thinking that one is worthy of the use of the divine eye
- thinking that by getting blessings, grace association, of a great yogi, one can use the divine eye
- having the wrong information about the eye from legends and information from people who became famous yogis

I can now declare that it is hardly likely that any yogi can develop the divine eye usage during the current phase of history. This is due to the lack of subtle perception and the enforcement within the mind of ideas and mental processes which discourage compliance with Patanjali's stipulations for the practice of yoga.

False expectations are the most common obstruction to the development of the divine eye. This happens because of arrogance and a high feeling of self-worth, where the yogi feels that he deserves to have the usage of the eye. After reading of its usage by great yogis in legends, stories, and biographies, a student may get the idea that he can realize and use the divine perception. This is a false expectation which dominates his meditation and keeps him from ever having the required experience.

A yogi may have the **wrong method** for practice of developing and using the divine eye. He/She may use that method for years and still not get one single experience with the eye. Yet, because of high hopes, he/she may continue the incorrect practice. Eventually when this yogi gets frustrated, he/she may resort to imagining that he/she has the use of the eye. Then because of a desire to become famous, that person may attract followers and give those persons the wrong method. They in turn may share that invalid process with others.

The **lack of recognition** of the divine eye may occur where a yogi has an experience of it, but is unable to identify it. He/She may trivialize the occurrence when it happens, such that during the experience, he/she dismisses apparitions, or visions, as being the normal mental inVisions in the mind, which occur randomly because of its shifty nature. It is not true that a rendering of the divine eye may only occur with clarity and proper recognition. It can happen that there is the operation of the divine eye happening simultaneously when the normal mental imaging and chaos occurs. A man in a brightly lit city may see a star and also lights from buildings simultaneously, but he may not discern that the star is a celestial body as compared to the light on a tall building, or the light of an aircraft which moves through the sky.

The **failure to comply with Patanjali's second sutra about termination of the mento-emotional energy (chittavrittis)** is a main handicap for a student yogi. In fact, this problem is ongoing and continues even for seasoned serious ascetics. This is due to the fact that as the psyche is so designed, it was manufactured for the rapid involuntary control of sensual operations. These tendencies work against the yogi, such that even if he advances in bits and starts, he will invariably find that he slides back to lower states where his mind is again filled with thoughts, ideas, and images, instead of being cleared of that mento-emotional debris.

Some ascetics begin their quest for yoga, or they soon develop it after they were introduced to it, with the idea **that one is worthy of divine**

perception. These yogis are arrogant but they do not realize it. If it is brought to their attention, they become sour in attitude to the practice, and towards the teacher, whom they feel deprives them of a natural right to have divine perception. Such persons have the presumption that they are naturally divine and should immediately resume the celestial status.

There are other yogis who **think that by getting blessings, grace of association of a great yogi** one can use of the divine eye. These students have no idea about working in meditation to attain divinity. They have no idea that it may take lives to attain a divine environment. As far as they are concerned the whole idea of a divine status has to do with being blessed by a deity.

Some ascetics have the **wrong information about the divine eye**. Their knowledge about it, is from legends and information from people who became famous yogis. Feeling that this information is the truth, they are unsubmissive to Patanjali, and feel that there must be an easier more natural method.

Rectum Malfunction

Hatha yoga has as an important part of it, the maintenance of the physical body, not as an end in itself, but as a way of keeping the subtle body efficiently toned, so that it is affected the least by the physical ailments. One problem which assails the physical body in its elderly condition, is the digestive and excretive tracks. These begin with the mouth and end at the anus.

There are many problems which could arise as the body ages but in particular there is slow evacuation which is a form of constipation. It is the lack of prompt removal of the food waste. The first step is to realize the ideal rate of travel of whatever is put into the mouth. A yogi should know the time taken for the transit of food through the stomach, higher intestines, colon, and rectum.

First one should know what the ideal rate of transit should be. One should know how to rectify it if it travels too slowly, or travels for a part of the passage, and then ceases to move.

A yogi should be attentive to this process in the body. He has a task to be aware of this on a daily basis. Worrying about the concerns of others is detrimental because the worry energy is limited. If he uses it for the interest in others, it will be reduced where he will not realize if he has problems with the colon and rectal inefficiency or system collapse.

What method should be used to get waste to exit the body promptly?

How often should waste be checked?

How does it affect meditation when the waste is not promptly evacuated?

Paramatma Meaning

The term *paramatma* consist of two words

- *param*
- *atma*

It is a Sanskrit compound word. The bare meaning is Supreme Spirit, Supreme Self. *Param* is simple. It is a superlative adjective for the highest, the greatest, the best. *Atma* has to be translated and understood according to the context.

There was a feud about this word in the debate between Mandana Mishra and Adi Shankara. In that debate Shankar ripped Mandana Mishra to shreds with the idea that *paramatma* means only that the observing self is superior to the intellect which that very self uses.

To support this idea, Adi Shankara cited the story from the Upanishad about the two birds on the tree, with one of the birds being superior simply because it neither eats nor participates in sensual acquisition, while the other bird, the inferior one, is always engaged in sensual quest.

Shankara presented the idea that it was not true that the superior bird, was the *paramatma* or God, and inferior one was not the limited self or *atma*. In other words, Shankara stated that the two birds cited in the Upanishads was not a comparison of the behavior of the God as compared to the limited self but rather it was a comparison of the self *(atma)* and its intellect.

If we accept this, it means that Shankara changed the meaning of the term *atma* where that is the intellect and the term *paramatma* was the self which does not get involved in sensual activities.

This makes no sense, and yet Shankara's arguments in the debate were so shocking, that Mandana Mishra was bewildered. In every argument they had, Shankara changed meanings of terms. Mandana was dumbfounded. Shankara successfully twisted formal meanings. He upended Mandana's reputation as the greatest debater of the time.

However, let us consider that if we accept the idea of Shankara, then it means that *atma* must be translated as intellect and *paramatma* as the self or particular self, as the governor in the body, the supreme factor, greater than the intellect.

Shankara's proposal also leaves us in a dilemma because on one hand we admit that we enjoy and are affected, but he declared that we do not. He said that the intellect enjoys. The self does not. That leaves much to be explained.

However, this article presents that if one uses the term *paramatma* for the limited non-involved self and one uses *atma* for the intellect which is involved eating fruits like the inferior of the two birds, then one should inform those novel meanings of the terms.

No standard Sanskrit dictionary will give that meaning. One must state it to be clear. In addition, in Bhagavad Gita, the term *paramatma* is used to mean the limited self but only once, in reference to the adjuncts in the psyche, where that self is not involved in the same way as the intellect. And this is a rare use of the word. Elsewhere in the same Gita the term *paramatma* means Krishna or God. That is the common usage.

Shankara was born to push the word *atma* into becoming the word *brahman*. He spent his life doing this. His conquest of pandits all over India, and of Mandana Mishra whom he humiliated, proves that. But no matter what he said, if one uses the term *paramatma* for *atma*, one should stop and ask this question:

What is the word for the detached observing self, if *atma* is the intellect.

Why is the term *param* being used if it does not mean superior or supreme?

Shankara's idea that there is no p*aramatma* Supreme Self, dismissed the majority of the Bhagavad Gita meaning for *paramatma*, where that special somebody, Krishna, is presented as the distinct Supreme Spirit.

Shankara presented an *atma* which is supposed to be superior to its intellect, where that *atma* does not participate in activities which are indulged by the intellect. The view of the Bhagavad Gita, that there is a limited self in each psyche, an *atma*, and another resident with it, is the Supreme Self, the *paramatma*, who detachedly looks at the involved limited self, is rejected by Shankara, who practically laughed Mandana Mishra out of the debate.

It was a low but effective punch by Shankara, who shamed Mandana into becoming Shankara's disciple. But the Bhagavad Gita which Shankara twisted into his submission, does not present a self and an intellect as a detached observer and an involved entity.

Gita gives us three realities beginning with the intellect, then the *atma* affected self and the *paramatma* unaffected supreme self. These three, not two, reside in the individual psyche, but with the *atma* affected self indulging, because it does not have the power to resist the allurements which are displayed by the intellect, and there exists side by side but in a different dimension, the *paramatma* unaffected supreme self who notices what the *atma* limited person is subjected to, but who remains segregated from the conundrums of the intellect which influences the limited person.

The great farce of Shankara is to suggest that the *atma* self is not affected by the shenanigans of the intellect, when in fact that is the very reason for the self's aspiration for liberation.

Waste Removal

Suppose, because of the elderly condition of the body, the muscular apparatus which transports the waste through the colon into the rectum malfunctions permanently. What should the yogi do?

How does one check to know if the waste quietly lingers in the lower colon and rectum?

If the muscular system no longer operates as it did in the youth of the body, what should the yogi do to remove the waste daily?

These are some considerations for a hatha yogi. In so far as the lack of removal of waste affects the consciousness experienced in the body, it is essential for the yogi to address these issues.

Kundalini Yoga / Pranayama Breath Infusion

Even though they are intimately related, kundalini yoga is different to the *pranayama* breath infusion practice. There are many methods of breath infusion with various focus. Hence, when one inquires about methods and their effects, one should ask someone who is versed in the particular practice of interest. No assumption should be made because each yogi may have a different method which cannot be figured merely by observing the physical part of the practice.

It is the same with *asana* postures, where when doing a posture, the outer appearance of two yogis may appear to be exactly the same, while in fact the mental and emotional processes within the psyche, are varied and may not be related.

Students usually want to get to the basic practice as soon as they can. This sets them in an attitude to harass a teacher for methods which are not displayed to physical senses, and which cannot be adopted unless detailed instructions are given. But even then, the factor of motive comes into play, where if one has a different motive, one cannot do a practice in exactly the same way as the teacher. The motive handles the result developed by anyone's practice.

There are two divisions of *pranayama* breath infusion. These are
- enrichment by increasing fresh air in the body
- enrichment by increasing used air in the body

These are broad titles for practice. According to the motive of the student he/she will practice one, or the other, or both. But these too, depend on motive which is culled from, and produced by, one's evolutionary status. This cannot be forced because it is regulated according to the previous births of the person, events which already happened and which cannot be adjusted at this moment.

Whatever one does now, will twist to produce a certain effect, that curls for an event in the future. One cannot force it to produce something else.

Kundalini yoga has many methods. Breath infusion is similar. Some persons raise kundalini merely by dancing. Some others by taking natural or man-made chemicals. Some merely by mentally enhancing their feelings. Some by shaking parts of the body. Some by becoming sexually aroused. Breath infusion is only one of the methods.

Even though breath infusion is a reliable method, still eventually a student should study what breath infusion does in terms of how it surcharges the subtle body, as well as its effects in the physical system. Then one can realize that breath infusion is a system all by itself, which can be used to accelerate kundalini yoga, and simultaneously surcharge the subtle body, irrespective of its effects on kundalini.

The value of estimating the effects on the subtle body, is that the student can prepare for a healthy upgraded subtle body, when the physical system is no longer responsive to one's willpower.

Rectum Worn-out

At the age of seventy-one (71), I report that from the age of sixty (60), the operation of the rectum was greatly hampered because of cell malfunction. If there was a biological warranty for the rectum, it was for fifty (50) years only, after which the warranty was void. Nowadays if one can pay for it in one way or the other, one may pay a surgeon to replace it with one from a recently deceased human or perhaps a pig, or even by cell replication.

Three functions of the rectum which concern its malfunction are

- wall lubrication
- muscular expulsion power
- wall sensitivity

When either of these malfunctions, the body is unable to evacuate itself efficiently.

The operation of the muscular cells which should convey the waste through the anus, is the obvious operation. The wall lubrication is not so easy to figure. In the first place most people have no idea about it. Usually, one understands the application of the downward compressing and pushing power.

If there is no wall lubricant in the rectum, then because the muscles are designed to operate with the assistance of the lubricant, the application of the muscles will not expel the waste.

But there is the aspect of touch sensitivity inside the rectum, where due to that knowledge, messages are sent to the brain when waste arrives from the colon and passes into the rectum. This sensitivity causes the brain to trigger the need for expulsion. If the sensitivity is lost, the impulse for expulsion will not be triggered, which will result in the waste arriving in the rectum, but with no information about the arrival reaching the brain.

That means that no attempt will be made by the person to reach a toilet. The waste will gather in the rectum and become compacted and dehydrated. These observations should be done by the yogi as part of the *hatha* yoga process.

Procrastination Enemy

Procrastination, which is the tendency to delay performing functions, is one of the most vicious and successful enemies of a yogi. Procrastination is also contagious, where it can move from the psyche of someone into a yogi, such that a yogi who does not have it as a habit, develops it by being in association with anyone who is habituated to it.

One dangerous *vritti* mental operation which Patanjali warned about, is memory. This function works in harmony with procrastination to defeat a yogi's objective. It makes a yogi into a hypocrite, where he/she pretends to be faithful, while in fact, he secretly cooperates with the delay tendency, which undermines the association he gets from the teacher.

There are so many students who do not adhere to the instruction of Patanjali in his second sutra, where he says that yoga means ceasing the *chittavritti* mento-emotional agitations in the mind. If one procrastinates, that is one way of undermining the process?

When something is to be done, when something should be promptly completed, when there is pleasure in the mind because one can delay a necessary action, at that time, there is an effort in the mind to store information about the delayed action. This storage is costly. The memory chamber logs the event, and creates a tag on it for future referral. The intellect notes that the action will not be committed immediately. To avoid negative consequences for the self, the intellect makes a deadline for when the action should be committed.

These psychological calculations cause mental and emotional inefficiency. That negatively impacts meditation because the intellect will have to interrupt a meditation session, and regular mental activity, to give alerts about the neglect of the action.

A yogi should not procrastinate. If possible, he should avoid associating with people who do. Procrastination is contagious. However, if one is unable to avoid someone who is habituated to it, one should be aware of the danger. It will negatively impact one's meditation. When one feels the influence of procrastination, one should promptly resist it by committing the action.

A yogi should implement methods for daily checking the rectum. One should do whatever is sensible to assist this organ as it becomes more and more unable to carry out the function of evacuation.

This is important because the accumulation of waste requires bio-electric power to be used for the maintenance of the waste in the body. The energy used for this will cause a reduction in the energy one has in the subtle body. That will cause a lower state of consciousness both in the waking and sleeping states.

Memory Failure

Alerts are given about memory failure, but these alerts appeared quietly and mildly in the psyche. Due to this the coreSelf misses the notation and acts as if it does not have to be concerned. The self thinks that the psyche will tend to the incidences as usual.

As the body reaches the elderly years from about fifty-five (55) years to its death, there is a reduction in memory capacity, such that the mind retains less impressions of events, and is less able to recall certain stored incidences.

One other observation is that some memories imprints are not stored in the psyche, such that a search for those events at a later time, results in finding no recall about them. This is called dementia.

A yogi can notice this happening in the body. He can notice that it occurs because of the deterioration of the brain, something that he cannot adjust but must succumb to.

One way out of this is to realize that the physical system, must by the law of nature, deteriorate. It is natural. One should not expect that it could be stopped. Another way to consider this, is to check to see if one can adjust one's assumptions, and learn to make notations of events in other ways. For instance, one can write of incidences, instead of being confidence that the mind will retain memory of them faithfully.

One may also consider if the incidences can be stored in the subtle body, rather than in the physical one. If it cannot, one may note it on the physical side, or make the decision not to store, and to release oneself from the need for recalling it in the future.

For instance, is it necessary to remember the characteristics of one's deceased father?

Memory failure is perplexing, and should be considered by a yogi. He should study what nature will support, and what it will refuse to allow one to recall.

What can one do with information about one's father, if it was stored in the subtle body? Can one use it hereafter in the astral world or when one assumes another physical form in the next body, somewhere somehow, where it is unlikely that one will again meet the father from this life?

Termination of Eating

A yogi should develop a diet schedule which is constant from day to day, except for exceptional occasions when it is necessary to honor circumstances which require eating at other times.

The main part of this is a daily time when the last meal is taken, where after that for that day, one eats no solid food. One may take water, or a beverage or milk, but not any solid foodstuff after the time for the last meal for that day.

If this develops, a yogi will find that there is a signal energy in the psyche, which gives a somewhat silent alert that one should cease solid food after a certain time each day. With this there will be a slight encouragement to break this regulation. This will feel as if it is permissible to eat again, and that there is no necessity for ceasing meals at a certain time.

When a yogi makes progress with this, it will help him/her to develop resistance to physical eating, so that hereafter the tendency for rebirth, just to have a physical body to eat physical foodstuff, will be removed from the psyche. The need for sex, and the need for physical food, are two of the many impediments, which may prevent a yogi from being satisfied with subtle existence hereafter. Hence their regulation and control are necessary.

Guru Now / Guru Then

My astral body went to a location which was formed by Kirtanananda Swami in the astral existence. He was the guru of the place. It was designed to his specification.

At first, I noticed that he created and conducted some religious hymns but none of these were the *Hare Krishna* chants which his guru, Swami Prabhupada, introduced while that swami was physical.

For persons like Kirtanananda there always will be music and singing. That is necessary in establishing and continuing a religious establishment. Kirtanananda had a *goshala* cow pen as well, something which Bhaktivedanta introduce, and which Kirtanananda loved to have.

He was in the process of building temple buildings, and large accommodations, just as he did at New Vrindavan in West Virginia. I met some persons there, whom I have not seen in over thirty years. These were senior people at the New Vrindavan place. Some are already deceased. Some use elderly bodies at this time.

Even though Swami Bhaktivedanta did not instruction Kirtanananda to produce this location in the astral existence, Kirtanananda attracted the other followers to this place. Recognizing each other, I was greeted cordially.

At one time, Kirtanananda wanted to weld some metal pieces to extend the supports for the *goshala* cow shed. Someone read his mind and brought a gas cylinder. The gadget was ancient. It was difficult to get it lit. One of his devotees tried but could not cause the gas to ignite.

Just them Kirtanananda arrived to do a ceremony. He gathered everyone before his honored seat. He sang. Unfortunately, no one knew the words to the holy song. It was not about Krishna. It was not any of the Krishna chants Kirtanananda practically compelled people to sing, when he used his last body, and was an authority under the auspices of Swami Bhaktivedanta.

Kirtanananda sang the song even though no one could sing the refrain. He did not have copies of the words to hand out. He sang and then signaled to one of his devotees to bring a sheet of paper. That person did that, but still no one in the audience knew or saw the words. Kirtanananda, a self-confidence person, sang on.

Soon after that I left his place. I considered releasing this information of something which happened on the astral side on October 9, 2022. It gives some idea of the activities of a departed religious leader.

Rebirth Pressure Point

Even though it appears that sexual pleasure is the highlight of physical existence, on close inspection, one will find that the actual highlight is the rebirth tube. That is a passage, a psychic route which runs from its entry vortex to its next potential entry vortex, such that on and on, as soon as a coreSelf successfully goes through the entry, it seeks to be flushed down the passage to the next entry.

Stated simply, once a coreSelf acquires a successfully opportunity for an embryo, that self will expect to go on the tour through the successful birthing of the embryo, to the development of the body through infancy and youth, then to adulthood and senior years, only to again seek a new entry vortex.

The self does not have a choice in this system. It is irresistibly attracted to this loop just as electrons in a wire are compelled to move when they are subjected to the influence of a magnet in an armature.

There is so much hype about the greatness of a coreSelf. Most of this conversation is such bragging, that it is not worth the consideration. It is best to carefully study the rebirth loop, and come to understand one's submission to it.

This life can be reduced to the loop of one rebirth after another. It is captivating. If one is attracted to another person sexually, that may seem to be a powerful impetus for a relationship, but an increase in electricity in a certain part of a circuit, does not mean that another component will not appear to be the most attractive factor at a later time.

It depends on where one is in the rebirth loop, as to who one will be attracted to, based on what one requires at that time, or on what force in the loop one is near to, and what opportunity one is compelled to indulge in at that time.

Other than the main entry, there are also compelling forces, which come from the environment. Through out the travel from one birthed body to another, one is pulled by the sexual transit energy. Other forces operate just the same, so that one seeks and relies on other relationships, with other persons at other times, with the sexual transit energy being superimposed or reduced.

Rebirth! Rebirth! Rebirth!

It is compelling. It is greater than sexual pleasure. It is the danger.

Romantic Notions Haunt a Yogi

On October 16, 2022, I trimmed some twigs from some ornamental plants. A deceased woman I used to know during the teen years of this body, arrived. She used a subtle body which was as bright and transparent as sunlight. If she stood before a human being, that human could not see her, because of the lack of contrast between the energy radiance of her body and that of the sun orb.

This is a person who was the age of my mother during my teen years. Recently within the past four years, I saw this person astrally about once every four months. Usually, we discuss events which took place around the year 1967. At that time, I was sixteen years of age. She had a daughter who was about fifteen years of age, a girl to whom I was attracted. In retrospect analyzing the energy of the time, it was a sexual attraction in part, and a friendly attraction in part. The thrust and force of the attraction, was that of the ancestors who lived in my body, and those in hers, in the daughter's.

Since that time, I have not seen this person, the daughter, but I heard some information about her from a friend who remained in contact with her through the years.

Anyway, this girl's mother, the lady who is now deceased, and who has a sunlight body, comes to speak regularly, at least every four months or so. It is still not clear as to how she can find my subtle body so easily but that is something which should not confuse anyone. The astral bodies have nature psychic powers which are baffling, when compared to a physical form.

When this sunlight lady arrived, she greeted me and immediately said this, "We could easily live together, you and me. We are compatible. Just as you tend plants, we could live doing that and other things, living a peaceful agreeable life. But that other woman should have no idea of this."

It is interesting that even when using a sunlight astral body, one can have cruel or hostile energy for some other person. People have asked me about similar incidences which were narrated in the *Mahabharata*, where in some heavenly world, someone develops a tension with some other person, which results in birth on earth to resolve the issue.

Just as she said the last sentence, about a person whom she addressed as that other woman, she began to transport my astral body to a place, where she felt we could live together, with no one knowing where we were. That effort failed. My astral form had a drag force because of how it was connected to my physical form.

I wanted to say something to her about her desire but I did not. I remembered a rule about the astral domains, that one should not say anything disagreeable to anyone while on the astral side.

I did speak however. I said this, "You cannot be sure that agreeableness in a romantic relationship will not flip to something which is undesirable. Even on earth we know that some relationships begin in a huff and a puff, with everything ready and set to go. Then something happens. There is an event or a mood. The situation of affection crashes. The partners then dislike each other, or one will remain attached, while the other will be callously detached.

"And conversely some relationships may begin on a bad note, like the case where one is born in a culture where one's parents pick the spouse for one. Then even though one had no say in the selection, and even though one knew nothing about the spouse-to-be, still, the relationship which began in cold romantic terms become bright, and was a source of fulfillment and fondness.

"How can we be sure that our romance will not flip."

After I said that, she looked at me with a curious expression. She thought, "There is always some wit and wisdom with you. I will get used to it."

It is interesting how this sunlight woman cut her daughter out of this, and did not want her friend to have any idea, that she was attracted in this romantic way.

Sexuality in Yoga

For some reason, it flashed in my mind, an incidence which happened some twenty or more years ago, when I was in Guyana. I was invited to a Diwali festival ceremony at a temple in Georgetown. At such functions there are usually only devout Hindus. It was unusual to be invited because I use a black body which was not caste assigned at its birth.

However, I got there before the ceremony began. I knew that if I arrived after, it would be awkward. Persons sitting in the audience would notice that I disrespected the schedule. When I got there, I was escorted to a row of seats which were reserved for specially invited guests. We were to sit there until just before the ceremony would commence, after which we were directed to sit near the central ceremony.

Suddenly I noticed an elderly lady approaching. I recognized who she was, but I did not feel that she would come directly to me. This she did. She smiled and said this, "Interlock every button especially the one at the top of the *kurta* (shirt)." I greeted her respectfully because she was the mother of an important *pandit* priest. She was highly respected for being born in a brahmin caste family.

I did as she instructed. There was also a mental energy which she radiated which was this,

"If the top buttons are not sealed, it would be a sexual invitation to certain females. That would be inappropriate at this place. Be sensitive to the way others view you. A saintly person *(sadhu)* cannot afford such mistakes."

Recently I remembered this twice. I know for sure that I would see this lady later in some heavenly world hereafter. At the time, I would thank her for the advice which I follow when attending similar ceremonies. Sometimes when students come for instruction, I may give an advice regarding the garments worn but over all I try not to get involved in such correction. Some students resent being instructed in that way, especially if the instruction may curtail their fashionable lifestyle.

Once when I instructed a student, he pitied my situation of having grey hairs. He felt that I could be pardoned because of having an elderly body. A yogi should be careful to reduce sexual attraction as much as possible. Once a sexual attraction is triggered for whatever reason, it is almost impossible to safely manage it. That is costly in time and energy for any serious ascetic.

Yogi Suckling a Breast

Once when doing breath infusion practice, a lady who is deceased but who does *pranayama* breath infusion and meditation *(samyama)* approached. She was there for just a split-second. When she vanished, I looked to see what force influenced her astral body. It was an elderly yogi who is a proficient teacher of meditation on the astral planes.

He called the lady. When she arrived where he was, which took only a moment, he assumed a childlike appearance like a six-month-old infant. She picked him up and placed him on her lap. He suckled her breast.

I recognized this great yogi because I take instruction from him from time to time. Using mind information transfer, without speech, I communicated to him like this,

"How is it that a great yogi of your proficiency, desires to suckle a woman? Why this?"

He replied with this,

"When I was an infant in my last body and in other bodies as well, I could not objectify myself to understand the suckling impulse. So much of one's life goes by with no integration of the actions and experiences.

"There is also the situation where if one has sexual access with a woman, one may indulge with her breast but usually it does not yield milk. If it does, which means that she was recently birthing a child, even then, one cannot access the energy as an infant would. One may understand the sexual experience of it, but not the nourishment feature.

"There is a need to know these experiences in their unmixed formats so that one can access what causes them, and how to utilize them without being damaged in the process. Why is it your concern if I suck a woman's breast? It is none of your concern. Continue your practice. Be astute to your behavior. Ignore others even other teachers, regarding what they do for studying the interactions in this existence."

Shoulder Kundalini Shattering

This is a shoulder connect to neck-base kundalini shattering. It is bright shining with jingling globules.

Taste Dominance

The sense of taste is a quiet but dominant influence in the body. It is supposed to assist the nutrition process, but instead it dominates and usurps the mission of the nutrition process, causing the body to overeat the correct diet, and gorge the wrong foods.

Due to the unity between the sense of taste and the nutrition need, the coreSelf has difficulty controlling diet regarding what to eat, and when to cease eating, on a daily basis. A yogi must sort the two functions, so that he can differentiate the call for food from the nutrition center, as contrasted to the call for tasting by the sense of taste.

If the yogi experiences these two functions as one urge, that means that he will overeat the correct food, and will ingest into the body unwanted foods because of a need to taste those products.

This tasting feature must be curbed so that the sense of taste only request tasting when the nutrition feature ask for food. Because the tasting sense is tyrannical, it cannot be trusted for making decisions about diet. It should only be involved in tasting as requested by the nutritional function. It should not be tasting just for tasting sake, for enjoying through the tasting organs in the mouth.

A yogi must split the joint energy of the sense of taste and the nutrition center. Then he will recognize when the sense of taste independently pressures the system to eat. This will give the yogi, the authority to rigidly control the tasting sense. That will result in freedom from overeating the correct foods. It will yield the power to cease the urge to eat just for the sake of tasting.

Yogi as Astral Baby

A yogi, I know, who lives on the astral side only, has a place where he continues the yoga practice. Sometimes students go there to get instruction. Most of them are there because they do not want to get into the loop for rebirth.

One day when I was to do breath infusion on the physical side, I noticed that a lady at that ashram, put a child on a cushion. She was aware that I would do the practice. She wanted to join the session.

I decided to question her about the baby, because on the astral side one rarely sees infants the size of babies. She replied like this, "It is the honored guruji. He requested that I should suckle him as a child."

Hearing this, I smiled. Sometime ago this yogi spoke to me about the suckling urge in the psyche, as to the secrets behind it. I told him that from my research it is an integral, built-in part of the psyche. At the time, we did not discuss the removal of it, nor how it influences anyone for rebirth.

After the session of exercises, the yogini left. Then, this guruji approached but in his young adult astral body. I confronted him. I said, "Why do that? What is the purpose? Sucking a woman's breast? What is written about encouraging that in the yoga text. There is a chance that you will take a body if you do this. What is your intention?"

He replied like this, "As you said before, that nutrition need is packaged in the psyche. I study what it is and how it operates. It is compulsive and involuntary. No one can stop it when it expresses itself as a need. Once it is triggered it runs a course of events. But besides that, I am studying it to discover a way to avoid its influence for rebirth.

"A yogi has to suckle a woman to understand it. One can contend that a yogi suckled in many previous births, even as births in animal bodies. Therefore, what is the need to suckle an astral woman?

"Theory is one way. Practice, real-life circumstance, may not confirm to that. Even though a yogi did this suckling in previous infant bodies, still he does not understand it. As an infant, one does not have the resource to research and be objective to it in the infant body. There is no impulse for understanding it there.

"I can study it now because the infant astral body has that ability which was missing in physical infant forms. Ultimately, it is no one's concern if I suckle the yogini or not. However, I study this feature because the tendency for it, is a dominant cause for rebirth."

Yogi Dress Code

What to wear if one does yoga practice?

Usually, I do not make suggestions on how someone should attire. I expect that an ascetic will dress as he/she likes. If during the practice, one finds that the garments are not suitable, one should change them. The idea for everything having to do with lifestyle, is to change anything which does not facilitate practice. Or change what once facilitated practice but which no longer does so, and is found to be obstructive.

The idea from the Vedic literature is for simple clothing. When we see drawings of Shiva for instance, the only garment is a loin cloth. When we see drawings of Vishnu, we see that he uses a dhoti and shawl. One can assume that there is a loin cloth under the dhoti. Shiva however is known to live in isolated regions like the cold uninhabitable Himalayan peaks. Vishnu is with a goddess, Lakshmi.

Hardly is Shiva described as a ruler, but Vishnu frequently is described as such. Some stories of ascetics list naked ones. For instance, the four Kumaras, some masterful yogis, wear no clothing. Their bodies remain in the boy state before puberty. They have no carnal knowledge or experience of sexual arousal. This means that they have no idea about using genitals for copulation or self-pleasure.

Even today some indigenous people go about naked or near naked, but we see that when they depart the jungle, and live in cities with the modern way of life, they clothe their bodies in the way which is acceptable. In some places appearing nude or near nude in public, could lead to being arrested for indecent exposure. This suggest that as humans shifted from clan life in jungles to citizen life with modern conveniences, it seemed that being nude in public was unacceptable.

For the matter of garment cleanliness, if a yogi lives in isolation, and is alone, or is with a few like-minded ascetics, he can do as he likes according to how garments augment his practice. He can even stop bathing. There are stories of isolated ascetics who ceased that for a time and it did not negatively impact their practice. However, if the yogi is not alone nor is isolated with other ascetics, the idea of not bathing may be a hinderance to the yoga practice. Others may object to it. The yogi will have to deal with that criticism.

As for clothing, if the yogi's garment is objected by others, then why should he not comply to clean the body and clothing daily. If a yogi lives in society, he benefits from that in some way. This means that he should compromise in return.

For years, I practiced the daily cleaning of clothing but there was a time when I was in Mississippi when I used a hamper for used clothing so that when the hamper filled, I machine washed the garments. This was a small hamper so that in two or three days the clothing was cleaned. In addition, the hamper was in an out-building and was not in the main residence. The odor from it was not in the residence. Even mentally, the vibration from it was in the out-building.

My opinion is that a yogi, even if he is in isolation, should wash his clothing daily. This should be done just after he takes daily bath. He should be near a fresh water source. If he is near salt water only, soap will be neutralized making it impossible to have clean clothing. A yogi should not under any circumstance feel that uncleanliness is satisfactory. It is not.

How will one go to higher dimension where the supernatural people live if one becomes accustomed to unclean body and garments? That is not sensible. It is suggested that cleanliness is next to godliness. Actually, cleanliness is listed by Krishna as one of the qualities of a brahmin. In addition, if a yogi has forms or images of a deity, uncleanliness may cause the yogi to go to a hellish place hereafter. That would be, because of subjecting the deity to an unclean place. Yogis who have deities walk a thin line, and are liable to hurt themselves, because of having no understanding about the restrictions in place, when deities are invoked.

शमो दमस्तपः शौचं

क्षान्तिरार्जवमेव च ।

ज्ञानं विज्ञानमास्तिक्यं

ब्रह्मकर्म स्वभावजम् ॥ १८.४२ ॥

śamo damastapaḥ śaucaṁ
kṣāntirārjavameva ca
jñānaṁ vijñānamāstikyaṁ
brahmakarma svabhāvajam (18.42)

śamo = śamaḥ — tranquility; damaḥ — restraint; tapaḥ — austerity; śaucaṁ— cleanliness; kṣāntiḥ — patience; ārjavam — straightforwardness; eva — indeed; ca — and; jñānaṁ — knowledge: vijñānaṁ — discrimination; āstikyaṁ — a belief in God; brahmakarma — work of a priestly teacher; svabhāvajam — based on natural tendencies

Tranquility, restraint, austerity, cleanliness, patience, straightforwardness, knowledge, discrimination and a belief in God, are the work of a priestly teacher based on his natural tendencies. (18.42)

Many yogis have deities, and think that it does not matter if the place, nor bodies in the vicinity, are cleaned. These yogis are ignorant, and think that they can use supernatural beings, without following the rules for Deity Worship. For such yogis it is okay to live like an animal if the deity worshipped requires animalistic habits to be used. Like for instance when using deities of Kālī or Bhairava which requires lower offerings.

If possible, a yogi should not keep a hamper of dirty clothing. I did that as described above, but it does not mean that because I said the sun set in the East, that it actually did so. It did not. My keeping a hamper does not make it acceptable. And I was particular while doing that to know that it was not. I kept it to a minimum.

When I was in Guyana doing austerities during two periods of my life, I took bath in the afternoon, then before I left the bath area, I soaped, scrubbed, washed, and hung the clothes I worn for that day. There was no washing machine. This was done manually. This is the ideal way.

If one keeps used clothing for a while, one is also saying to oneself that uncleanliness is acceptable. The unclean or worn clothing carry a negative vibration. These are more difficult to clean because the pollution of sweat, skin debris and anything else in the fabric will emit odor. That will increase day by day. That is not good for a yogi who has aspirations for transfer to heavenly places.

In cases where a yogi became successful doing austerities, where he ceased bathing, or where he wore no clothing, that person transferred or was transferred from his physical body consciousness. His mind was completely removed from the physical level. He was no longer participating on this side of existence. That is a different achievement. It is not that such a yogi wore no clothes, or wore the least clothes, and took no bath, and also lived in society. What happened is that he successfully extracted his consciousness from the physical body. He lost track of its condition.

A good example of this is Buddha. But another example was the criminal yogi, Hiranyakashipu, where he extracted so much of his consciousness from the physical body, that ants eat his body except for the bones. They made an ant hill using the bones as the framing. Such a condition however is not the same for a modern yogi. Recently we heard of no yogi, extracting consciousness so completely.

nilaGanga

On November 6, 2022, I saw Swami Shivananda at Yogeswarananda's ashram. He happened to be there when *nilaGanga* Yogini was present. She is deceased. Seeing her and sensing that I knew her previously, he mentally said this, "This lady is like a blue-black Ganges. She is a parallel to *anuGanga*. Give her the title of *nilaGanga*.

After this he expressed a desire to find a mother on the physical side. There was no sexual interest in the energy but in any case, for that to happen, there must be some sexual expression, at least in the likely parents.

I did not question him about what happened from he left his body so long ago. However, there was a gap in his psyche which allowed me to check it. After not having that physical body when he was a recognized guru in India, in the astral world, he completed the remaining yoga practice required for entering long samadhi trance states. He was in that phase of existence for many years. Now suddenly he resumed a subtle existence in a subtle body which looked youthful and which was filled with a hazy white light.

Feet / Elderly Yogis

The feet will give trouble to elderly yogis, just as they do to elderly persons who do no yoga. I noticed that as some yogis endure the elderly years, their *hatha* yoga practice consisting of *asana* postures and *pranayama* breath infusion becomes reduced. In fact, some elderly yogis are encouraged to relax and not practice, except for doing meditation, and entering trance consciousness phase-outs.

The image below is supposed to be the feet of a yogi who lived 125+ years. He may or may not be alive today. The point is that there are signs of decay. There is surely a look of not getting fresh blood circulation. These indicate arthritis and osteoporosis.

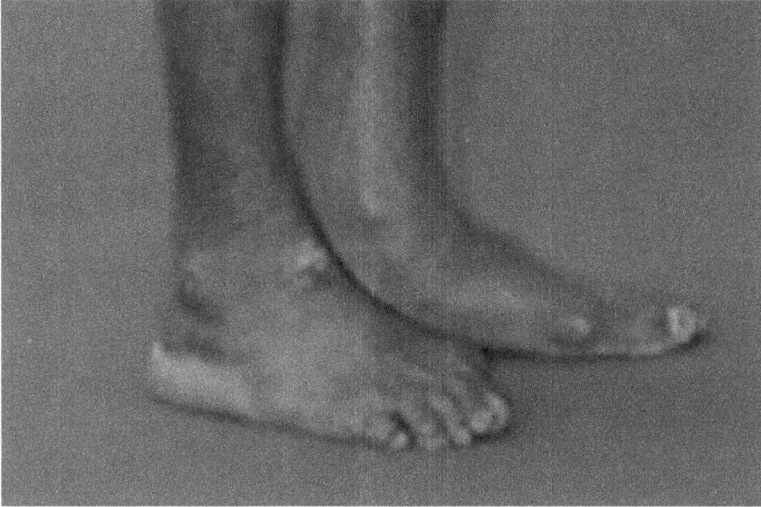

A yogi should not be superstitious where he/she feels that due to doing *asana* postures, the body will not deteriorate as the years proceed. It certainly will. Hence one should do the best at caring it. The toes are the most extreme places in the body. They are like a dead-end junction at Land's End. Whatever goes there must either turn back or park as is.

The problems arise when the transportation gates, which allow polluted blood to return to the lung for poisonous gas expulsion, no longer operate in an efficient way. Some valves no long hold the polluted blood which is pumped above them. The result is that this polluted liquid falls back to the toes which eventually become gangrene and infected.

It begs the question:

What can yoga not do for an aged body? Are the claims about yoga, mostly hype?

Compassion's Other Side

Some time recently, I met a lady on the psychic side. This is someone I used to know but whom I did not see recently. This person has a spiritual practice. In an astral conversation, she said this, "This person, a woman, asked me to be her parent. I wondered what your view is about this. If anything, if it was possible, I would do it if you were the father of the child."

I replied, "How would that be possible. The age of my body makes it near impossible. As for yourself, age is also against a wish like that. Or is it that you are considering rebirth, not just yours but mine, as well. What is the idea? I take birth. You take birth at approximately the same time. We fall in love. Then we have this person as our child.

"That is risky. In the meantime, until we could achieve that, and it is a tall order to request from Cruel Fate, this woman who is deceased, would have to wait on the astral planes, and greatly restricted her associations. Otherwise, she will be drawn into being an embryo for another mother and father.

"Compassion?

"It is not a trustworthy influence. It should be checked closely."

After this the person who made the request for the body, shifted from the scene. She did not use a form that resembled a body. She was in a form which was like a five-foot long sixteen-inch-diameter colorful mineral which had streaks of blue, brown, white, yellow, and crimson.

Taste Orb

I met an advanced yogi in the astral world. He was in the process of curbing the taste orb. This feature of the subtle body is very difficult to control. It evades the willpower grip of the yogi. It acts as something which is slippery, difficult to grasp.

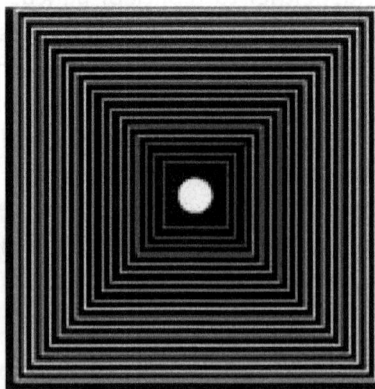

This yogi showed that it was located in the central mouth in a tunnel. Even if a yogi eliminates this orb or makes it disappear by some method, it again appears magically. It continues functioning the way it did previously. For some reason this orb is reinstalled in the subtle body each time it is eliminated by the yogi. The only way to avoid its influence is to satisfy its justifiable needs, or to transit to a higher dimension where in the subtle body, it is absent.

Sexual Issues on the Astral Side

I was at Yogeshwarananda's place on the astral side, when I heard two yoginis discussing a monk who goes there now again. One yogini said this, "It is not known but he loves me more than he does anyone else."

Then the second lady replied, "Why are you saying this? How can you estimate the degree of his love for you as compared to his affection and concern for any other person?"

The first lady defended her view like this.

"I know what I know. Have you ever seen the way he looks at me with such eagerness. What do you think would happen if he was not a monk? Obviously, we would have sex. And if we were in the physical world, there would be children as a result. What do you think? You feel that I miscalculate this. Actually, even though you are female, you do not know the particulars of love.

"It is a totally different energy. But in any case, what I said was for your ears only. Others would fall apart if they caught wind of it. Keep it secret. But do not worry. You have my word that it will not convert into sex."

At this point in the conversation, I looked at the yoginis. They understood that I heard the conversation, and I would not repeat it except for teaching purposes, when their names would not be mentioned, either on the astral or physical sides of existence.

Anxiety Hell Hereafter

On November 27, 2022, I was in an astral place where there was constant ongoing anxiety about floods. This is a place for permanent residents who are anxiety prone, in reference to flooding. Say for instance people who live in the Mekong delta, or persons who reside in Bangladesh, in areas which are habitually flooded, due to seasonal weather of intense rapid rainfall.

If while living on earth, one becomes habituated to a certain anxiety, it is likely that hereafter one will reside in a place where one is in constant, day in day out, anxiety in relation to the same natural, or unnatural phenomena.

In that place the people expected a flood and waited for it for many days. Finally, the flood came. It destroyed their residences and roads. Then it receded. They quickly built their places again in a matter of moments. They had a mystic ability to do this. Then they sat. They worried that the rains would again come. The flooding would resume.

There were only mud/clay roads and wooden houses. There were no automobiles. There was no idea that one needed to eat. One's attention was focused on thinking of the impending flood. All houses were elevated on posts to protect from ground floor flooding. There were exterior stairs, where women sat waiting for the flood to arrive, thinking about it on and on. This is a hereafter place for those who have a particular anxiety about a natural disaster which recurs unexpectedly.

Silent Reactive Mental Actions

There are many silent reactive mental actions committed in the psyche from day to day, almost continuously, with very few pauses where the mind is silent, and does not emit responses to whatever it detects, either in the physical or psychic environment.

Most of these are irresponsible expressions which will bring negative consequences. However, the coreSelf rarely detects, tracks, analyses, and assesses these, as being dangerous to its wellbeing.

The kundalini lifeForce and the intellect are ever operating, to express responses to whatever the self is subjected to, by the in-sucking actions of the senses. By constant practice of the *ashtanga* eighth staged yoga process of Patanjali, especially in the higher practices of *pratyahar* sensual energy withdrawal and *dharana* inFocus, the yogi gets clarity, where he/she can see what occurs in the mind, where he/she does not self-identify as the doer of everything that happens in the psyche.

Decisions made in the mind may be thoughts of someone other than the coreSelf, where those decisions convert into subtle indulging suggestions for certain actions, which if sanctioned by the core, will bring unwanted consequences, where the self will be forced into future circumstances, where it can become involved in instances, which are not to its liking.

The insensitivity of the coreSelf, where it cannot determine which thoughts are authored by it, and which are authored either by tenants in its psyche, or by non-tenants who project thoughts into the psyche, is costly to the self. The self is held responsible for those psychic actions, and for any physical ones, which occur as a result. This could mean having to assume an embryo in the future, and living through a lifespan in the new body.

Tenants are people who live in the psyche of a yogi, either in the mind part of the subtle body, or in any other sector. These silent entities are not silent in the least, but a coreSelf may experience their presence as an absence, where that core greedily assumes that whatever occurs in its mind, as an opinion or feeling, is its energy and should be acted on urgently.

Sometimes when a yogi is in a circumstance, an opinion is given by someone in the physical environment. Then, one or more silent tenants who live in the psyche of the yogi, may express an opinion, and desire that a view be expressed physically, as an objection or assertion in response to what someone else said.

The yogi, if he/she is not alert, and does not identity the idea as being that of someone else who resides in the subtle body, may render that opinion physically. That is how the yogi becomes responsible for the concepts of others.

If, however, the yogi recognized that a tenant in his subtle body, expressed that idea, he/she may resist expressing that view, and save the self from having to interact further, and from having to indulge with that person, somewhere else at some other time or during the event. This further isolates the yogi, and screens him/her from unwanted whimsical events, and the people who indulge there.

It is an achievement when a yogi learns to avoid or ignore influences from other physical people. It is a greater feat when he/she recognizes, and avoids the view of tenants in the psyche, people who live in the mind of the yogi, who have a right to reside there, but whose influence should be resisted, and carefully tagged from moment to moment. Having to live with others in the psyche, is reason for resisting their views, especially when those opinions may result in having to take rebirth, or having to indulge mentally in ideas which are of no spiritual benefit, and which deter the yogi in spiritual progression.

Part 3

Naad Link

Yogeshwarananda instructed that I explain what he termed as the naad link. He said this, "Even though the tendency is to focus visually is a practice in its own right, for the greater part, that is based on the addiction to the visual sense. Humans have that addiction. In some animal species, the predominant sense is the one of smell. One can observe how a cow is dominated by the smelling sense. It will not eat a vegetation if its nose does not recognize the grass as edible. Even if it is edible, still, if the nose does not give a favorable opinion, the cow will reject it. That applies even if it is starving."

"In humans it is the visual sense which is predominant. Due to that an ascetic may be addicted to, and preferential to, seeing psychic or divine lights. I wrote a book about my experiences with this. However, one should consider that it is easy to reach naad sound resonance. From getting access to naad, one can slip to the visual field and focus there. Naad can assist with the quest for psychic or divine lights.

"First the yogi should become anchored to naad resonance during meditation. He should observe how he shifts from it, and is positioned to resume normal random thought sequences in meditation. After some years of practice, a yogi may get an understanding of how his mind works, so that when he is stationed listening to naad, either by being in it, or by being near to it, he can observe how he finds the core to have shifted from naad, and to be viewing something else, somewhere else in the mindspace."

"After mastering this observation, one will find that during some sessions of meditation, there is no shift from naad, while in some others there are frequent shifts. One yogi may control the core to make it remain absorbed in naad. Because of a weak willpower, another yogi may not have the control."

"When the core finds that it is easy to remain in, or focused towards naad, it should study the hearing sense, as to how that sense is aware of, and becomes fused to naad. When this happens, the core should remain stationary in the mindspace. Being absorbed in naad, it should check the visual sense. Usually when this is done, the ascetic will realize that the visual sense is closed. It is as if it is non-operative. It will be as if the self is in a closed container such that it cannot see an environment. The self should then open the two psychic eyes.

"This action may cause the appearance of a space which has indistinct lights in the distance. There may be a general glow of light in every direction. That is focus on inner light meditation."

Memory Helper in Psyche

In a discussion, I tried to recall the name of a building but could not. After some seven minutes, a psychic boy of the age of eleven, handed me an impression, which was the forgotten name. He was a person who lived in my psyche.

When I could not recall, he dove through the neck of the subtle body into the chest. He thumbed through the packed memory files until he found a particular incidence, which had the name of the building.

One does not live alone in the psyche but one hardly realizes this. Even though usually one takes credit for whatever happens in the container of the self, others serve as well. It is just that one has limited objectivity, and does not perceive the subtle activity clearly.

Miniature Inhabitants

There are miniature persons in the psyche. These may be as small as half inch in height. These have full intelligence just as someone would, who has what we consider to be a normal human body. Sometimes during meditation, one may see one of these persons somewhere in the subtle body.

Once during a meditation, a yogini appeared. When I noticed this, she assumed a miniature size. She descended through the psyche to the bottom of it. Her form was only half-inch. There was no verbal communication but there was chakra bridge or linking which occurred in split seconds, rapidly. This type of relationship is involuntary. The yogi does not make a decision for it. It occurs with such rapidity that he/she may not influence it.

Some experiences like this occur in a flash, so quickly that if one has no keen awareness, one will have no idea that this occurred.

Chakra bridging or linking is when the chakra from one subtle body links to that of another. This is mostly an electrical connection. It may be through space like when radio signals are passed through the air or through a wire. Some linking occurs through superimposition by the interspacing of one subtle form on the other, like for instance when in electrical circuits, a magnetic field from one component crosses that of another component, and has some effect.

Physical Body Part of Yoga

It is important in yoga, that the physical body be kept in tip-top shape. This may be interpreted as a cover for the desire to have a healthy human body for materialistic purposes. Like for example the yogi or yogini, who has a desire to be the most handsome, or most beautiful person in the world. It is a fact that many persons who do yoga, have an underlying reason which motivates practice, which is that *asana* postures and breath infusion methods will cause one to have an attractive body.

However, the reason for body fitness in yoga is to cause the subtle body to give less and less energy for the maintenance of a physical one. The point is that in monitoring the use of subtle energy by the physical system, a yogi notices that the more energy required by the physical body, the less one will be successful in meditation.

Excessive demands for energy by the physical system, stresses the subtle situation of the self, with the result that meditation is deterred. The progress is decelerated in real terms. The real problem however is that the person is fooled because of noticing that the physical system is healthier than before. He/She assumes this as spiritual advancement.

Take for instance the yoga practice of tracking the daily digestion and evacuation. As time goes by, the intestinal track and rectum become inefficient. There is slower movement of what is eaten, such that the daily termination of the digestive process occurs later than it did in the early years of the body, when the intestinal peristalsis movements were the best.

However, it is a fact that the alerts, which were given at the optimum stage of the body, are reduced. The self becomes more and more unaware of the digestive system, even more than it did before. Hence the time for transit for food, from the mouth to the anus, increases.

The yogi must note this, and do whatever is necessary to assist the involuntary actions, which slowed because of the age of the body. For instance, one should know that food eaten at a certain time, should be in the rectum, and cause a trigger for evacuation in a certain time. If the system does not give the expected alert, or if there is silent alert which is ignored, something should be done to complete the evacuation.

In the event that an attempt to evacuate results in no excretion, some action should be taken to cause the evacuation. What action? That must be decided by the ascetic. For as long as stool linkers in the rectum, or at the top valve of the rectum, this will be a deficit of energy for the subtle body. That will result in decreased psychic perception, which negatively impacts yoga.

There was an experience, where once there was no evacuation at the expected time, after some four hours, still there was no evacuation, even though attempts were made to excrete. To check physically, I used the properly pared middle finger of the left hand. First it should be the left hand because the right one should be reserved for cleaner tasks. This middle left finger should be pared of protruding nail. There should be no sharp edges. It should be pared and filed.

It should be lubricated with anti-bacterial cream. It should be made damp with germ free water. Then it should be inserted into the anus which is the lower valve of the rectum. There one should check for waste.

When I checked, I notice that the rectum was filled with waste. After, removing this waste with the left middle finger, I noticed that there was some waste, a smaller quantity above the rectum, in the lower end of the colon, above the valve which is at the connection of the colon and rectum. Thus, a small quantity of stool was shifted through the top valve by a muscular action. Then it was removed by the left middle finger.

To understand this, one must accept that the system of the stomach, intestines, colon, and rectum become inefficient as the body ages. The sensors in this food passage become insensitive. The alerts for evacuation from the nerves are given with less frequency. In fact, some alerts are not given. Where there are alerts, some may be so slight, that they are unnoticed.

A yogi should check this system and use methods to assist in the process. A youthful body can process certain foods efficiently, which the same body at an older age, cannot efficiently handle.

Because of the increase in digestion time, which is due to the slower transit of waste, there is dryer stool, which an older body is not equipped to expel without assistance.

A yogi may consider using a non-aggressive laxative, like senna or prune juice. This should be used to the minimum. There is a risk of infection or bruising, if a finger is used to extract waste from the rectum. To be sure that the finger nail does not cut or bruise the walls of the rectum, a finger condom (rubber glove), may be used, but it should be lubricated with antiseptic lubricant.

Light Access by Powerful Yogi

On December 14, 2022, Yogeshwarananda took control my subtle head. This was unusual because it was done in the astral existence, while I practiced with the physical body. It is possible to get yoga instructions, and to practice accordingly, after one is deprived of the use of the physical system. More and more, a yogi should transfer interest and association to the astral plane. Eventually one will be shifted there, regardless of whether one is prepared for that or not.

In the astral existence, suddenly Yogeshwaranand was high in the sky. I could not determine the distance. He was in another plane and was in a supernatural realm. I was in a cloud of energy which surrounded me on all side. He was outside of that in a sky which has sparkling light in all directions.

At first Yogesh was at a distance. Then, in an instant he was near. He did not enter the cloud of energy which enveloped me. Instead, he remained in the supernatural environment. He squeezed some of the cloud energy which was near my face. At that time a slit opened in the cloud energy. Then a star appeared where the cloud energy split.

Later, Yogeshwaranand said that for many disciples, it is difficult if not impossible for the teacher to elevate them. Even if the teacher is inclined to that, still the power required is great. Students fail, he said, because they are unable to challenge the adjuncts effectively.

Taste Dictatorship

Each morning for years now, to break the previous day's fast, I use one glass of water. This serves the purpose of washing the kidneys, where they can release harsh chemicals (urine) before the day's digestive activities.

There is one consistent experience which occurs morning after morning, which is that the sense of taste objects, or approves of the action. It analyses the taste, temperature, and texture. It gives approval, or files a complaint, and grumbles about it.

If it is in disapproval, regarding the flavor of the water, or the texture (feel) of it, or even its temperature, it will assume a disagreeable attitude. It releases a discouraging influence, with intentions to stop the intake. The tasting sense will corner the coreSelf to file a grievance. If it gets no satisfaction, it will attempt the hurt the core.

No consideration is given for the requirements of the stomach, or of any other gland, or organ, in the body. No regard is felt as to if some other organ is in need of the water. The sense of taste is a ruthless dictator, which only cares about its satisfaction, above everything else

Desires Continue Hereafter

Those who feel that desires are done, once someone passes from the body, are mistaken. The desire energy persists. I was in an astral place with a person who followed a Krishna devotional movement. He was disgraced when found guilty of having sexual relations with a male student, who was in his care in a boarding school.

This offending teacher was ostracized from the devotional sect some years ago. However, he maintained his confidence in the religious process of the sect. On the astral planes, he still visited temples and locations, where the deity of the sect was worshipped.

At one such place, he was summoned by a sannyasi leader, who was also rejected by the devotional sect. The teacher went there for an official ceremony, for the assumption of sannyasa, official full renunciation of every obligation, besides duties assigned by the religious institution. This is a coveted status for anyone in that society. Someone who is designated as a sannyasi is regarded as an authority.

Somehow because I knew these persons years ago, my subtle body was summoned there. After the teacher was awarded the status, he was presented with some clothing which signified his status. He immediately glanced my way to inform me that it was done, he reached the coveted status, which he longed for so many years ago. There was no chance of him getting it on the physical side of existence but he achieved it on the astral level.

At that time, I became aware of the fact, that somewhere else this new sannyasis had a child one month ago. Then from his energy there was a response which stated, "That does not matter. One who takes sannyasa is not obligated to anyone from the time prior, not even to a wife, not even to a child. I am only obligated to the sect and the leader. All previous obligations are void."

Yogi and Breasts

A yogini who is resident on occasion at Yogeshwarananda's astral ashram, one named, *NilaGanga*, met me astrally to complain about an advanced yogi who approached her with a request to suckle her breasts. I was a bit surprised that this yogi was interested in doing this, but I did not have a reply for the yogini, except to say, that I would query the yogi about it.

The problem with this type of request, is that the nurturing tendency is packed with the reproductive urge, which has an aggressive pleasure aspect in it. It is near impossible to sort the nurturing feature from the reproductive one. That urge also has two features, which are inexorably combined like the strands of a cord. At every part there is the wrapping, such that at no place will one find one strand, without the other. Any interference in one has effects on the other.

If a yogi makes contact with the nurturing tendency, if that is his singular interest, it will be dangerous for him, because nature does not recognize that tendency as being distinct, and apart from the reproductive urge, and its offshoot, the sexual pleasure.

Of course, we find that children may suckle their mothers with the nurturing feature remaining in isolation, without it invoking the reproduction feature, and the sexual pleasure spread. But it is also a fact that when an infant suckles its mother, that action may cause sexual arousal in the parent.

When I met the yogi in the astral existence. I questioned him about the yogini's complaint. He said that his only interest was the nurturing feature. His statement was that even though he reached an advanced level in yoga, still the need to be nurtured remained in his psyche. He claimed that the reproductive and sexual pleasure aspects are absent and there was no possibility that it would convert to the sexual urge.

I told him however that the yogini was offended by his request. Her opinion was that in her psyche, the breasts simultaneously feature the nurturing and erogenous zones. The two features are mixed to such a degree that an arousal of one, immediately causes a strike or urge of the other.

When I met the yogi again, I explained the situation. I give a suggestion that he should find another yogini who had the features isolated in her psyche, or one in which the sexual pleasure feature was absent. He did not like the idea. He replied like this, "I did search for someone. I could not find that type of female ascetic. The more important consideration is that I need to do it, to someone to whom I am attracted, as one would be attracted to a mother. Then I can study the need for nourishment in my psyche and get to the bottom of it."

At this point, I was stern with him. I said, "Do not approach this lady again. Find someone else. There is someone else. This person is a disagreeable. That must be respected."

Naad as Reference

On January 1, 2023, Yogeshwarananda said that I should again stress the importance of naad absorption in meditation. He claims that naad will convert into the reference, the steady anchor during deeper meditative states.

His situation was that when he used a physical body, he would sometimes steady the mind of a student. This allowed some adherents to develop confidence in the process, and to learn how to keep the mind from its innate habit, which is to drift from one topic of interest to another.

Even if at some stage, a guru helps with the mental instability which is natural, still the student must endeavor, or bring the mind into a stability, where steady focus on an objective can be attained. The last reference which is natural is the naad sound vibration which is heard in the head of the subtle body.

One should make the listening to naad, and the hearing of it, to be the objective. Later when naad becomes the addiction of the mind, then it can be used as the stable focus. When that is attained, one should, from the link to naad, or from being in the naad influence energy, focus on the objective, while keeping naad as the underbasis, the reference which is maintained.

No-Food Astral Zone

In preparation for being exempt from rebirth, Yogeshwarananda has a place on the astral side, where yogis/yoginis can become accustomed to not eating food, even psychic foodstuff.

At this place no food is prepared or served. Yogis who reside there feel no need for eating or tasting. The subtle body takes nourishment from the atmosphere of the place. There is energy exchange between the subtle energy in the body with the subtle energy in the psychic atmosphere there.

I discovered this place when I visited on January 10, 2023. At first, I was at the astral ashram of Yogeshwaranand, a place where yogis may go if he permits. The practice of yoga in terms of breath infusion or meditation can be continued with full focus while one lives there.

Someone whom I knew, who lived there, was absent. When I wanted to inquire as to why that person was missing, that person came from high above but in a sunlight body. Coming within fifty feet, that person beamed without speaking. The expression was that she transferred to another location where food was unnecessary.

Later Yogeshwarananda said this to me, "They practice to develop the resistance to the desire to eat. The subtle body should lose that tendency."

Evacuation Inefficiency

In *hatha* yoga practice there is a section dealing with digestion and evacuation, as to the efficient processing of food and food waste through the track which begins at the mouth and terminates at the anus. Of the various methods known, few consider evacuation efficiency to be important. For that matter, people who are obsessed with meditation, may not consider the condition of the stomach, intestines, colon, and rectum, to be significant. They feel that if the track malfunctions it has no significant impact on anything.

Even some famous gurus who mastered some *asana* postures when they had youthful bodies, abandoned the physical practice as soon as their reputations as great yogins became established. Especially in the elderly years, these teachers sat to meditate only. They did no postures nor breath infusion as they did early on.

To their view, it is not something to consider, and it has little relevance to *samadhi* absorption states, or to what one would attain hereafter. Some profess the infinite. Others, the oneness of whatever there is. Some advocate the heaven of a deity. Others speak about existential demolition. Some are aggressive about erasure of the personal self, which they earmark as a persistent, but bothersome shadow which trails the real.

For those ascetics who do *haṭha* yoga, malfunction of the stomach, intestines, colon, or rectum is an impediment. It negatively affects the practice. When there is an inefficiency in the operations of the physical body, the subtle form is affected, whereby there is decreased psychic perception, and reduced clarity for the yogi.

In addition, unless the yogi can scrap the subtle body, its condition causes positive or negative feedback to the core. The yogi should be sure that the physical body requires the least amount of subtle energy, so that the subtle form is highly energized, and does not have to give extra focus to the physical system.

As the physical body ages, it becomes more inclined to inefficiency in its operations. This means that it will take more energy from the subtle form for maintenance. A yogi must ledger this accounting, so that he can do whatever he can, to keep the energy expenditure of the physical body to a minimum.

If any part of the digestive and excretive functions become damaged, the physical body will act inefficiently into two ways.

- longer processing time
- decreased nerve sensitivity

A **longer processing time**, means that consciously or subconsciously, the yogi will be involved mentally with ideas, and opinions relating to the damage done, which caused the increase in application, of the attention to the cause.

Decreased nerve sensitivity will make it impossible, for the yogi to know what to do, to assist in the efficient transport of food and food waste. The lingering of the waste in the colon and rectum, will attract more consciousness to those areas of the body, resulting in constant thinking about the condition. This will steal time and focus energy, which should otherwise be invested in meditation practice.

There is a risk that the subtle body will run a parallel ailment, where the energy which surges through it, will be obstructed, causing a lower level of psychic force to flood the corresponding part of the psyche.

On the physical side, there will be constipation. Or there will be addiction, developed from the chronic use of laxatives, enemas, and massages. As time goes by, over a period of years, the yogi may or may not sense the deterioration of the muscles, and nerves of the track, such that the transport of food waste through the colon, slows down considerably, making the passage slow, and causing the sensory alarms about the effort to evacuate be so silent, or be totally absent, where the yogi/yogini does not know, that the waste was transported to the end of the colon, or into the rectum.

Waste will linger somewhere in the passage. Due to insensitivity of the nerves, the yogi will have no information about it. Even for those yogis who are alerted sensually, there may be such a loss of muscular control, that exerting the body to discharge the waste, will result in no outward movement. Physical means like digital (finger) extraction will have to be made, or enemas will have to be done for each evacuation session. This will continue until the body is deceased. In fact, the muscular, and nervous systems of the track, will deteriorate more and more as the body ages. Hence even with stomach churning exercises, and other postures, and movements which crunch the intestinal pack in the abdomen, still the yogi will experience a sluggish transport, and a lack of sensitivity as compared to the youthful days of the body.

Lotus Posture and Yoga

Lotus posture is not necessary for mastery of yoga. It sure helps in the achievement of mastering the *asana* postures which are known to be part of yoga, but it is not an absolute necessity. There were many advanced yogis who did not do the *padmasana* lotus posture. Some did it sloppily, and still attained spiritual advancement and mystic achievements.

We read about Buddha where in the last section of his life, he reclined and gave discourses from that posture. There is also the case of Ramana Maharshi. If one looks at pictures of this yogi, one will realize that his back was curved even in his youthful years. He did not sit in a tight lotus. Yet, he is accredited as an advanced ascetic.

When one sees pictures or figures of advanced yogis, usually these sit in lotus posture. The leading yogi for all time, Shiva, is regularly illustrated in lotus pose. Hence one may derive the idea that to meditate one must sit in lotus. However, when defining yoga, Patanjali did not list *padmasana* lotus pose as a necessity for yoga.

There is a misunderstanding where *asana* postures when done in final poses by anyone, is regarded as mastery of yoga. However, Patanjali listed *asana* postures as one of the eight requirements for yoga. In terms of meditation, he only listed the three higher subjects. These he grouped as *samyama*. While practicing that, one may or may not be in lotus posture

I had many mystic experiences of significance which occurred when my body was in some other pose, even in a reclined position, or even when it was fast asleep, folded or crumpled. On occasion, I did full lotus and did not have significant experiences.

What then is the ideal posture for doing meditation?

Let us use a reply from the *Yoga Sutras of Patanjali*.

स्थिरसुखमासनम् ॥४६॥

sthira sukham āsanam

sthira – steady; sukham – comfortable; āsanan – bodily posture.

The posture should be steady and comfortable. (Yoga Sutras 2.46)

Liberation as a Whimsy of a Conditioned Being

Sometimes there arises the question as to if liberation is necessary or desirable. This happens when one dreams in deep sleep, where one finds oneself to be in a wishfulfilling world, where the situation is at one's creative command. But if liberation is a whimsy, what is the use of gurus? Why bother or even talk about superior beings?

This brings to mind a story from the life of Gautam Buddha, where two of his prominent disciples were tracked to their desire in a former life, eons and eons ago. The question is: Can the idea for liberation appear in one's mind because of influences of others or because all by itself, one's mind composed the desire?

In the book, *Great Disciples of the Buddha* (Thera and Hecker), it is explained that eons ago, *Sariputta* and *Moggallana* met a previous Buddha named *Anomadassi* who checked the future potential of this world, to see if

Sariputta and *Moggallana* could become two chief disciples of a future buddha. He saw the probability, and consented them to be the two primary disciples for Gautam Buddha, some one hundred thousand eons hence, an incalculable age.

Those two persons could have attained arhatship perfection from *Anomadassi* Buddha but they stalled themselves because somehow, they were distracted by the desire to be prominent disciples. In other words, instead of being liberated during the time of *Anomadassi,* when they would be liberated, but would be unknown, they wanted to be liberated, when they were known as primary disciples of a buddha, any buddha. That little adjustment of desire caused that they would take birth for one hundred thousand eons before they could be liberated.

What a wonderful power is desire! How does one know if one will be influenced by someone to desire liberation. Desire can enter the psyche, and make one serve it to fruition at great expense, even for a length of vast time, for eons, where one has to wait, until conditions perfectly match the wishes.

To become liberated, and not be known, is much easier than to become liberated and be known as a prominent disciple of an extraordinary spiritual master.

Buddha's Whereabouts?

I was asked about the location of Buddha after his *parinirvana*, his situation after the death of his physical body. This is technical. It applies as well to the location of any other type of spiritualist, who is believed to have reached a certain location, or no location, hereafter.

In plain and simple language, the question is:

Where is the Buddha?

Did his existence dissolve into nothing?

Was it transferred into a habitat where everyone who achieved that place, became as nothing?

Is he somewhere where there is absolutely no personal existence, no possibility of reversals or approvals of any type of desire?

Here is an answer given by *Mahakassapa*, a senior disciple of Buddha who explained it to *Saraputta*, another leading disciple during the time of Buddha. This is from the book. *Great Disciples of the Buddha*.

On another occasion *Sāriputta* asked *Mahākassapa* whether the *Tathāgata*, the Perfect One, exists after death, or does not exist, or (in some sense) both exists and does not exist, or neither exists nor does not exist. In each case *Mahākassapa* replied:

> "This was not declared by the Blessed One. And why not?
> Because it is of no benefit and does not belong to the

fundamentals of the holy life, because it does not lead to disenchantment, nor to dispassion, cessation, inner peace, direct knowledge, enlightenment, and Nibbāna."

"But what, friend, did the Blessed One declare?" "This is suffering—so, friend, has the Blessed One declared. This is the origin of suffering...the cessation of suffering...the way to the cessation of suffering—so, friend, has the Blessed One declared. And why? Because it conduces to benefit and belongs to the fundamentals of the holy life, because it leads to turning away (from worldliness), to dispassion, cessation, inner peace, direct knowledge, enlightenment, and Nibbāna." (SN 16:12) Relations with Fellow Monks (page 123)

We have no explanation why Sāriputta posed these questions, which for an arahant should have been fully clear. It is, however, not impossible that this conversation took place immediately after Kassapa's ordination and before his attainment of arahantship, and that Sāriputta wanted to test his understanding; or perhaps the questions were asked for the sake of other monks who may have been present. (page 126 in some editions, 122 in others)

It may help if I explain the term **parinirvana** (parinibbana). In Hinduism, a similar term is mahasamadhi which has two primary meanings.

- the condition assumed by a departed soul who was liberated either before death or at the time of death
- the tomb of a reputed spiritual teacher

The problem with these technical terms used in the various spiritual societies in India, is that each sect issues its own definition or issues a vague meaning which is difficult to decipher.

In Buddha's case, if we take what is presented in the original texts (canons), it would mean that he attained *nirvana* early in his life and attracted disciples. Then he lived for many years where eventually his body succumbed to death. At death he was supposed to attain *parinirvana* or the total shift from any situation where there is suffering at any stage.

It is obviously from *Mahakassapa*, that the question regarding Buddha's location after death was taboo, not to be inquired. Why? Because it was not relevant to their path as render to them by Buddha.

The problem with Buddha is that he did not declare a location, habitat, or dimension in which there would be no suffering of any type. He only branded every place, local and remote, as rendering various degrees of trauma to anyone. Thus, the idea of his going to some other place is whited out. In their cosmology, there is the earth. There are hellish regions. There are heavenly worlds. And there is the attainment of nirvana, where a transiting being shifts out of existence, in such a way as not to ever be in existence with sensitivity to any earth, hell, or heaven.

Eons of Practice

A frequent query of ascetics is about the length of time, and the amount of practice, one must do to make advancement. Some people read about the accomplishments of proficient teachers of the past and present. Then, expecting to make rapid advancement, they set out to follow a method described, but only to find that the result intended, does not happen in their case, as quickly and as deeply, as that of some other yogi.

Some question:

How long will it take for one to advance?

When will one get a significant experience?

Why does it take so long, more than a week or a few years, to get a fantastic vision?

In the book, *Great Disciples of the Buddha*, (page 56 in some editions), Buddha's primary disciple, *Sariputta*, who practiced spiritual ascetism and righteous lifestyle for one hundred thousand eons, was praised by Buddha, just after Sariputta passed away and entered what Buddha termed as *parinirvana*.

Imagine having to practice for an incalculable period of time of one hundred thousand eons before one could become a primary disciple of someone who is rated as a Buddha, and attain *nirvana* as it is defined in the Buddhist literature.

There are more details about Sariputta in their literature, about how he was blessed some eons before by another Buddha just to fulfill his desire to be a primary teacher under a Buddha. Why the formality in a path which should eliminate the need for having to stoop to anyone for anything, especially for attainment of Buddhahood, one's existential privilege as that sect defines?

Tenants in the Body

Sometimes there is double vision where someone else, or a group of disembodied individuals, use the physical body. These folk may influence one's selections. They may even use the speech power to express their opinion.

However, it is not easy for a yogi to know when this happens in the psyche. Most yogis are oblivious to this. They live by the convention, which is that in the body, there is one entity who makes decisions, who has preferences, and who commands what sensual exposure there should be.

When a light is superimposed through, or into, another light, the imposing one may or may not realize its dominance. The occupied one may not know that it was dominated. The influence is such that the mix is similar to when milk is poured into by water. The milk is diluted but it may not understand that it is.

I wondered for sometime now about certain decisions which were made in my psyche, in regards to what should be seen or focused on, during the course of the day. As for instance, if there is a red object to the left and a blue object to the right, while driving, which one should be given preference?

Is such a decision made by the sense of sight itself? Is it made by some other entity who inhabits the psyche, and who has the power to operate any one of the five senses, and even the focusing sense which engages a particular sense?

After studying this for some years, I conclude that in some instances, the sense itself makes the decision. However, for the most part, it is made by another entity who resides in the psyche, but who is positioned invisibly, whereby with the normal consciousness, one cannot segregate that person. Instead, one feels that one is that person, and that his/her decisions are those of oneself.

The pressing concern of a disembodied soul who inhabits the psyche of someone who is embodied, is that of rebirth, the acquirement of another embryo. Since that is the priority of the disembodied inhabitant, he/she focuses on rebirth opportunities, especially on the turnstile aspect which is the womb of females. It is in the womb where the final developments are made for a new body. The womb is like a transportation hub where all trains entering or leaving the city are tracked. It is a busy place. It is useful to everyone.

Those disembodied persons who inhabit one's psyche will have as the priority, sensual targets which indicate a womb. The system of existence compels the senses to search for and acquire this.

Since the primary resident of the body, the central coreSelf, has a body, he/she does not in the immediate sense need an embryo, hence the attraction to a womb is misinterpreted as being attraction to sexual pleasure. In addition, nature encourages this misidentification, which in turn accelerates the forces, which set pregnancies into motion.

Buddha's Death

On occasion someone asks about the death of a great yogi. People are curious about the details, about the actions of that person when that happens. In the literatures there is not much about this. However, there are descriptions in the Puranas about some great yogis transiting to higher places. There is however a description of the passing of the Buddha. This is given in *Great Disciples of the Buddha* (Thera-Hecker page 177 in one edition).

And once more the Master turned to the assembly of monks to give them his final words of farewell: "Now, monks, I declare this to you: It is the nature of all conditioned things to vanish. Strive for the goal with diligence!"

After the Exalted One had spoken these last words, he entered into the four *jhānas* and the formless spheres of meditative absorption, until he attained the stage of cessation of perception and feeling. While the Master was in cessation Ānanda said to Anuruddha: "The Blessed One has attained final *Nibbāna*, venerable sir." He no longer addressed him as "friend," but as a senior monk, although both had been ordained on the same day. Anuruddha, however, had the divine eye and corrected him: "The Buddha is in the state of cessation, but has not yet passed away." To recognize this last subtle difference of a state of mind was only possible for an *arahant* like Anuruddha, who was skilled in clairvoyance. Subsequently the Buddha entered the nine stages of concentration in reverse order, back to the first *jhāna*. Then he rose again through the *four* jhānas, and during his absorption in the fourth *jhāna* he passed away.

At the moment his life ended the earth quaked and thunder roared, just as he had predicted. The *Brahmā Sahampati*, who had induced the Buddha to teach and who himself was a non-returner, spoke a stanza which pointed to the impermanence of even a Buddha's body. The king of the devas, *Sakka*, a stream-enterer, spoke a stanza which repeated the famous lines that the Buddha had proclaimed during his own discourse: "Conditions truly are transient." Anuruddha gave voice to two serene verses. But Ānanda lamented:

> Then there was terror, and the hair stood up, when he,
> the all-accomplished one, the Buddha, passed away.

Time as presented by Buddha

There is some idea of how Buddha regarded time, as to its past and future. This is from Buddhist Dictionary by Nyanatiloka Thera.

> Kappa, (Skr. Kalpa). 'World-period', is an inconceivably long space of time, an aeon. This again is subdivided into 4 sections: World- dissolution (samvattakappa, dissolving world), continuation of the chaos (samvatta-tthayi), World-formation (vivatta-kappa), continuation of the formed world (vivatta-tthiiyl).

"How long a world-dissolution will continue, how long the chaos, how long the formation, how long the continuation of the formed world, of these things, O Monks, one hardly can say that it will be so many years, or so many centuries, or so many millenniums; or so many hundred thousands of years" (A. 4 156). A detailed description of the 4 world periods is given in that stirring discourse on the all-embracing impermanence in A. 7. 62.

The beautiful simile in SN 15:5 may be mentioned here: "Suppose, O Monks, there was a huge rock of one solid mass, one mile long, one mile wide, one mile high, without split or flaw. And at the end of every hundred years a man should come and rub against it once with a silken cloth. Then that huge rock would wear off and disappear quicker than a world-period. But of such world-periods, O Monks, many have passed away, many hundreds, many thousands, many hundred thousands. And how is this possible "Inconceivable, O Monks, is this samsara. (q.v.), not to be discovered is any first beginning of beings, who obstructed by ignorance and ensnared by craving, are hurrying and hastening through this round of rebirths."

Compare here Grimm's German fairy-tale of the little shepherd-boy; "In Farther Pommerania there is the diamond-mountain, one hour high, one hour wide, one hour deep. There every hundred years a little bird comes and whets its little beak on it. And when the whole mountain is ground off, then the first second of eternity has passed."

When considering Buddha's disciples, names like Ananda, Sariputta and Moggallana come to mind. There were others of importance like for instance Anuruddha. One of his peculiarities was the development and positive use of the divine eye, not just after he became a monk but even prior.

I was questioned about the divine eye. Here from the book, *Great Disciples of the Buddha* (Thera/Hecker), pages 188-194, there is some information about the definition and use of it in the Buddhist literature.

The Struggle for Arahantship

The divine eye is the ability to see beyond the range of the physical eye, extending in Anuruddha's case to a thousandfold world system. This faculty, which we will discuss more fully below, is of a mundane (lokiya) character, one whose acquisition does not necessarily entail that its possessor has gained realization of the Dhamma. Anuruddha attained the divine eye before he became an arahant, and to reach the heights he still had to overcome many inner obstacles. Three reports in the canon tell of his struggles.

Once, when the Venerable Anuruddha was living in the Eastern Bamboo Park with two friends, his cousin Nandiya and the Sakyan noble Kimbila, the Buddha visited them and inquired about their progress. Anuruddha then told him about a difficulty he had experienced in a very sublime meditation he had been practicing. He had perceived an inner light and radiance and had a vision of sublime forms. But that light and vision of forms disappeared very soon, and he could not understand the reason.

The Buddha declared that when he was still striving for enlightenment, he too had met the same difficulty but had discovered how to master it. He explained that to experience these subtle states in full and obtain a steady perception of them one should free oneself from eleven imperfections (upakkilesa). The first is uncertainty about the reality of these phenomena and the significance of the inner light, which might easily be taken for a sensory illusion. The second is inattention: one no longer directs one's full attention to the inner light but disregards it, evaluating it as unremarkable or inessential. The third imperfection is lethargy and drowsiness; the fourth, anxiety and fright, which occurs when threatening images or thoughts arise from the subconscious. When these imperfections have been mastered, elation may arise, which excites body and mind. Such exultation is often a habitual reaction to any kind of success. When that elation has exhausted itself, one may feel emotionally drained and fall into inertia, a heavy passivity of mind. To overcome it, one makes a very strong effort, which may result in an excess of energy. On becoming aware of this excess, one relaxes and falls again into sluggish energy. In such a condition, when mindfulness is weak, strong longing may arise for desirable objects of the celestial or the human world, according to the focusing of the inner light which had been widened in its range. This longing will reach out to a great variety of objects and thus lead to another imperfection, a large diversity of perceptions, be it on the celestial or human plane. Having become dissatisfied with this great diversity of forms, one chooses to contemplate one of them, be it of a desirable or undesirable nature. Concentrating intensely on the chosen object will lead to the eleventh imperfection, the excessive meditating on these forms.

Addressing Anuruddha and his two companions the Buddha thus described vividly, from his own experience, the eleven imperfections that may arise in the meditative perception of pure forms, and he explained how to overcome them.

When Anuruddha had perfected himself more and more in the jhānas and in those refined meditative perceptions, he one day went to see the Venerable Sāriputta and said: "Friend Sāriputta, with the divine eye that is purified, transcending human sight, I can see the thousandfold world system. Firm is my energy, unremitting; my mindfulness is alert and unconfused; the body is tranquil and unperturbed; my mind is concentrated and one-pointed. And yet my mind is not freed from the cankers, not freed from clinging."

Thereupon Sāriputta replied: "Friend Anuruddha, that you think thus of your divine eye: this is conceit in you. That you think thus of your firm energy, your alert mindfulness, your unperturbed body, and your concentrated mind: this is restlessness in you. That you think of your mind not being freed from the cankers: this is worrying in you. It would be good, indeed, if you would abandon these three states of mind and, paying no attention to them, direct your mind to the deathless element, Nibbāna."

Having heard Sāriputta's advice, Anuruddha again resorted to solitude and earnestly applied himself to the removal of those three obstructions within his mind.

Sometime later Anuruddha was living in the country of the Cetiya people, in the Eastern Bamboo Grove. There, in his contemplations, it occurred to him that there were seven thoughts that should be cherished by a truly great man (mahāpurisavitakka):

This Dhamma is for one with few wishes, not for one with many wishes; this Dhamma is for one who is content, not for one who is discontent; this Dhamma is for one bent on seclusion, not for one who is gregarious; this Dhamma is for one who is energetic, not for one who is lazy; this Dhamma is for one who is mindful, not for one who is confused; this Dhamma is for one who is concentrated, not for one who is unconcentrated; this Dhamma is for one who is wise, not for one who is dull-witted.

When the Buddha perceived in his own mind the thoughts that had arisen in Anuruddha's mind, he appeared before him in a mind-made body (manomaya-kāya) and applauded him: "Good, Anuruddha, good! You have well considered seven thoughts of a great man. You may now also consider this eighth thought of a great man: 'This Dhamma is for one who inclines to the non-diffuse, who delights in the non-diffuse; not for one who inclines to worldly diffuseness and delights in it.'"

The Buddha then said that when Anuruddha contemplates these eight thoughts, he will be able to attain at will the four meditative absorptions. He would then no longer be affected by worldly conditions but would regard the four simple requisites of a monk's life—robes, alms-food, shelter, and medicines—in the same way as a layperson would enjoy luxuries. Such simple living would make his mind joyous and unperturbed and thus be helpful to his attainment of Nibbāna.

In parting, the Buddha advised Anuruddha to stay on at the Eastern Bamboo Grove. Anuruddha did so, and during that same rainy season he attained the consummation of his striving: arahantship, the undefiled liberation of the mind (AN 8:30). At the hour of his attainment the Venerable Anuruddha uttered the following verses, in which he expresses his gratitude to the Master for helping him bring his spiritual work to completion:

Having understood my mind's intention,
The unsurpassed Teacher in the world
Came to me by psychic power
In the vehicle of a mind-made body.

When the intention arose in me,
Then he gave me a further teaching.
The Buddha who delights in the non-diffuse
Gave me instructions on the non-diffuse.

Having understood his Dhamma,
I dwelt delighting in his Teaching.
The three knowledges have been attained,
The Buddha's Teaching has been done.

ANURUDDHA'S SPIRITUAL PATH

The Venerable Anuruddha's spiritual path is marked by two prominent features: first, his mastery of the divine eye and other supernormal faculties; and second, his cultivation of the four foundations of mindfulness (satipaṭṭhāna). We will discuss each of these in turn. The divine eye (dibbacakkhu) is so called because it is similar to the vision of the devas, which is capable of seeing objects at remote distances, behind barriers, and in different dimensions of existence.

The divine eye is developed by meditative power. It is not a distinct sense organ but a type of knowledge, yet a knowledge that exercises an ocular function. This faculty is aroused on the basis of the fourth jhāna, and specifically through one of the meditative supports called the light kasiṇa or the fire kasiṇa, a visualized circle of light or fire. After mastering the four jhānas through either of these kasiṇas, the meditator descends to a lower level of concentration called "access concentration" (upacāra-samādhi) and extends light to the immediately surrounding area, thereby bringing into view forms that are ordinarily imperceptible. As the meditator becomes progressively more adept in this ability to radiate light, he can then suffuse increasingly larger areas with light and project the radiance outwardly to distant world systems and to planes of existence above and below the human plane. This will reveal many dimensions of being that are inaccessible to the ordinary fleshly eye.

The characteristic function of the divine eye, according to the texts, is the knowledge of the passing away and rebirth of beings (cutūpapāta-ñāṇa). This knowledge was achieved by the Buddha on the night of his own Enlightenment and was always included by him in the complete step-by-step gradual training, where it appears as the second of the three true knowledges (tevijjā; see, for example, MN 27) and the fourth of the six superknowledges (chaḷabhiññā, see MN 6). By means of this faculty the meditator is able to see beings as they pass away from one form of existence and take rebirth elsewhere. But it is not only the actual passage from life to life that the divine eye reveals. With the appropriate determination it can also be used to discover the particular kamma that brought about rebirth into the new form of existence. In this application it is called the knowledge of faring on in accordance with one's kamma (kammūpaga-ñāṇa). At its maximum efficiency the divine eye can illuminate the entire panorama of sentient existence—spread out over thousands of world systems and extending from the highest heavens to the lowest hells—revealing too the kammic laws that govern the process of rebirth. While only a supreme Buddha will have absolute mastery over this knowledge, disciples who have perfected the divine eye can perceive regions of the sentient universe that elude our most powerful telescopes.

The Venerable Anuruddha was designated by the Buddha as the foremost bhikkhu disciple endowed with the divine eye (etadaggaṃ dibbacakkhukānaṃ; AN 1; chap. 14). Once, when a number of eminent monks living together in the Gosiṅga sāla-tree forest exchanged views on the kind of monk that could beautify that forest, Anuruddha characteristically replied that it was one who, with the divine eye, could survey a thousand world systems, just as a man standing on a high tower could see a thousand farmsteads (MN 32).

Anuruddha also helped his own pupils to acquire the divine eye (SN 14:15) and in his verses celebrates his skill in this faculty:

Absorbed in five-factored concentration,
Peaceful, with a unified mind,
I had gained tranquillity
And my divine eye was purified.

Standing on the five-factored jhana
I know the passing and rebirth of beings;
I know their coming and their going,
Their life in this world and beyond.

The other major facet of Anuruddha's spiritual path was the arduous practice of satipaṭṭhāna, the four foundations of mindfulness: "Here a bhikkhu dwells contemplating the body in the body ... feelings in feelings ... mind in mind ... mental phenomena in mental phenomena, ardent, clearly comprehending, and mindful, having removed covetousness and grief in regard to the world. The practice of satipaṭṭhāna is sometimes taken to be a quick, "dry" path to enlightenment which bypasses the jhānas and superknowledges, but from Anuruddha's words it is clear that for him, as well as for those trained under him, this method of meditation could be used as a vehicle for the acquisition of psychic powers and superknowledges along with the final fruit of liberation. Whenever the Venerable Anuruddha was asked how he had gained proficiency in the "great superknowledges" (mahābhiññatā), which include the five mundane superknowledges and arahantship as the sixth, he always replied that it was through the development and cultivation of the four foundations of mindfulness. It was through this practice, he says, that he could recollect a thousand past aeons, exercise the supernormal powers, and directly perceive a thousandfold world system

Anuruddha also said that satipaṭṭhāna enabled him to gain that perfect control of emotive reactions called the "power of the noble ones" (ariya-iddhi), by which one can regard the repulsive as nonrepulsive, the nonrepulsive as repulsive, and view both with equanimity. He further stresses the importance of this practice by saying that whoever neglects the four foundations of mindfulness has neglected the noble path leading to the extinction of suffering while whoever undertakes it has undertaken the noble path leading to the extinction of suffering; he also declares that this fourfold mindfulness leads to the destruction of craving just as the river Ganges would not deviate from its course to the ocean, in the same way a monk who practices the four foundations of mindfulness could not be deflected from the life of renunciation and made to return to the worldly life.

Once, when Anuruddha was ill, he surprised the monks by his equanimity in bearing pain. They asked him how he was able to bear up as he did, and he replied that his composure was due to his practice of the fourfold mindfulness (SN 52:10). Another time Sāriputta came to see Anuruddha in the evening and asked him what he now regularly practiced so that his face always radiated happiness and serenity. Anuruddha again said that he spent the time in the regular practice of the four foundations of mindfulness, and that this was the way in which arahants live and practice. Sāriputta thereupon expressed his joy at Anuruddha's words (SN 52:9). Once, when questioned by Sāriputta and Mahāmoggallāna about the difference between those who are still "in training" (sekha) and an arahant who is "beyond training" (asekha), he said that they differ in the practice of the fourfold mindfulness: while the former accomplishes it only partly, the latter does so completely and perfectly.

Anuruddha also claimed to possess, through his practice of right mindfulness, ten lofty qualities elsewhere called "the ten powers of a Tathāgata" (dasatathāgatabala). These are: the knowledge of what is possible and impossible; the knowledge of the result of the acquisition of kamma by way of stage and cause; the knowledge of the paths leading to the different destinations of rebirth; the knowledge of the world with its many diverse elements; the knowledge of the different dispositions of beings; the knowledge of the degree of maturity in the faculties of other beings; the knowledge of the jhānas and other advanced meditative states; and finally the three true knowledges. The commentary says that Anuruddha possessed these knowledges only in part, as in their completeness they are unique to a Fully Enlightened One.

No-Food Zone

On February 5, 2023, I was informed by a friend that a mutual acquaintance who has a terminal condition, ceased eating for seventeen (17) days. It is assumed that this person will not resume eating in his physical body. He has terminal health issues.

This information reached me at a time, when I made some observations about a no-food zone in the astral existence. Some persons who were at a hermitage, created by Yogeshwarananda in the astral world, were shifted by him to a higher astral place, where the subtle body has no tendency for eating food. Instead, it exists there in a bliss condition, being infused by white-gold light energy, from which the subtle body gets nourishment.

I find this place during breath infusion practice, when the subtle body and the physical one reaches a stage of saturation, with fresh subtle energy and fresh physical air. At a certain stage during a session, this happens. Then I become aware of that level of existence which is the no-food zone. I usually perceive one or more of the yogi/yogini people who reside there.

On some occasions, to do breath infusion, one of these persons will descend to a lower level in the ashram. When I questioned a yogini about this, she explained that when they are in the no-food zone, after some time, after some days, weeks or months, the subtle body develops some lower astral energy, which forms in the lower trunk of the subtle body, in multicolored beads. These, if left there will get heavier. They will be of such weight that they will cause the subtle body to shift from the no-food bliss zone, causing the yogi to come to a lower astral plane, from where an embryo may develop.

To avoid this rebirth possibility, yogis who are in the no-food bliss zone, frequently shifts back to an astral plane where breath infusion using *bhastrika*, or *kapalabhati pranayama*, can be done. This diffuses the beads, after which the subtle body is shifted upwards again.

There is a question:

What do the yogi/yogini do when residing in the no-food bliss zone?

The answer is: Meditation, with an objective of going to a yet higher level.

Spiritual absorption practice (*samadhi*) is better on the no-food level. The attention energy which is used involuntarily, to acquire and use subtle food, is reduced during practice on the no-food phase. Absorption will be more intense and focused, if there is no tendency for eating.

If a yogi/yogini fails to develop the subtle body to its no-food astral zone, that means that rebirth is necessary. The impulse for eating will cause the subtle body to seek out an embryo, where it can begin the eating process through a new baby form.

How does this relate to not eating when the body is terminally ill?

Actually, there is no relationship because the terminal condition prohibits the person from using the physical system to cause a transfer to the astral no-food bliss condition. Some yogis who develop resistance to physical eating, and to subtle body nourishment from physical eating, can in the terminal stage of the body, shift to the no-food bliss zone, but that is after long practice from years of digestion and excretion control. In the Puranas yogis who achieved this, were mentioned. Gradually over years, they ceased solid food, then liquid food, then air intake was regulated. They ceased taking nutrients which related to the physical body.

It is the connection of the physical to the subtle one, that is the issue. The subtle body depends on subtle energy which is in physical substances. First one must cause the subtle body to cease its dependence on subtle energy which is generated from the physical system.

Electricity is not a physical substance, like for instance, a rock. And yet currently for the generation of electricity, engineers use physical substances like copper and iron. This shows that there is a dependence on physical materials for the creation of even subtler things like electricity. Thus, the mystery concerns how to eliminate the need for the physical body.

The nature of Nature

Observe and adjust!

That is what someone can do when he/she realizes that this creation is preset and full of limited possibilities. The big threat is death of the physical body. No matter what is offered even if the events are infinite in number, someone is limited by the very nature that he/she has a perishable body.

To change this?

No substantial impact is possible.

On a small planet, near a small sun, in a small galaxy, what can someone do?

Act as a vantage point?

Feel that one has command of a moment?

The nature of this Nature?

What is it?

It arrived in the scan of time, as this.

This fizz of flaws?

When it began, it formatted to become this?

The root disappeared.

It left this?

Thought Generation

Thought generation occurs in the mind. It is twofold in origin.

Either it is generated in the psyche, where it is illustrated; or it is generated in another psyche and then transmitted into the psyche of the viewer.

Psyche generated thoughts are of two kinds.

- deliberate
- indeliberate

Those thoughts which were generated in another psyche and which were transmitted into the psyche of someone else, may be voluntarily or involuntarily transmitted into the mind of the receiver.

The sender may be compelled to transmit the thoughts. Or he/she may deliberately transmit the ideas.

When a thought is generated in the psyche, it may or may not be fully observed by the person, such that this person may not be aware of the thought, but may have some subliminal idea of it. Regardless, the person would be affected. As to what agency in the psyche is involved in the manufacture of a thought, there is the following creative agencies.

- illustrative intellect
- architectural intellect
- lifeForce creative energy
- coreSelf deliberate construction using intellect as a scribe tool
- memory suggestive power dominating the intellect

The intellect has two functioning abilities. These are.

- illustration of ideas presented to it by the lifeForce, memory or coreSelf
- illustration of ideas which it creates by itself. It does this as an architect would design buildings

If the intellect fails to illustrate, no thoughts appear in the mindscape. Instead, there will be a blank mind which is void of ideas. Even though thoughts may be created by some other adjunct or upon command/need of the coreSelf, still if the intellect fails to initiate construction of the seed-ideas, there will be no illustration in the mind. The intellect is the essential instrument (adjunct) involved in thought production.

During meditation, thought generation is an unwanted feature of the mind. The cessation of thoughts is an absolute must for deep meditative states. Since however there is more than one cause for thought generation, the solution for cessation of thoughts varies, according to how, and by which adjunct the thought was produced. That is the scientific way to view the issue. However, many meditation systems by many teachers, advocate that it does not matter how a thought was formed. They claim that the solution is to remove interest in the thought.

This, however, shows that because the self does not have the power to totally squelch an idea, it is not likely to terminate a thought. If the solution to the issue of unwanted thought production, is that the self should simply observe or ignore the thoughts, that indicates that the self does not have the power to give a command which will eliminate the thought. Is this the situation?

Divine Eye Unlikely

It is unlikely that most of the people who aspire to experience the divine eye, will do so. There are many uses of the divine eye but to put it simply, it is not an eye like the visual experience we are familiar with. The physical vision system relies on two eyes. The divine eye is one orb but it may be a complex set of visionary equipment which are psychic stuff and not biological materials.

By itself, the divine eye is the intellect when that adjunct functions as a vision orb. Otherwise, the divine eye is that same intellect interlocked with the brow chakra mechanism. The rendering of reality by the intellect is a subjective perception which requires keen and sensitive detection.

The divine vision rendered by the intellect when it is interlocked with the brow chakra, results in what is termed as the third eye which is a singular vision orb. This may be experienced as a portal transmission, or access, to higher dimensions. For this, the yogi finds himself peering, or directs himself to look into other worlds. This is an objective perception as compared to the subjective view which is rendered when the intellect is used by itself, and the brow chakra is not involved.

The intellect by itself is constantly used in the matter of thought illustration or projection. For this the brow chakra is not necessary. In fact, most people use the intellect or stated more precisely, most people are used by the intellect. And yet if one tries to use the intellect to peer into other dimensions, usually one is unsuccessful. It gives easy access only to things which concern the physical world.

Most yogis practice meditation but do not experience the intellect as anything but a thought creation, idea projection, and memory illustration mechanism. Even to realize this is difficult. Patanjali suggested, in fact, required, that the yogi cease the thought functions of the intellect. This is because the higher uses of the intellect cannot be experienced, if the yogi does not close the operation of its lower functions, which concern thought production.

One factor of the intellect which makes it difficult to cultivate its higher functions, is the fact that the intellect spontaneously operates to reach lower dimensions and to illustrate factors from this physical level. It rarely shifts upwards. If it does so, the perception is without contrast, and is so subtle as to be imperceptible.

This means that any valid practice, for using the intellect in its higher modes, may seem to be useless, because what it renders from higher planes is not seen, because of the lack of contrast and the subtlety.

When the intellect shows something from the physical level, or from a lower plane, the yogi may undervalue that perception. That will discourage the development of the psychic operations.

A transparent person from a higher or lower dimension, who sits with a yogi, and who converses, may not be seen by the ascetic. At least not until there is a contrast, or if the yogi can recognize transparent reality. Unless one has a sensitive mind, one cannot use many functions of the divine eye. Again, Patanjali's instruction about ceasing the normal mental operations, is vital. That is the method for developing the required sensitivity.

Honesty in Yoga Practice

Honesty is a part of yoga practice, but only in so far as one can maintain that without risking self-endangerment. There were exceptions where an ascetic shared a truthful rendition of an event, and suffered terribly, or even died as a result. On the other end of the spectrum some ascetics were known to deny information, or to distort an opinion, to save their lives. To save one's life, which is better? To be totally honest? Or to be outright dishonest?

There is no clear-cut universal answer. It depends on the time and place. To determine the value of the speaking truthfully, omitting facts, or denying information about what he witnessed, an ascetic must be knowledgeable of the past, present and future.

Cheating is part of the physical existence which we currently endure. How did someone come here? From where did someone transmigrate to this place? Whose idea was it that a woman's orifice would be the terminal place for the embryo?

What kind of place is it, which is the tracing point as one goes backwards to the father's body? Who planned the journey? Did it happen spontaneously, with no biological engineer on a mystic plane, designing it?

But even in there, in the mother's lower part, one is dishonest. Even there one hides. As for instance, when one is in there and one is fearful of a loud noise, or of violent strike to the mother's abdomen. One may have this idea, that one should be as small as possible, to stop the mother's abdomen from becoming distended, where someone being aggravated by the protrusion, may strike, and kill the growing shape, during the embryonic state.

And then the force which pushes one out. The fear of it!

This creation is filled with numerous energies and their resultant mixes which renders as live events. The pressure is on to honor the energies by absorbing, promoting, and facilitating. A yogi should respect the operations but at the same time, he/she should, if possible, sidestep, avoid, and be neutral to most of them. Even the positive ones should be regarded with caution.

If you see a grenade, do not pull the pin from it. In fact, do not take it. Leave it as it is with the pin preventing detonation. Do not try to disarm it. In some instances, the attempt to disarm it, even by an expert, caused it to explode in his/her face.

Even though you know that it is dangerous, and that some ignorant or informed person may be killed by it, leave it where it is. Seeing it does not give one the right to changed its location, nor to activate, nor disable its trigger.

Suppose however you need it to blast some part of a mountain? Should you take it, place it in the mountain and blast the place?

Suppose you saw a grenade, but it was an old one which did not detonate for some fifty years. It is rusted and encrusted with grit. The rain fell and exposed it. You know a man who is a miner who needs it. Should you take it to him?

Of course, you would not stress that it may explode to his face. That is a possibility, but you want to avoid speaking of that because if you do, the miner may turn away. He may not buy it. Why not sell it to him. Be sure that you get a handsome amount for it. Or if you are in a good mood and do not need the money, give it to him but do not warn him. After all, if it exploded untimely, he will be dead. If it explodes as he would like it to, he would be happy.

Yogic Contraception

As to the matter of how parents can circumvent the begetting process, the question is regarding what to do if one has a child and does not want to have another, or wants to stagger the children' births so that there are years, after each delivery of an infant.

In the animal kingdom, each species must comply with whatever timing Nature decrees. The animals have no way of using contraceptives to bar or inhibit pregnancies. This means that Nature does not allow their freewill decisions.

When an entity finds itself to be a physical body, that entity discovers itself with certain abilities, and with the lack of certain controls. In the modern situation, however, human beings discovered ways of blocking pregnancies. For instance, males may use a process of extraction of their genitals from a female orifice, just before those males would release sexual fluids into the female passage. Can a bull or billy goat figure this?

Extraction of the male organ before ejection of sperm, is a simply act. Yet we do not find the lower animals carrying out that action. In the human society, there are liabilities for pregnancies. These cause the males and females to consider contraceptives. However, there is another aspect which most humans overlook. It is the reaction from Nature if one effectively blocks a pregnancy. There is, also, the social mores to be considered. In some societies, some person in power may created and enforce laws, to penalized would-be parents for interfering with Nature's begetting process.

The male genital extraction process has a down side, where the female involved may be dissatisfied by the action. It would end the sequence of events, such that the female may be unhappy, due to not enjoying the activity sufficiently at that time.

Should a yogi/yogini use another means of contraception?

If a parent takes a surgery which causes the body to become incapable of contributing either sperm or egg, towards a pregnancy, that parent would be blocking at least one ancestor, a person who is disembodied and who has rights to rebirth. What to do?

Such an action may not cause the reduction of sexual desire. In fact, it may increase that, which would result in more frequent sexual release in one way or the other, tormenting that person, whose body became incapable of contributing to the formation of a fetus.

If a parent takes an action, with medication which makes the body hostile to sperm or ovum, then for that day or week, an ancestor would be frustrated in trying to have an embryo. Who would have to absorb that frustration and/or disappointment?

According to the medical information, a woman who bottle-feeds a child, will resume ovulation in 15 weeks (a little over 3 months) after delivering the child. This means that such a woman has an infertility period of only 15 weeks before her body could begin developing another infant.

In comparison if the child is breast-fed, the lady will take 36 weeks on the average before her body will produce another child. This is an average. The fact is that it may be between 15-36 weeks, depending on the genetic attitude of the mother's body. That varies as per the individual with every woman having a different rate when checked.

What is the best course to prevent a pregnancy early on, if one wants to have other children, but do not want them rapidly as Nature would have it. An obvious recommendation is abstinence. That is impractical in most cases. Sexual compulsion does not allow it.

What should one do?

- Reduce sexual stimulation
- Reduce viewing sexual media

If proximity increases sexual arousal, sleep in separate rooms.

Let the infant which was recently born be the conjoint focus of the parents. Instead of focusing on each other, each parent should focus on the child (children) and guide their affectionate energies and nurturing needs to the child and not to each other, nor to someone else.

Affection and nurture quickly convert into sexual attraction. A yogi/yogini should be aware. He/She should act in a social way which does not easily permit that conversion to take place.

I cannot recommend contraceptive methods unless I want to be responsible for giving the advice. I am disinclined to absorb negative reactions. However, the information above may be useful to some ascetics. More or less, Nature has the situation covered. I could not find a loophole which I could utilize and safely consent to.

Currently the society is not designed to support abstinence. There is that question as to why I recommended that. The answer is that despite the lack of support, that is the only method that makes sense but even that method is flawed.

Any type of contraception is a violent act to the perspective person(s) who would have a body if that abstinence was not in place. However, in the case of abstinence, the would-be parent does not enjoy the reproductive energies in a sexual intercourse. In other words, the parents are not taking the enjoyment-payment, and will incur less unwanted reactions as a result.

In terms of negative returns, abstinence is the best method. If you cannot do it, if it is impossible in your case, then the choice is yours about another method. But certainly, I would imperil myself if I suggested an alternative.

Death Location Objective

When considering the current difficulty for attaining yoga objectives, it is best to be realistic, and to plan for the next level of achievement, rather than to aspire for full success.

In relation to what situation, level, or location, one desires after losing access to the physical body, the idea of aiming for the highest achievement is not a practical way. Why?

Due to the fact, that under the present conditions, it is hardly likely that one could achieve the highest level according to one's view of it. What is realistic?

To aim for a situation hereafter in which one may continue the practice, and will not hanker for physical access. You may recall that independent life for the present physical body began with the need to prevent suffocation and satisfy hunger. It began with acquiring air and suckling liquid food either from the mother's nipples, or from a bottle, or spoon. That basic need for physical food should be eliminated while one lives as a physical body.

Then one may experience a subtle body, which does not have the urge for physical liquids and solids. What will be left is air, physical air. Since that is to a degree subtle when contrasted to drinks and physical foods, it is a good place to start, to reorient the self to acquiring nutrition from subtle matter.

This will help considerably to offset the constant need for physical access, which most disembodied people feel, once they are deceased.

I was with a friend who recently departed. On the astral side, we did breath infusion in several postures. We discussed the *agnisara* stomach infusion practice. He did not complete it before he lost access to his last physical body. The result is that there is the formation of a digestive, excretive mechanism in his subtle body, just as there was one in his last physical form. Now he must endeavor to eliminate it.

Once when I ate physical food, this friend came on the astral side to partake of it. I said to him. "What is your need for this? You are no longer a physical being."

He wanted to eat. The tendency to take and process subtle energy from physical food was present in the subtle body, as a mandatory urge. This feature of the subtle body should be eliminated before the physical system dies. Otherwise, it is likely that one will crave physical food, and will become a humbug, who will harass relatives and friends to eat through their living bodies, such that one may derive subtle nutrients through their digestive system. This is a sure induction to becoming an embryo again.

For safety's sake, one should constantly check the subtle body, to be sure that it eliminates whatever it acquired as a habit, which it derived because of developing a physical form, and having to manage physical tendencies.

Astral Nude World

Just as the animals do on this planet, there are several astral planes, where humans move about with no clothing. In contrast there are astral levels where humans are active with clothing, and with the ability to change the fabric and colors on the spur of the moment, simply by thinking or desiring.

While in this world, if someone does not like the color of hair on the head, he/she may dye or bleach it. In some astral places, the color changes instantly just by the desire to alter it.

Once when doing a session of breath infusion, two females appeared. Each was nude but it was without sexual stress. Noticeably were their breasts which were firm and full, exuding the energy of motherly nurturing, with some slight sexual energy, which was supportive of the nurturing tones. I questioned about their condition, and about why they descended to the lower astral level, where I could see them. One, the senior of the two, said this.

"Where we reside, there is hardly any need to eat. Sometimes we eat there but the food looks like sparkling gems. None of it is sour. None of it has salty taste. We rarely evacuate. When we do it is in small amounts, and looks like colorful granite material which is soft to the touch.

"As for sexual intercourse, it rarely occurs there. No one thinks of it. If somehow someone does, that person is transited instantly to another astral plane, where coitus is enacted."

I asked about their breasts which exuded a milky substance. One pair produced a milky white-orange liquid. The other produced a milky white-yellow liquid. When I tasted it, it had a neutral taste which was due to my tasting sense, which could not taste the flavor which was experienced in the dimension, from which these beings were native.

The one who spoke, explained this.

"My breasts exude milk when there is a feeling from someone somewhere with whom I had a relationship. Based on the relationship, a specific type of milk would flow. To fulfill this, I shift to the dimension where the relationship person resides. As for instance, by coming to you, my breasts exude milk, which is based on maternal feelings for you specifically.

"When we are in our realm, there is no idea about life on earth. It is dormant in the psyche but only as a distant memory, which is like a faded imprint, or like an ancient script which no one currently understands. Still the energy may cause a transfer to a lower plane, where someone exist, with whom I had a relationship at some other time, even in some other place."

These persons were from a place where there are angelic beings whose subtle bodies have only the *sattva guna* clarifying energy. These are not yogis in the way we are. They do not do austerities. The people who are on the plane of existence from which they hail, do no austerities. Still, they are not attracted to rebirth or physical history, or liberation even.

Because of a release of a memory energy in their psyches, they came to visit. I was reported as being absent from that place. I was traced to where I am currently. This was a reminder that I have other associations in other places, and should not create more links to anyone or anything on this earthly plane. Such earthly relationship would further stall my return to those other places.

For some time now in this body and before, I endeavored to break from earth history and to terminate relationship accounts. This visit provides. more impetus to end my interest here.

Violence as Product of Desire

Desire is a permanent feature of this creation, such that it cannot be eliminated. It may be suppressed, suspended, or expressed, but it cannot be eradicated. This gives desire the worth for investigation, as to its origin, impulsion, manifestation, or frustration.

One feature of it, is violence. That is one of its productions. When a desire is frustrated, violence is produced. Its bleeds violence in one way or the other. However, it also bleeds violence when it is expressed, and the expression is impulsive, where it cannot be contained sufficiently by the person.

Desire as we are currently familiar with it, is an impressed force which carries in it, its own way of expression and containment, such that to the person expressing it, it seems to be impulsive and personal. Most desires however are impressed on the person. As for instance, the way a branding iron impresses a mark on the back of a bull. The situation of the bull does not allow it to resist the violent heat of the iron. The mark in the animal's hide cannot be removed by the animal.

Over time, desires which were imbedded in the psyche, surface and command the psyche to act for fulfilments. If the situation is not responsive, there arises a feeling of frustration. This, if not contained, swells into violent activity.

To curb this influence, one should become detached from the desires which are embedded in the psyche. Without thinking that one can eliminate desire, and understanding that one may suspend or de-energize it, one may squelch one or the other desire. Otherwise, one will be compelled to endorse its manifestation. Then, if nature does not facilitate, one will commit violence. That is unfavorable for yoga practice.

Purpose for Asana Postures

Asana postures are the third stage of the *ashtanga* yoga process, which is divided into eight parts. This is according to the definition given by Patanjali in his *Yoga Sutras*. There are however many yoga teachers who give definitions which are at variance with Patanjali.

In inSelf Yoga™, the asana postures make the physical body more conducive for doing the psychological practices in yoga. This is due to the fact that the linkage between the physical aspects of psyche, and the psychic features of it, are more efficiently coordinated, if the physical body is healthy.

The stage of yoga which is higher than the asana postures, is the *pranayama* breath infusion. That feature of yoga is for targeting the subtle body. At first this is a physical practice with noticeable health benefits in the physical body. When some of the breath infusion is mastered, the student realizes that he can target the subtle body while doing the physical breathing process.

Some students who are space bound, do not realize the subtle body. Instead, these persons focus only on the physical system and derive benefits in the physical way mostly. Their conclusion is that yoga is primarily *asana* postures.

This happens because of not practicing the fifth stage of yoga, the one which is higher than *pranayama* breath infusion. That is the *pratyahara* sensual energy withdrawal practice.

Scattered Subtle Energy / *Vikshepa Chitta*

One puzzling event which happens frequently, is the inability of a yogi to ceases the scattering attitude of the mento-emotional energy in the mind. I feel that Patanjali did not go into sufficient details about this type of incidence in meditation. It may be that during his composition of the *Yoga Sutras*, the atmospheric energy around planet earth was more conducive to meditation (*samyama*), where the scattering of the energy in the psyche was not prevalent as it is now.

Many meditators begin with the premise, that even though for the time being, it appears not to be, the self is absolute. Then, there is another set of meditators who deny that there is a self. Thus, there is no need in their view to consider the self as a target of scattering energy.

For inSelf Yoga™, one begins with the premise that there is a self which is subjected to desired and unwanted states of mind. Another important admittance is that there is an environment in the psyche, in which the self lives or resides. Then there is yet, another admittance. There are environments which surround and affect the psyche. Some of these dimensions, facilitates meditation. Some obstruct it.

Those yogis who begin with the idea that the self is absolute, do not consider that it can be obstructed by an environment which is outside the psyche. Their premise is that if something is absolute it should not be affected by anything besides itself.

Then there are the yogis who have the idea that there is no self which could be targeted by anything. These persons also conclude that since there is no self, there cannot be anything which will adversely effect the self. Their defense is that something which does not exist, cannot be targeted by something else.

However, for the purpose of inSelf Yoga™, the self, a limited principle, can be targeted by what is in the psyche as well as by what is exterior to it. There is scattered energy in the psyche. It may block attempts to meditate.

This happens as well if there is scattered energy outside the psyche. That energy causes the energy in the psyche to resonate unreasonably.

This can happen because of the relativeness of a self. Hence in some meditations no matter what the yogi does, he/she may find that a scattered state persists. Because of the dominance of the scattered energy, a quiet state is not experienced.

Breath infusion before meditation accelerates the state of high energy quietude in the mind. In some instances, this process causes a partial increase in the scattered condition. In others one notices a full or near-full quietude,

The suggestion is that one must have internal as well as external assistance, in terms of the type of energy, which is current during the meditation session. One should practice regardless but one should not expect that in every session one will have the ideal inner or outer conditions for meditation.

Condition of Subtle Body after Death

The physical body is at the forefront during the physical life. This is evident even for spiritualists who claim that they are not concerned with it, and that it is temporary and useless. When all is said and done, we find that even people who spend their lives ridiculing the physical body, remain concerned with it until it dies. At that stage, one may have no idea what his position is. That is if one has no psychic perception, where one can track the hereafter condition.

Recently, in his eighty plus year, a friend passed away. His body had a cancerous condition, which cause it to malfunction to the point that eventually, it ceased processing food. Gradually it starved to death. In the meantime, the cancer progressed.

I saw him on the astral side. What happened is that I did some *bhastrika* breath infusion practice. He approached to join the session. At the time, he noticed two ladies who were undressed but who did some of the exercises. When they noticed him, they moved into a position astrally where he could no longer perceive them. He asked me about them because earlier in the day on the astral side, these two ladies were in a condition of emotion, where their breasts emitted milk which flowed from their nipples.

He wanted me to explain the reason for this. I told him that there was no explanation. These things happen frequently on the astral side, where there is some activity by someone which is unexplained, and which would not have occurred on the physical side. He then switched the subject saying that his neck was somewhat hunched, and some of his tendons were stiff. He said he needed new bones.

I told him that after death, it is normal for the subtle body to mimic the condition of the last physical form. However, if one does *asana* postures and *pranayama* breath infusion on the astral side, there is the likelihood that one can adjust the condition of the subtle body to one's preference. Over time the subtle body will change if one does this. He replied that during the life of his last physical form, he did not pay attention to the condition of the subtle body. He regretted this.

"It is so stupid to focus on everything besides the condition of the subtle body. In the end when the physical system which one identifies as dies, one will be left with the subtle body. Then, if it is not in a preferred condition, fixing it will become the priority."

Sex Enjoyment in Yoga Practice

Sex enjoyment as everything else is part of the existence which we currently experience. It should be monitored just as anything else. A careful study of the psyche and its habits should be done by each yogi. Irrespective of what books inform, or what teachers profess, each yogi should study his/her habits and work, for expansion or contraction of habits, in a way which better facilitates the practice.

There are restrictions mentioned in books about what facilitates yoga, and what deters it. In the final analysis one should examine one's individual habits, and fine tune the behavior of the subtle body, so that yoga realization is increased.

Most of the literature about yoga, points in the direction of *brahmacharya* which means a behavior which focuses on and is absorbed in *brahman* which is a general term for the spiritual level of existence. Somehow that word was used in another way to mean celibacy. Actually, its original meaning in that context was not celibacy as a general aim, or achievement but celibacy as it is experienced, before sexual maturity.

Celibacy after sexual maturity and after having sexual experience (carnal knowledge), is not the same as celibacy before sexual maturity. To understand this, imagine what it would be like to go through the years of a body to its elderly state, and not have that body reach sexual maturity. How would that be? Is that the same as not having sexual experience after the body reaches sexual maturity?

The ideal *brahmacharya* state is the one where the body does not reach sexual maturity, but it develops in every other way. It looks like an adult form but it remains in the juvenile state, and it does not have sexual arousal.

Consider if you had a love for someone of the opposite sex, just as you had already in this life span, but there was no sexual response in that emotion. Can you experience that? If you can, you may understand the true meaning of *brahmacharya*.

What is the big deal about not having sex? Why is it given such appraise in the literature. In the first place some writers mean childhood and adult restraint from sex, as celibacy. We should read about it, knowing the meaning for each writer.

What I wrote above is theoretical only. We know that Nature causes sexual development involuntarily. It does not allow anyone to command such development. In each childhood body, it causes the sexual development to happen, regardless of whether the individual desires that or not.

Thus, if someone desires to cease sexual indulgence, that cannot happen completely. Partially one may do it by restraint, by surgically removing the genitals, by pretending that one is not sexually engaged or by some other means. But the fact is that sexual expression is mandatory because that is Nature's way. It is a joke when monks speak about their celibacy.

Not a single monk gives a guarantee that he/she does not have subtle sexual activities. For that matter, if a monk is not aware of every subtle act, he cannot truthfully state that he is celibate. He may declare that he has no sexual engagement physically but he cannot be certain if he does so during sleep or in dreams.

What should he do if someone has a sexual attraction for him? How does he deal with that projection of energy?

For those who want to be honest, my advice is that one should quit sexual behavior on the physical level as soon as one can. For the subtle level, that is a difficult, almost impossible, achievement. For that one may strive to reduce the frequency of it.

Cease physical sexual activity if you can but be practical in achieving this. Do not think that a religion's declarations and promises can guarantee this. Nature does not care about religious dogma and ideas. Face up to the need for sexual participation. Over time reduce it if you can. Study how nature operates it.

Brahmacharya, or celibacy as not having sexual experience, is a wonderful idea. But here in this world, Nature does not allow it. It is not available except for the early years in a body, and then only as a transit for the development of full-blown sexuality.

Ghost of the Past

A ghost of the past, a man whose daughter I was attracted to and was perhaps crazy over, during the teen years of this body, found me last night on the astral level. When I was in love with his daughter, he was against the relationship, and guarded his daughter to be sure that I could not sexually access her.

Later, here and there but infrequently, perhaps every five or ten years when I met him on the astral level, he was hostile to me. However, now he is friendly and jovial. He said this.

"How do I know whom she is? What was her identity in the last three lives before this one, when you approached her with sexual interest? These circumstances with our responses to them is silly in a way. We do not have the proper information to make informed decisions, regarding who should have sex with whom."

I did not reply with a lengthy brief. Instead, I said this.

"You were being responsible for the young lady who happened to be positioned as your daughter in that case. Looking back, I conclude that your objections to the relationship were in order. Why should I begrudge you for it. Suppose you encouraged such a relationship, what would be the outcome? Who would take responsibility for progeny produced. When all is said and done, a fruitful sexual relationship reaches the situation called pregnancy. Which teenager is prepared to fund that?"

After this he inquired about yoga practice. He expressed a desire to learn it.

The ghosts of the past will haunt a yogi. Not this one, but most of the others are concerned to hold me to account for what they consider to be my irresponsible acts. Some others want me to extend my socially acceptable acts. Either way, if their desires are fulfilled, I will remain time bound.

Leadership Role in Yoga

Perhaps the most corrosive desire in yoga, the one that hurts the most and sets back the aspirant, is the one where a student aspires to be a leader or founder of a sect or lineage.

Anything created by anyone must be abandoned by that creator. This happens because of locational shifts. Since Nature always shifts at every moment, nothing is stationary, nothing stays put. Whatever is created by whoever will be confiscated by Nature, as it will shift the position, and cause a rupture in time, which separates the creator from his/her creation.

When someone is motivated by the desire to be in a lead position, that person is set for stress and disappointment because of the shifting way of Nature, which does not allow anyone to keep anything for any indefinite length of time.

Sooner or later, a leader will be dead and gone, with nature confiscating his monopoly. That will cause distress because the running credits will disappear from the leader's view, pushing him in a position, where he must again endeavor to be in a choice position. It is similar to a child who builds a sand castle on the beach. Within twelve hours, the tide advances and demolishes the construction.

The child may cry for it. Or he may accept the demolition as a challenge to his creative prowess. He may again construct the building as soon as the tide recedes. Day after day, twice each day, he may reconstruct the building.

Those who come to study yoga, and who have a need to be a leader, will fail at the practice. This will happen unless they abandon the leadership need which is a manifestation of dishonesty and arrogance.

Someone comes along. He hears about a leader of a yoga sect. He figures he will learn the practice from this exceptional person. On checking closely in his psyche, one may find that there are subconscious motives, which will disrupt progress. One of these undesirable aspects is the need for leadership. It is corrosive to yoga practice.

Part 4

Contrasting *Asana* postures and *Pranayama* Breath Infusion

There are *asana* postures as a practice on its own. Many mistake this as the culmination of yoga. It is not so, however.

There are *pranayama* breath disciplines. Some who master this are of the opinion, that this is the way to establish the foundation for interiorization and spiritual absorption. Interiorization is called *pratyahara*. Spiritual absorption, as a conjoint practice, is tagged as *samyama*. *Samyama* is segmented in three stages as *dharana*, deliberate focus, *dhyana*, effortless focus, and *samadhi,* extended effortless focus.

Asana is not the culmination of yoga but it is necessary if the physical body is not flexible, and does not have efficient blood circulation. Spiritual achievement is not a physical process but it is related to that attainment of yoga. A lack of efficient circulation, causes increase consumption of attention from the subtle body. This robbery results in a lower vibration subtle body. That reduces spiritual perception. *Asana* postures should cause efficient circulation so that the subtle body expends the least possible energy to maintain the physical form.

Pranayama breath infusion is concerned with increasing the quality of energy which is circulated in the physical body and the corresponding subtle one. While *asana* is concerned with circulating the energy which is in the physical and subtle bodies, the breath infusion is concerned with the quality of the energy.

A low quality of energy even if circulated efficiently, will not cause that energy to be improved in quality. This is why *pranayama* is required. It increased the oxygen in the physical body and increases the subtle energizing energy in the subtle one. Hence what is circulated is of a higher quality which results in brighter subtle perception and more shifts to higher planes.

Some yogis practice *asana* postures as the preliminary practice. When these are completed, they switch to *pranayama* breath infusion. That should result in automatic interiorization because as soon as the subtle body has a hyper charge of energizing energy, it internalizes.

Once this happens the meditation on higher planes of consciousness can occur as a natural progress, or as one which requires very little effort to hold the attention of the coreSelf.

The *asana* postures can be combined with breath infusion. When this happens, the yogi can cause the infused energy to be circulated through the entire physical body and the subtle form very efficiently. Otherwise, one may do *asana* postures, and then do breath infusion, to conclude the preliminary preparation for interiorization and meditation.

Shining Face Yogi

I met a yogi on the astral planes. He was long passed away, over one hundred years, but he did not assume an embryo. After being unable to assume himself as his last body, he delved into a high samadhi state, where his subtle body remained immobile, with the senses and adjuncts turned inward intently.

Due to this action, his subtle body progressively shrunk, and became reduced to a round shape of about ten inches in diameter. After being as that round shape for some years, that total psyche appeared as a shining face. He was in a moonlight *samadhi* bliss state, in which there were continuous waves of icy twinkle bliss. He smiles at every moment and cannot cease this. It is an involuntary state of consciousness.

He became aware of my meditation practice because I was posted to an astral place which Babaji occupied and which I assumed as a substitute lineage teacher. This is what he appears as.

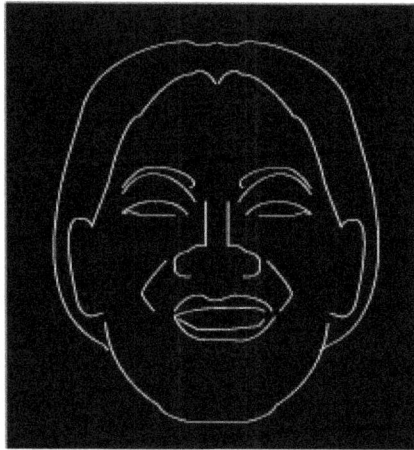

The Long Wait

Success in meditation, success on a consistent basis, happens after a long wait. In the Puranas, there are tales about yogis who succeeded in achieving their mystic objectives. Most of these made achievements after many years of practice, and after many lives.

Why the long wait?

The point is that whatever reason there is for a delay in an achievement, that is irrelevant. The fact is that one has to be steady, patient, and consistent. One must also redo a practice which was performed carelessly early on.

There are preliminary skills required for every advanced practice. If one overlooks the initial achievements, one will find that after a time practicing, one makes no progress. Or one makes irregular progress which does not tally for success. That may cause discouragement to such an extent, that instead of correcting an incorrect practice, one abandons it.

For success in meditation (*samyama*) one must be fully introspective (*pratyahar*). The mind must be calm with no flashing of memories, thoughts, ideas nor images. If the mind is preoccupied stubbornly flashing this or that event or symbol, one must have an effective practice, which can bring the mind to silence and blankness.

Once the mind is silenced, the long wait begins. One waits for a breakthrough, the opening of a portal to higher dimensions, the communication with a deity who is a supernatural or spiritual being, or a transfer so that the energy content of the mind is spiritual bliss.

Holding Breath

When doing *pranayama* breath infusion, one must be careful when holding the breath in or out. Any action for suspending breathing is dangerous, and should be carefully monitored. Suspension of breathing means that the body cannot continue its normal breath routine. Thus, the person who suspends breathing for any reason, takes responsibility for any mishap which occurs in the lungs, brain, or body, because of the system being unable to expel carbon dioxide (polluted air), and to absorbed oxygen (fresh air).

When doing *kapalabhati/bhastrika pranayama* breath infusion, the suspension of breathing should be done for one reason only, which is to facilitate the distribution of accumulated air. The assumption is that due to the rapidity of inhaling and exhaling, there will be excess oxygen in the lung cells. This excess should be distributed. That is the reason for a cessation of breathing. It is not for the purpose of holding the breath. The breath should not be suspended if there is no excess air in the lung cells which should be distributed.

If someone does several rapid breaths, the rate of ingestion of fresh air will be higher than the lung's ability to move that air into the blood stream. This means that the air will be compacted into the blood cells (alveoli) in the lungs. This reservoir of oxygen should be collected and transported by the red blood cells, which travel through the arteries.

There is a practice for holding the breath so that the body becomes conditioned to existing on stale air (carbon dioxide and other negative gases, ketones). That process is not the one which is practiced in *inSelf Yoga*™. For this yoga, retention of breath is only for distribution absorption, such that as soon as the excess oxygen moves from the lungs, into the blood stream and is distributed somewhere in the body, normal breathing is resumed, or rapid breathing is begun. Then again as soon as there is excess fresh air in the lung cells, there is retention of breath on an inhale or exhale, and there is immediate and intense focus, on the distribution of that excess air through the body.

The **danger in suspending breathing** is that the kundalini life force may switch its reliance from fresh air to stale air, from oxygen to carbon dioxide. If that happens one is likely to lose control of the body. Intake of carbon dioxide by the brain will cause the cells which support objective consciousness to enter a dull state, which will produce swoon, fainting, or unconsciousness.

As soon as the body needs to resume breathing, it should be allowed. Normal breathing should begin or rapid breathing for more infusion of fresh air should be initiated.

Desires control the Selves

On a close inspection of the interaction of desire formation and the self, one may safely draw the conclusion that the self is controlled by desires. There is a saying that *where there is a will, there is a way*. It suggests that providence will assist in manifesting a desire, provided the person involved exerts sufficient self-power (attention) into the idea.

This indicates that even if something is impossible by the laws of physics, it may be possible for a person who thinks of it and applies sufficient will-maneuverability. I tested this theory, and found that because there are so many dimensions, something that is impossible in one place, may be possible in some other niche, such that even though it is out of the question in a location, it would happen somewhere else in psychoSpace.

Early on in this life during its juvenile years, a pastor of a Christian church conceived of the idea of my becoming a pastor in my adult years. For no reason, without my permission, this preacher felt this way. He transferred the desire into my psyche.

Just yesterday, some sixty years after, his desire was fulfilled in the astral existence. I found myself as my subtle body in an astral place where this preacher, who is now deceased, and who even took another body with another profession beside religion, ordained me to be a Christian preacher.

Some years prior, I was pulled by him into a church service where he intended to ordain me. I resisted and escaped from that astral circumstance. This time however, there was no energy for escape. My subtle body went through the motions cooperating with whatever he desired.

He had a wish for my becoming a pastor. That desire is now fulfilled in a psychic world which facilitated his idea. I did not have to spend the major part of a lifetime being a preacher. It lasted for only about ten minutes in earth time. It was fulfilling for him such that the desire energy was dissipated completely. In his psyche the need for me to be a pastor is now fulfilled. In my psyche the energy he injected during my juvenile years is neutralized.

In his new physical body, he may have no conscious memory of the occurrence. This is because energy from the psyche of someone may be used, to enact the fulfillment of a desire, when that person has no idea, that the desire was processed.

Reproduction with Seduction

The main drive in a physical body is reproduction. Even in the case of infants and the elderly, where either has no reproduction capability, the reproduction urge is present. It is hollow in either case but it is there nevertheless, like having a ghost instead of a physical person. The ghost has psychic register which verifies its reality.

From day one, from the moment one is discovered to be an infant body, there is the representation of the reproduction energy. This manifest as the need to eat, to suckle. With it, is packed a small bubble of energy which is the seduction force. At that time, its appeal is rendered by soft skin and soft noises. These soft sounds charm the mother. These are an introduction to the seduction force. It is disguised as being pleasant to the touch sensation, which is an ally of the seduction power.

A question arises as to why Nature packed the seduction force with the reproduction aspect. What was the necessity? Did this happen accidently or indeliberately?

The sad part is that no one can rout or abolish this force. The entire speech about eliminating the reproduction/seduction power is nonsensical. There is no logic in the discussion.

The ascetic must allow it to happen because he is not in a position to thwart it. The battle is won by Nature. As a humbled warrior, the ascetic must put down his weapons, and leave the battlefield in shame. Because of the inability to bring the reproduction/seduction forces to order, one by one, each ascetic will do this. A truce is declared by Nature, not by the ascetic. He/She must hang his/her head in shame, having lost the challenge.

The reproduction force stands there. It is infallible. For millenniums it fought the battle. It suppressed the ascetics. It repeatedly proved its superiority. And yet some fanciful ascetics were of the view that they could topple it. What a shame!

Yoga is affected by Hard Feelings

Yoga practice, especially high-end meditation, is drastically affected by the hard feelings (resentments) which others hold for a yogi. These include whimsical differences which are of little consequence, but which occurred, and left unfavorable impressions in the psyche.

In the astral world, I met a lady who divorced her first husband, because they found to their dismay that they were incompatible. This lady was in the upper part of a residence she created in the astral world. She sat on a luxurious couch. Soon after this, her first husband appeared. He carried the energy of being her spouse.

They wanted me to be a witness to their conversation. The man said that early on, his life with that lady was haphazard. He admitted that many mistakes were made. He was immature, and could not at the time, make the proper decisions.

The lady for her part, wanted to live with him again. She said that she felt unfulfilled. She needed to be with this man, to reenact their life style in a perfect way.

After this experience, I considered writing about the incidence to explain that whatever hard feelings, one has, that will dictate one's future. The resentments and unfulfilled feelings which remain in the psyche, will be used by Nature to create new circumstances, where one may rectify the circumstance to one's satisfaction. The problem with this is that the attempt to change it for the better, will invariably cause new disagreements, in an endless loop of events, one to the other, with perfection of action, and mood, never being attainable.

For a yogi, it is ridiculous to think that in the future, somewhere, somehow, one will fix all resentments or hard-feelings which one was involved in, either as the target or as the agitator. Nature funds these events. It is the energy of Nature which drums up the disputes. The self's energy is used, but that self is not the creator of the energy which is stirred. A yogi should step aside and let Nature resolve events in whichever way it fancies.

Family Life Disagreements

A yogi should be careful not to become habituated to disagreements with friends and relatives. This applies even to those who are renunciants, but who reside at religious establishments, where maintenance of the residence is shared with other members of the sect.

As far as Nature is concerned, there is no difference between family members, and sect members who reside together, and share in social responsibilities. Under the cover of a religious organization, some ascetics are of the view that their associations are exempt from the laws of Nature, but that is not the reality.

Social interactions of every type are rated in the same way by Nature, in the way of tagging one for each involvement. Even the God, Krishna, during his life on earth, as reported in the *Srimad Bhagavatam*, dealth with social clashes, even with relatives who were rated as divine persons.

One should avoid being involved with factors and events which cause resentments and disagreements to arise. These energies will be logged by Nature, so that one will have to resolve them in the same lifetime or in the future. Disagreements and resentments bruise the subtle body. Some cause rashes in it. These damages itch, scratch, and irritate the psyche. Some rupture like abscesses which squirt pus.

Some yogis can fix these hurts in the subtle body, without having to take another embryo. One must understand that even if one was the victim, the person who was correct in the incidence, still it may bring a bruise on the subtle body.

Chit Akash Access

On April 29, 2023, during a discussion with the subtle presence of Yogeshwaranand, the topic of *chit akash* access was mentioned. This yogi facilitated many disciples to reach the *chit akash*. His method was to have a student stare into his eyes. From this Yogesh gained entry into the subtle head of the person. He strengthened and aligned that person's focus allowing vision into *chit akash* sky of consciousness.

Since he used a subtle body, and I used a subtle one which was interspaced into my physical form, the access did not require my staring into his eyes. Instead, I reached his psyche by projecting attention from my psyche to his. The first try was a failure. So was the second one. On the third attempt however, there was success with him being transferred to the right of my coreSelf in my psyche. Just then there was a blinding light which entered in a double blast, like the light on a dark night, which appears due to a lightning strike.

This did not remain for a long time. Perhaps it was there for nine seconds for the most. It was definite however. Yogeshwaranand said that the difficulty was to have the access remain open for the student. That does not occur unless the student has a tight *samyama* meditative focus meditation.

Yogeshwaranand confided to me that he did not transit to the *Krishnaloka* place nor did he have a full transfer to *chit akash*. He said that his original need was to use the inSight vision to peer through his physical and subtle bodies. Perhaps, that objective was not enough to granted access to the deity domains, the *devalokas*.

Need for Physical Energy

I was with a long-deceased yogi, who was very advanced in yoga practice in his last life. Suddenly, he asked if he could clasp my hands. I said there was no objection. He explained that recently he felt the need to be physical again. It was as if there was a need for physical energy, from someone who had a physical body.

Grasping my hand, he clasps it tightly. I felt energy leaving my forearm bones and moving into his subtle hand and forearm. Then I said this to him.

"It is a wonder that after becoming so advanced in practice, and having passed away for many years, also attaining higher levels of consciousness, still there is this need to be physical, and to have the subtle body needing physicalness. It is astonishing. Why is there the recurring need?"

He did not explain it. After some minutes when his forearm was filled with the subtle energy which flowed from my hands and forearm, he released his grip.

Meditation Wait

Yogeshwarananda explained that in some cases, a meditator who achieves a blank state, with a few ideas arising now and again, should continue for some time, for at least fifteen minutes. If perchance the yogi can do *pranayama* practice before the meditation, then it is likely that he/she will stay in the blank state, for a longer period, and with little or no effort to remain there.

In that state, one should wait for developments. The question of how long arises. The answer is that, if necessary, one should be prepared to wait forever. In the Puranas, we read of ascetics or even lower deities, who went to an edge of reality, and waited, or called for a superior personality to speak or appear. The wait for this in some cases was thousands of years, a period of an era, a long time.

The demigod Brahma may wait for several eras of time, for his guru, Lord Vishnu, to appear. Or Brahma may only hear a word or two spoken by Vishnu. He may not see the deity.

If during meditation, the yoga guru appears in the mindspace of the yogi, that is wonderful, but one should not wait in anticipation that this will happen. One does not know how the communication will be expressed. If one has an expectation, that may cause stress, which will prevent one from reaching higher planes.

During a meditation session, when Yogeshwaranand entered my subtle head, he instructed that I gather the focusing energy, which was randomly sprinkled in the mind. This was like gathering dust which floated on water. When this is done, a yogi should focus on the collected energy. He should keep the attention there. This may cause one to gain access to *chit akash* sky of consciousness, or to a supernatural plane of existence.

Cluster Focus / Divine Eye

In the effort to develop the divine eye, Yogeshwarananda mentioned that the *pratyahar* closing of the senses is to be mastered first. The yogi should spend hours in meditation, struggling to cause the senses to be retired. This will be known, because in meditation, there will be darkness with the visual sense not operating, not being alert, not wanting to be manifested nor expressed. The hearing sense will be active, but will only react to inner sounds, especially to naad resonance.

Once this retraction and inner closure is mastered, the yogi should peer forward to be sure that there are no ideas, images, and memories occurring. If that is the situation, the yogi should peer forward mildly. He/She should check for a speck of light, or for a portal to a super-dimension.

If there is only darkness or a blank condition, the yogi should make an effort to remain with it, with no ideas, images, nor memories. If he/she can be stable in that, the yogi should settle in that and do the long wait. This is a condition of waiting for a portal to open to a super-dimension, or the announcement of a deity from a transcendental place.

If after waiting for a time, in many meditations, for months or years of daily practice, and still not having access to a super-world, the yogi should consult with an advanced teacher about having someone enter the psyche, to provide guidance from within it. This is similar to asking a carpenter to enter a house, to observe a defect in it.

Once a guru is invited, provided he does enter the psyche of the student, he may advice the yogi in what to do to advance further. All depression or disappointment felt by the yogi, should leave the psyche when the guru enters. The teacher may offer a solution.

Yogeshwaranand told me that it is difficult for a yogi to access and use the divine eye. Even if the yogi gets the opportunity, there is no guarantee that it will be a permanent faculty. It may occur for a short bit, for seconds only.

He suggested that once the dark space is attained, the yogi should peer forward into it, grasp a cluster of that energy, and place the focusing ability in the cluster. If somehow the cluster which is grabbed evades the grip of the yogi, he should grab another cluster as soon as one eludes his grasp. This should be done repeatedly as if to give the mind a repetitive task. Over and over and over again, this should be done until there is the manifestation of a portal to higher dimensions, or a light from such places, or the appearance of a divine being from those zones.

Teaching Yoga

Last night, May 21 2023, Arthur Beverford appeared on the astral side. This person was my first yoga teacher. He said to inform a student that he should teach on the military base. I asked Beverford for details of what should be taught. He said that it should be *hatha* yoga and deep breathing with meditation in the end.

In that case *hatha* yoga means *asana* postures with stomach lifts. Deep breathing is that only. It does not include *kapalabhati/bhastrika*. The meditation is third eye focus which is done at the end of the session for about 15 minutes for the most.

I explained to Beverford that nowadays one has to be certified by an established institution before one can teach on a military base. Once years ago, around the year of 1976 when I was in Thief River Falls, Minnesota, Beverford came there. Money was hard to come by. He went to a college and spoke to a dean who hired teachers.

In a meeting with the man, Beverford was hired on the spot. Suddenly out of nowhere, Beverford pointed to me and told the Dean that I was an expert at yoga and should be hired. I almost froze in my seat. For one thing I use a black body, and the place was devoid of other-than-white bodied people. Luckily the Dean shook his head to indicate that he would not hire me.

Anyway, the point is that Beverford did teach yoga formally on US bases, and even without paperwork about this expertise. His real certification was Japanese martial arts which he learned at a monastery in Japan.

Rebirth Prep

Yogeshwarananda discussed the problem of rebirth. This is of interest to yogis. Whatever happened during the life of a physical body, may cause a yogi to get serious about liberation. The question is however: What is liberation?

How is it attained?

Is there a guarantee for it?

Is there a process which yields it?

How many years of practice are required to make sure it happens before or at the time of death of the physical system which currently one identifies as?

Yogeshwarananda said this.

"Tell them to prepare for rebirth. Any ideas about liberation are far fletched. All we know for sure right now is that rebirth will happen. Who knows otherwise? Who has that control. There was birth before. We know that. There was death before. Some of us are sure of that. Hence let us prepare for rebirth.

"Somebody said that he will transit to a deity's world. Really? Who told him that? Where is the heavenly place? England is to the north, south, east, or west, but where is that heaven?

"We know about the astral place. We access it in dreams. We travel from here to there during sleep. It will be the same at death, except that we will return to the physical side after months or years and not just within twelve hours or less.

"Study that. Prepare for rebirth. Did you see the woman you prefer as your next Mommy? Did you see a possible father? What about education? Which school will you attend? What will be the college degree?

"Who will be the wife after puberty?

"Do not be funny. Speak about it! Talk to me! I wish to hear nothing about liberation."

Deity Worship

The question arises as to if a yogi should do deity worship. The answer is that it depends on the need for it and also on the stage of advancement. Isolated yogis are not expected to do classic full deity worship. That is done in temples under opulent circumstances with time laid out for the ceremonies.

Deity worship is painstaking, detailed and requires precise focus and actions, which usually a yogi cannot commit, unless he was familiar with it from childhood. That would require being born in a family, where from birth he heard sacred Sanskrit mantras, and became familiar with worship procedures, handling of sanctified articles, saying special prayer for each action committed, and respecting senior priests who may or may not be related to him.

What to do if one did not take a body in a priestly family?

One should then apply for training in a lineage which is expert at deity worship. Provided they accept one as a student, one should learn the methods gradually, and gain their permission to do worship on one's own.

Alternately, without training, someone may get an image, a sculpture, a poster, or some art format of the deity which one is attracted to and feels to worship.

One should make a commitment to oneself or to the deity, to do certain actions where the deity is the daily focus. For instance, one can agree to present at least one flower if not more, daily. Or one may agree to do that, and also offer five minutes or more of one's time to sit before the deity quietly, or to do so while saying prayers in Sanskrit, or in any other language.

One may be committed to clean the area where the deity is located, on a daily or weekly basis, as much as one feels one can maintain. In time, doing this, one may add more obligations, provided one maintains the previous commitment, and do not skip nor neglect it in any way.

Above are a pair of Rukmini and Krishna deities. Before them and behind them are flowers which were specially acquired for them. The flower before them is changed on a daily basis. That has a pleasing fragrance which is preferred.

Every action which is added by the yogi will involve more time for the daily involvement. Hence, one should not whimsically make promises which one cannot maintain.

Dietary Control

Control of diet with the restriction of the time of eating, is an important part of *hatha* yoga. Because of making excuses for wrong diet and ill-placed eating times, some students neglect to discipline the self about food consumption. Usually, one becomes addicted to certain tastes, and time of eating, during the infant and juvenile stages of the body. These habits may be deep rooted, not just from the parents, but from the past life of the yogi, where the tendencies for eating disorder, surface in the mind as a definite need.

Some students resent a teacher who makes suggestion about diet. Due to not wanting to oppose the teacher openly, such students maintain a sharp-edged grudge, because of suggestions made about changing the diet and adjusting the time of eating.

Actually, the teacher has little to do with it. One should act for self-preservation, which means to act in one's long ranged interest. For instance, when this body was in the boyhood stage, there were no objections made by its seniors, as to eating many sweet or over-ripe fruits. The short-ranged result of this was the pleasure of sugary food. The long-range effects could be a diabetic condition in the elderly years.

There are many instances for resentment for either dietary restriction or the lack of it. Here I list three examples.

- resenting seniors for not providing sweet fruits during infant and adolescent years
- resenting oneself for not ceasing the sugary foods intake during the adult years after the seniors relinquished their social control
- resenting oneself or parents for the negative results which manifested as incurable diseases in the elderly years

It is difficult to nudge these resentments. They are instinctual in formation. They bully the self as mandatory urges. A person rarely understands how these energies are formulated. There is little objectivity when they gush out of the self, with intentions to hurt someone else.

One is born with a sense of taste which is involuntary. Who can conquer the tendency?

Divine Eye Development

Divine eye development is a complex discipline which may take years, if not lives, to be available for usage. I did some research into this. Recently I endeavored under the tutelage of Yogeshwarananda, a person who in his last body would energize some students, and even arrest the willpower of some disciples, and cause them to have the use of the divine eye.

When questioned about this arresting of the willpower, he did not have an English vocabulary, to further define what he meant by willpower. He restrained the wayward and erratic willpower of some students, but it was unclear as how to better define what exactly he arrested in their subtle heads.

After checking and checking, I determined that he arrested the focusing power of the person. One other word which would help is attention, in the sense of when the attention is focused, or when there is intention to focus it, and it becomes alert.

The other part to this is the object of focus. There may be gathering of the focusing power, or positioning it as a beam being directed. But there must also be an object of focus, or no object of focus, with the focusing power's alertness being itself the object of focus.

My report is that when the focusing power is not alert, it is in a relaxed condition, where it is either subjected to an influence, or it loses self-objectivity. It fades, with the self assuming a blurred consciousness, a lack of definition.

Any of this was arrested by him, in students whom he engaged in that way. I determined this by his presence in my psyche, while watching his actions through the sense of identity, which is itself the focusing power in conscious subjectivity.

Once when he moved in my subtle head, he ceased movement. Then he meditated with intentions of gathering the *chitta* subtle energy in my subtle head. His intention was to gather all or part of it and focus into that energy. In some cases, this action produced access to the divine eye but with limited usage, according to the intention of the person, who had sufficient concentration and gathering control. This ability is then transferred to the student.

It happened in my case, that the *chitta* energy in the subtle head, resisted his gathering action. It began to compress inwards on itself, but then it stopped and compressed no further.

On another occasion when he entered the subtle head, he went to the right back of it. I went to the left front, collected some energy in a narrow oval shape which was like a bullet or mini cylinder. Then for a split second an opening appeared there. It accessed an environment which was all-pervading milk-white light. This is a *chit akash* spiritual zone.

Yogeshwarananda clarified that dimension, to be a supernatural perception, which was different to his experience with the divine eye. In fact, as we discussed this, we were not sure as to if there was more than one divine eye. His experience was a specific one which he described in his books, like *Science of the Soul*.

The concept of the divine eye only happening at the third eye chakra is false. It can arise anywhere in any location in the psyche. It does not have to be in a specific place. However, most ascetics of the *kriya* lineage, and the *Bhagavad Gita* itself, attests to it being there. This is due to the fact that the center of the eyebrows is itself a third eye, which can be used by itself, or in conjunction with the intellect, which is inside the subtle head.

There are at least six means of using the divine eye.

- Center-of-the-eyebrows chakra
- intellect analysis thought-producing orb
- crown-chakra penetration energy
- sense-of-identity attention powers
- combination of intellect and center-of-eyebrows chakra
- transparency-intuition subtle tool

This means that an ascetic should be broad minded in his/her desire to use the divine vision. One should expect any opening or availability of the divine eye. It does not have to be this or that. It can be any of those listed. Or it may be something else. If one is hard set with only one method, that attitude may cause more frustration in the effort to attain supernatural or divine perception.

It is likely, that the divine eye may happen spontaneously, when one least expects, and irrespective of one's interest in it. It could occur involuntarily with the person having no control of it, as to when the access begins and ceases. There is sufficient evidence that sensual perception did not form, due to any limited person's willpower or forced desire. It developed through a natural process, irrespective of the demand for it by an individual. For instance, who can say that he knew he wanted a spherical eyeball, or a pin-like eye, as in the case of an insect?

If one did not create any sense of the physical body, how practical is it, to think that one will produce a divine perception visual access.

It is explained in the history of some ascetics and powerful yogis, that they accessed the divine eye, and perceived the movements of the subtle bodies of others, regarding developing embryos, then growing as adult bodies, then being disenfranchised from those bodies, then living in a psychic dimension hereafter, then again become embryos elsewhere.

The question is. How did that divine eye function? Was it a visual perception which rendered understanding of colors? Was it an accurate intuition, where the ascetic instantly knew the whereabouts, and motivational energy of someone?

I saw people moving to get rebirth in the astral dimension, but in most of the perceptions, such persons were perceived as transparent subtle bodies, where their destinies travelled with them as psychic energy. I could absorb their destiny format, and know details about their past, present and future. Is this a use of the divine eye?

Agnisara Abdomen Demolition

Agnisara is an abdomen control and demolition practice. It shows results in the physical and astral bodies. The thrust of it is on the astral side but it is necessary for any yogi using a physical body to achieve progress in the physical body as well. Once it is alive, the physical body affects the astral form. It is important to control diet, digestion, and excretion. This control yields efficient use of subtle energy such that the subtle body supplies the least energy for the maintenance of the physical one. Such conservative transfer of subtle energy benefits the psyche, where it remains in a brighter condition, and does not dim because of energy inefficiency.

There is a sharing exchange between the physical body and the astral one. That entails dimming or brilliance in either form. Improper diet, digestion, and excretion, causes dimming.

On May 27, 2023, I met a yogi on the astral side. This person has no physical body. He departed over sixty years ago. Since then, he was preoccupied expanding and protecting the spiritual society he established with his last physical body. He was interested in the *agnisara* practice and said that even though he mastered meditation in his past life, he did not pursue much practice of yoga *asana* and *pranayama*.

His lineage did not stress it. Instead, they spent hours in still meditation within the mind. His last physical body became bloated. His subtle body mimicked that condition. It remains in a barrel shape even to this day. He wanted to do the aggressive breath infusion as *kapalabhati/bhastrika pranayama*, to bring his subtle body into a fit condition.

He was also concerned with toning the energy in the thighs, legs, feet, and toes. He said his thighs were enlarged like those of a woman. He wanted to change that. As I did an hour of breath infusion, he did whatever I did. He smiled much because of feeling the effects in the subtle form. He studied the way I infused, compressed, observed, and directed the accumulated breath energy in my subtle body as well as what it did in my physical form.

One can begin yoga *asana* postures and *pranayama* breath infusion after one loses control of the physical body, and is left with only the subtle form.

However, it is better, if one began these disciplines while using the physical body. That effort would result in a fit subtle form.

Sexuality in Yoga

In yoga practice sexuality should be closely monitored just as diet and some other aspects must be checked. Sexuality is a big factor in the practice of inSelf Yoga™ but not in a fanatical and dogmatic way. Rules about expression, suppression and even the elimination of sexuality are present in most religions and spiritual disciplinary practices, but generally these ideas are dogmatic.

History has shown however, that the dogma and stimulations repeatedly prove to be impractical. When one considers the factor of physical masturbation and astral sexual activity, the theories about celibacy are absurd beliefs for the most part. This is because what the individual professes may not be endorsed by Nature. Whatever moral rules the institution claims to enforce may be broken by overpowering urges.

The sexual urge is such a compelling impulse, that an individual or instruction, cannot override it, merely by making promises, or by stamping rules. For the purpose of *inSelf Yoga™* the policy is that sexual restrained must be studied individually. Pledges and rules must be adopted to the individual's practice but Nature's power must be taken into consideration.

Unless it is a limited pledge that is easily maintained, no one should take a vow of absolute celibacy. There are so many ways for Nature to disrupt any vow, that one would be foolhardy to make one. It is best to deal with sexuality day by day, as to its challenges, and as to if one can be exempt from it. As a limited being using physical and psychological equipment manufactured by Nature for its own purposes, it would be silly to make a rash vow.

There is the problem of definition. What does celibacy mean?
- Is it a physical restraint?
- Is it a physical restraint with psychological expression on the psychic side of life?
- Is there no chance that the individual will be compelled to express sexually?

If there is uncertainty in any such area, the celibacy effort is an effort only. In whatever field an ascetic makes a commitment for total restraint, he will be the ridicule of others, if he does not comply. The reality is that his pledge to whatever principle or practice, was done with little regard for his limited power.

It is not that Nature only encourages indulgence and does not foster celibacy. Nature does honor total restraint but she does that on occasion only. There are times when she is downright against it, when she works to destroy any notion of the possibility of it. But there are times when she upholds it flawlessly, where there is no conversion to sexual relationship within the physical or subtle bodies.

One should note this. One should cherish the experience of celibacy which Nature affords it. One should astutely study Nature's rejection of celibacy, and how she dismantles it during certain occasions.

A newborn has no sexual arousal. Even if there is an erection in the male infant body, still that is not accompanied with sexual feelings. The concept of sexual movements is not present in its psyche. In fact, this lack of sexuality persists continually for some years. That is a celibate condition. One may, in meditation, reach that infant consciousness which did not have a sexual urge. To get a deeper feeling of it, one may contemplate it for a time. One may wish for a change in psyche, where the adult format is replaced by the infant sense of gender.

Even in the elderly years, especially for males, sexual expression is drastically reduced. In time it is reduced to near nil. The whole idea about sexual expression vanishes. One is no longer reminded of it. There are no more arousals. But this is if one is in an environment which lacks sexual forms and media.

Imagine what life would be, if the infant condition continued through the whole life of the physical body, where there was no stage at which puberty manifested. That is an issue. Who would want to live forever in a sexually neutral body? Can one be certain that the adult status of the physical body with its compelling sexual urge, is the desired condition of gender? Does anyone aspire for a perpetual condition of existence, as a sexually neutral expression of self?

When as the body ages, there is reduction in sexual urge, some persons become anxious that a vital part of the self is being cancelled. I once knew a man who was fearful of old age. He felt that it portended bad luck, because it initiates sex reduction hormones in the body. He dreaded the day when he would not have sexual arousal. He pitied older men who found that at a certain age, they lost virility, and could not have erections, nor sexual emissions.

One's existence is not threatened by Nature's refusal to continue sexual activity, in the form of malfunctioning sexual organs, which cannot assume a condition for some type of sexual pleasure activity. One's existence continues regardless of suspension, or elimination of sexual capacity. Hence why be dissatisfied if the same Nature which developed, and explored sexual indulgence, took steps to reduce, and eventually eliminate it.

Is life without sexual activity a dismal reality? A man I knew once spoke to his nine-year-old son. He probed, "What is the name of your girlfriend?"

The son abruptly replied that he had no girlfriend. He was startled by the question. He answered as if he had no idea what a girlfriend was, nor any view that such a person was required. What about remaining in that state forever?

Arrest of Focus

Yogeshwarananda explained that the use of the divine eye is based on the ability to control the willpower. However, this use of the term *willpower* is different to the normal meaning for the word. Willpower in its frequent usage is mental control of physical or subtle events. It is the ability to execute a determined act.

When I checked the details of what Yogeshwarananda described, it was the control of the focus of the coreSelf. This is the control of the focus of the sense of identity, which is a relational connection between the coreSelf and any other subtle or physical object. In this case the object is something psychic. It could be a zone of energy, a space, an atomic dot or point, or a color which is in the mind's energy field.

According to Yogeshwarananda the ability to maintain the focusing energy of the coreSelf on another part of the mind, or on the core itself, will result in divine eye access.

This is easier said than done, because it is unnatural in our present condition, for any limited being to maintain such focus for any length of time. Usually someone may begin the focus on a desired psychic location or object, but then as soon as the focus is applied, it is shattered. The person does not shatter it, it is shattered by other energies in the mind.

The effort is to upset the shattering factor, so that the focus is continuously maintained. What normally happens is that the student applies a focus, and keeps it for a moment only. That focus is shattered, and another involuntary focus begins. This new focus may be acceptable or unwanted. Regardless, the matter we are concerned with, is the shift of the original focus. How did that happen? Can that be prevented? Which is the yogic discipline which curbs the mind from this shifting habit, where it breaks the resolution of the yogi?

I spoke to a man recently about a topic which he eagerly inquired about. During the conversation when I explained the detailed answer, he dozed. He could no longer focus to hear what I said. Something in his mind shattered the focus. He assumed a drowsy condition, in which there were several ideas shifting in and out, with his focus on either one being diminished.

After he dozed for four minutes, he resumed attentiveness on this physical side. By then he completely forgot our conversation. Instead, he began a new topic. He acted as if that was the conversation before. What causes this?

Nutrition ~ The Central Issue

On close examination, time and again, year after year, in my research into the forces of attraction and repulsion, in the sensual quest of the psyche as one experiences it while using a physical body, and even when there is no such form for usage, I concluded that the main attraction is the need for nutrition.

There are and were many proposals with proofs given by many other ascetics and spiritual teachers of renown. Most of them have issued no such conclusion. Why? It all depends on the angle of perception, and the state of mind while doing the investigation into the cause of attraction and repulsion.

Separately, there is the issue about what sponsors the drive. Why it is so compelling? As for the idea of eliminating it, that is mostly fantasy. There is no scope for the limited individual to rid himself/herself of it.

Nature manufactured the urge for nutrition but it runs through specific conduits. These passages cause the self to derive incorrect ideas about the objective. From day one, from the time the embryo is pushed from the womb, it finds itself with the urge for nutrition, something it must fulfill to continue living on its own. It was concerned with nutrition while it was in the mother's body but that concern was met moment by moment. It was connected to the placenta tubing which channeled the liquid substances it needed.

Once the placenta ceased transporting nutrients, there was a gap in fulfillment which cause the nutrition urge to panic. At first its gasped for air. Soon after it checked for liquid food. Ideally it was transferred to the mother's breast, where its sucking impulse was activated.

All of this was done from a blind condition, by mere sensing through feelings, and its innate ability to judge without seeing. The sense of touch was present, as well as the sense of smell, the sense of hearing and the sense of tasting.

With no developed sight, there is the subtle need for seeing. These energies collectively form and seek out developed sense perception. With that the entity pursues color which is the hint of form. The attraction to color is a dominant sense in the human body. It is can be misleading, where the effort to procure it, does not result in the fulfillment of nutrition. Still, it remains the dominant impulse for pursuing nutrients.

Enjoyment is involved in this quest but that is not the issue. Nature misleads one into thinking that enjoyment is the objective. It is not that. It is the need for acquiring nutrients, for the convenience of nourishing whatever form one uses.

Reluctance to Practice Yoga

Today, July 3, 2023, Yogeshwarananda said that he was disappointed by the high percentage of yogis, who become reluctant to practice. After they are introduced to methods, and shown these in detail, it seems that they continue for a bit, and are then overcome by a retardative braking force, which causes them to cease, and to continue making excuses for not making the effort.

He said that eventually such stalled yogis, abandon the practice. Usually, they secretly go away from advanced association. They resume normal life with superficial spiritual interest. Their resistance to materialistic association makes a sharp dip from which they rarely recover.

He asked me if I noticed this. What could I say? Of course, I noticed it. For some years now doing yoga in this body since at least the year 1973 when I first taught some of the practice, I noticed that most of the students, even those who begin with an aggressive strong interest, gradually are neuralized by other influences.

Some students are ardent readers of yoga books. Some do not read. They prefer to associate and participate in discussion. In either case, there is a power struggle between the interest of yoga and other energies which counteract the need for the practice.

This conversation with Yogeshwarananda brought to mind, the situation of why I had the idea that a physical body would be useful, for the purpose of discovering methods of yoga, which were proven in this time and place, to be productive of mystic perception.

Before taking this body, I had the view that being physical, practicing methods to see their effectiveness, and teaching the same, showing by example, that many students would benefit, and would sustain a practice. However, this idea is put to question because the majority of people whom I somehow or the other introduced to the practice, did not continue to do it.

My physical presence is just as good as if I did not assume physicality. Why become a body to do something, and then discover that the risk of being physical was not worth it. If one is present in the physical history of this world, and even then, one has little or no impact on humanity, what is the value of going through the birth process, from being made sexual fluid, then being male-female sexual combination, then embryonic, then newborn stage, then infant stage, then juvenile stage and so on?

At some point one is faced with realization that this world will go its own way, with no regard for anybody, not for a great yogi even. And where does God fit in? But even if there is an argument to show that God functions, still then, the limited self who tries to make an impact, finds itself to be irrelevant to Nature's plans for human development.

Psyche Inhabitants

Over the years, one after another, I discovered some other persons living in my psyche. In most cases, the discovery was made after an occupant was in the process of leaving the psyche. Rarely have I discovered anyone who stayed in the psyche after being confronted. In addition, usually I was unable to interview the person. There was present, a hesitation energy, which stalled the mind as soon as an inquiry about the identity and purpose of the person was made.

This occupant whom I discovered during a meditation on July 9, 2023, was a supernatural being. He resided in my right hip. When he was discovered, I instantly realized that he was resident there for some years, for at least ten years. His format was weightless, so that I could not know of his presence. His energy was invisible except that it became known as a sex polarity force some years ago. Then, after a few years, after the first detection of the polarity force, it became known, when a woman I knew was present.

It is clear that the supernatural being was wrapped in a neutral energy, like a worm wrapped in a silken cocoon. The idea was for me to become this person's father, with a specific female being his mother.

At the discovery, suddenly the surrounding energy disappeared. A lust energy manifested. That diffused so that only a neutral energy was present, with this occupant being released from my psyche. It is to be understood that other entities may live in the psyche. These persons may be unknown to the primal occupant, and he/she may influence one's behavior, with one not knowing that one is controlled.

Guarantees for Salvation

On June 19, 2023, I was speaking to a famous Vaishnava swami, who is now departed. He wanted to discuss the accusations which some of his living and deceased disciples made about him, concerning his promise that if they adhered to his methods of spirituality, they would attain the spiritual world where his deity resided. This deity is Krishna of the *Bhagavad Gita*.

The Swami said this.

"I give those guarantees on the basis of the *Bhagavad Gita* primarily, regarding what Krishna said there. Some part of the assurance is based on what was said by Lord Chaitanya.

"When I reconsider the incidences, how many white-bodied persons came to me, and were assured by me about this method of salvation, I see that I confidently made certain guarantees, which were not serviced by providence, where these people who submitted to me, did not get the result intended.

"I indicated to them that if they followed the words of Krishna in my translation of *Bhagavad Gita*, they would definitely go to Krishna's place, back to Godhead, as I declared.

"To consider this now, there were other factors which needed to support the warranty. For instance.

- God would have to agree to do it.
- Nature (Maya) would have to agree to support parts of it
- My understanding of Krishna's promises in *Bhagavad Gita* would have to be absolutely correct.
- Provided that the guarantee was valid, the disciple would have to meet the standard to qualify.

"Any mishap in any of those conditions would result in failure of the warranty. I was overconfident at the time. I did not think in any way that there could be a defect. I was assured by my authorities in the lineage in India. I was self-confident. I radiated that idealism. The disciples absorbed that. With myself and the disciples being saturated with the assurance, I could not predict, nor know, that there would be failure, and not a single one would attain the salvation promised.

"One other thing is that when I said that a disciple should surrender to Krishna, that was a mix of actions which included Krishna. It meant surrender to myself, first of all, because the disciples were not before a physical speaking Krishna. They were present with me. The idea that they should do as Krishna instructed really meant as I instructed, which in some circumstances may be at variance with how Krishna would have directed.

"One area where I had doubts about my instructions but where I was not self-critical, was the area of disciples being married. As a religious head, some disciples were married by me. Many of those marriage did not endure. My blessings to them, the official religious ceremonies with rituals, and deity services performed, did not prevent the divorces which followed.

"This means that my blessings for marriage did not apply for any length of time, not for the lifetime of those two disciples. Nature did not support it. Krishna did not cause it not to dissolve in a short time.

"This guru business is not a good thing. It is best not to be a guru, at least not in the way of having wholesale control of the disciple's lives. One should advice someone, and let that person work out the social details like marriage. Otherwise, one will give a guarantee which Nature and God may not service.

"And the final question is this.

"Why did Krishna not support the promises made?

"The answer is that the promises were flawed. The incidence is to be regretted. I am sorry about it. Unfortunately, I cannot reverse it. It is now part of history."

Discharge of Pleasure Energy

As I read one of Yogeshwarananda's book in the series of *Beads of Sermons*, someone approached. It was a deceased lady whom I knew some years ago. She is departed. I see her every so often when she desires to discuss something. She used to be at Yogeshwarananda's astral ashram and was known there as ruchiSindhu. Because of attachment to physical social life, her subtle body left the hermitage.

She was in a state of pleasure, unbearable pleasure which needed relief. As I attempted to speak to her, she mounted my thigh and then collapsed so that her spine was not erect but the rest of her body was in contact with my thigh, but with her vulva pressing against my thigh. Because she is on an astral level, where no clothing of the body is present, she was nude.

I realized that she was relieved of a high pleasure state which accumulated in her subtle body. I kept reading the book. After some minutes she moved from the collapsed position and sat on my thighs, while hugging my body. With no words being said, she expressed a happiness, because of discharging in a circularly wave motion, the pleasure energy which saturated her body to the point of exhaustion.

The subtle body may accumulate pleasure energies from time to time, such that one will have to find a way to gain relief from it. For those who practice *pranayama*, they should practice to disperse accumulated kundalini lifeForce energy or sexual energy expression. This will cause the kundalini to disperse itself continually, where there will be no accumulation of sexual needs or of any other type of pleasurable or unpleasure force.

Tobe Terrell's Astral Place

Tobe Terrell welcomed me at his astral place (July 20, 2023). He has a large wooden building which was spacious. The back yard is a small beach on a black water river. He even had paint on hand and requested me to paint one room. The paint was old-fashioned linseed oil-based paint.

To be consistent with his way of doing things, I requested a caustic soap for washing the floor of the room, which has twelve-inch wide roughly sawed one-inch timber. He wanted to know if a dear friend of mine, Sir Paul Castagna, would come there. I assured him that Paul would be glad to do so.

If one has a resistance for taking an embryo, if one wants to avoid doing that, it is likely that one will have an astral place which closely resembles the physical surroundings one had, just before passing from the recent physical body.

One noted feature about Tobe's astral surroundings, was the bright sunlight which was present there, not a sun orb, just sunlight in all directions. There were children there, and some persons who were compatible with Tobe when he was on the physical side.

Friction: Woman to Woman

A lady who was long deceased but who did not become an embryo as yet, came to see me on July 28, 2023. She was eager to speak.

She said this, "I was surprised that everywhere I went in the astral existence, there are some negative features of physical life which remain the same. For instance, I noticed while I was alive physically, that women are covertly and openly competitive to each other. This is in regard to their relationship with men, where a woman who feels sexually attractive to a particular male, will do her best to foreshadow or push away any other woman who comes in the vicinity of that man."

"On one side, men are sexually aggressive. Men are expected to be competitive with each other in terms of partner choices. But women also have a constant rivalry, even though that is not as obvious as the males. For instance, when there is a public occasion, women exhibit their rivalry towards each other in the way they attire themselves. This includes the use of cosmetics.

"Sometimes when I meet a group of women in the astral existence, I find that the competitive energy between us arises with even greater impetus, than when we were physically alive. This realization that the tendency for sexual rivalry continues hereafter, is disappointing. I did not expect this.

"Why would a female friend, whom I knew during the teen years in my dead body, be hostile to me and express suppression energies, because she liked someone who spoke to me, when we were in high school so many years ago, when we were physically alive."

My reply was this.

Whatever tendency one has, whatever ingrained feeling or urge, that will remain as is, when one passes from the physical body. There is no change in the psyche when the physical system dies. What may happen is that a certain tendency may be muted for a time. Or it may be suspended. But it remains intact somewhere in the psyche. Some aspects remain under a spring-loaded psychological pressure. It is like a time bomb. It is in a harmless state, until a trigger is released by some action.

This means that whatever tendency one had during the physical life, that will be triggered sometime somehow in the future. That teen friend had those feelings so many years ago, but was unable to bring it to your attention. She suppressed it, or it was suppressed by an involuntary force in her psyche. The pressure of it remained like a corked bottle of aged alcohol. If one removes the cork, the gas force within the bottle will be released.

When this person met you in the astral existence, the pressure in her psyche was released, because the social condition which caused the suppression of the resentment towards you, was no longer present.

From one perspective, it is good that it was released. Otherwise, it would still be covertly present, and would increase in pressure, and would in the future explode with even more violence.

Design of the psyche

A perplexing and very daunting challenge for yogis, is the study of the design of the psyche. A big question which some ponder, is: Who or what designed it?

The identity of the designer as Nature, or a personGod, is hotly contested among some yogis but after the argument is relaxed, that issue fades because the challenge remains, which is: How can one alter the design?

Speaking about it using obvious features, means that one began as an embryo which was itself predesigned by Nature, or by an unseen personGod, or by the influence of both Nature and God. But certainly, the entity did not create its embryo.

Usually, it is in the adult stage of a body, that the person begins to realize that the body and its psyche operates in a way, which that someone would not have designed. But there are features of the body and psyche which are approved by the person.

More important, why is the person blamed for the way the psyche operates?

Why is someone held accountable for the urges which the psyche produces involuntarily?

For instance, someone who was a theistic yogi had a contentious argument with another ascetic. The theistic one claimed that his guru was God incarnate. The other yogi who was an atheist, contested that. He said, "If your guru is God, he had better not evacuate waste from his body. That is a foul activity which God would not tolerate. With God there is enough power to stop unwanted habits. Does your guru evacuate? I would accept him as God if he does not."

This argument illustrates a point, that one has a psyche which one cannot control, or which one can control in a small measure. All liberation processes should include the information that the psyche was predesigned by some personal or impersonal agency. The yogi must work with the already-created design.

Some aspects of the psyche cannot be changed by the person. Some can be suppressed for a time. Some go into dormancy and resume at another time. Most operations in the psyche are involuntary. For instance, breathing on the physical level is involuntary. One cannot change that feature of design.

Sensual quest is involuntary, which means that one is compelled to pursue and procure specific objects. Some slight alteration may be installed but the main design cannot be changed.

A simple feature like the appearance of a certain color will give a specific response in the psyche. Even if one trains the psyche not to sprout that response, there is an underlying predesign response, which remains in the psyche, and which arises repeatedly, even if one does not want the psyche to operate in that way.

God Experience

On August 1, 2023, Yogeshwarananda shared with me his experience of God. This is not a person form of a deity but at the same time, it is not an imperson either. What is it?

It is the all surrounding and penetrating influence, which is the underbasis of whatever can be experienced in this physical world and its psychic counterpart. This is a mental energy which is supportive of whatever happens, whatever happened, and whatever will occur, where as the support of this, its presence is necessary for this to occur.

In the experience, it felt as a person with a face which is near to everything and everyone, but then it felt as a smiling person who is the producer of this manifestation.

In the experience, this is both personGod and non-person source Ultimate, but with no pain or repercussion being transmitted to that source, where the trauma we endure never afflicts that Absolute, even though we are subjected to unpleasant feelings and events.

There is the feeling that this Basis produced this situation, both the physical and non-physical portions of this. But this Source has no liability for this. It is never subjected to being responsible for this. It is beyond reproach for this. Yet It is essential to this.

Yogi in a Compromising Position

An agnihotra priest whom I knew some years ago, and for whom, my friendly relationship was terminated, due to rivalry and disagreement, came on the astral side on August 2, 2023. He acted as if there were no disagreements. He spoke to continue the friendly relationship as before.

There was however, a favor which he wanted me to render. With a distressed face, he said this.

"I will need you to render a favor, my friend. If you can, please be seen in public, in a compromising position with that woman."

I questioned him, "And what would that do, if I am seen with the lady in a sexually compromising behavior?"

He replied, "O no, you do not have to actually be in a sexual act with her. The supernatural people are sensitive, where even if you stand near to her, or even if you attempt to kiss her but do not actually do it, that would be sufficient."

For more clarification, I said to him, "And what would that immoral behavior, do for you friend?"

He replied, "From the day I was confronted with accusations about speaking to that other woman, every bit of my pious activity as a Vedic priest, prior to that time, was lost for me. In addition, my wife who assisted me during that time, will be unable to receive her pious credits.

"As it stands, because my wife and I were jointly engaged doing the Vedic rituals, she cannot reap the rewards singly, and I cannot be reimbursed due to being with the other woman.

"An astral authority said that if I could get a mystic yogi to absorb the relationship with that other woman, my wife and myself could jointly get the merits."

After saying this, he left.

The question is. How did I become implicated in the activity of this priest and his wife who assisted him, when he rendered priestly duties before his wife accused him of an affair with another woman?

My involvement happened when his wife complained to me. She had evidence of phone calls made between this priest, (her husband), and the other woman. Because I heard those accusations, I was implicated. Helping others, hearing of the troubles of others, can be hazardous for a yogi.

Should I help him?

What is your advice?

Morality in Yoga Practice

Yogeshwarananda, on the astral side, dived into the chest region of my subtle body. This was on August 5, 2023. He retrieved a memory incidence which happened over fifty years ago, during the teen years of this body. When he surfaced from the chest, and entered the throat, he displayed the memory. He examined the events.

During a conversation, he said this.

"Previously I did not consider the ancestors' parts in this. Previously, following the Vedic literature, I regarded it as a moral breach only. It is more than that. The puzzle is that one rarely sees the ancestors who are the integral motivating force of this. Nature pushes this ignorance. One's insight is disabled, because of not having the applicable discrimination to sort this.

"The world will go the way it is, with the colossal ignorance on the part of most persons. This will continue. However, let us discuss this as a talk between a celibate yogi and a sexually involved one. There is some need for this discussion. Like for instance, if I took another body, and Nature made conditions in my youth where I become a family man. How would that play out? What about the discrimination? How much of it does one have? It seems that Nature disables the aptitude. It causes one to see the urge for sexual intercourse and the avenues for coitus. What is your opinion about this? In the present body, you passed through events for this."

Since he requested my views, I explained this.

"The incidences which you retrieved from my memory were buried long ago. Until this moment when you retrieved it and showed it, I did not have an active recall. You were a celibate yogi in the immediate past life. Now you have an interest to understand the forces behind the sexual impulses.

"This much I can say. Most of it is a matter of fate but that is a combination force. The person concerned, in this case, myself, has very little to say in what happens. Yes, as you realize, the ancestors are the major part, but with Nature operating the overall plan and course of events.

"First of all, the development of sexual impulse is not done by the entity who is identified as the body. He or She does not create the events. Society may blame the individual if there is a pregnancy or otherwise even, but still the offender and the victim, neither of them are actually the creators of the incidence.

"The ancestors have more to do with it, but they are compelled as a lust force by fated circumstances, which are beyond their control. Still, if a yogi can understand the role of the ancestors, and perceive their influence, he/she may have some objectivity, and be released from the influences.

"In the incidence which you saw in my memory, the young lady in question became known to me through a relative who was a friend of hers. Initially there was a slight attraction between her and myself. That was not enough to draw us into a sexual interest relationship. However, after seeing her once more, the sexual interest spontaneously developed.

"Based on that force, I arranged to take her to a friend's cottage but when we arrived there, this young lady hesitated to enter the residence. After this, we got transportation. She returned to her parents' place. Later her parents got wind of this and complained to my parents about it.

"The incidence was constructed by ancestors, where some of her ancestors were hesitant for her to have a relationship with any young man. But there were some ancestors on her side who did not mind the event. Those persons were willing to take the risk of having teen parents who had no income or property.

"On my side, the ancestors in my psyche were eager to be the children of the young lady. They were in control of my psyche, at least the sexual aspects of it. I had very little control of the sexual potential of my body at that time. I did not consider the risk involved.

"My ancestors were reduced to being a sex desire force only. They had no rational faculty. Their consciousness at that time, was only an urge for finding their way into a young woman's sexual passage, with no idea about the social circumstances of the young lady. From my perspective at the time, I was on a journey, on a need conveyance which went somewhere. I did not consider the social liabilities."

Yogeshwarananda replied with this.

"Morality is a social idea of people who are in control of making moral stipulations for the convenience of those who are elderly. We see more and more, that the older generation lose control. This is due to the advancement of science. The elderly persons become irrelevant, because of the invention of many devices, which change the spread of the liabilities, as for example birth control which prevents pregnancies. Women can get rid of pregnancies. Once they occur, they are not forced to complete them."

Rivalry

In every area of relationship among the selves, rivalry is natural. Each self aspires for prominence. Fortunately, Nature throttles the clashing energy which we know as fate. This is done so that the rivalry is expressed in a reduced condition with less violence than it would be if it was not regulated.

In the astral existence, I was with some women at a meeting of acquaintances. These females were in elderly bodies on the physical side. They met in their elderly years on the astral side to compare their career successes. For a split second, I got a vision of what would happen if their desires were accelerated, so that they would attempt to fulfill their wishes all at once.

In that astral place, war began. They hacked at one another with severe violence. Each scrambled to best the other. Each tried to get this or that item of value which the other one reached for, and thought she deserved. The most violent scenes occurred when each wanted to have the same man as a lover. They shouted profanities at each other. One threatened to disfigure the other. One cursed and said, "I will fix your fucking face, you ugly bitch. He is my man. Get away. I will sever your lopsided breast. I will push a hot poke up your cunt, you whore."

The whole thing was grievous to witness. I also saw how Nature spreads these antagonistic energies in the psyche of each individual, so that someone who would hate another person, may appear to love that somebody under certain circumstances. But in fact, there was only a rivalry between the two selves, with Nature keeping them apart, by regulating how they could meet as physical bodies, and where they would interact, and for how long.

This physical existence and its corresponding psychic plane are terrible situations indeed. As one prepares for death, one should investigate and experience the domains of the hereafter. Where will one go? Who will one be? How will one participate in events after being deprived of the physical body?

After this, I had another vision which showed some contradictory emotions of one person to another person in different lives, where different relationships were configured by fate. In one life, this lady was the daughter of this other woman, but then in the next life they were school friends who intensely disliked the other. Once as school friends, when one liked a male, the other was in love with that man. A fight ensued between them. In the hostility, the daughter now being a rival, kicked and abused the other, who was humiliated.

The question is. What is the true basis of a relationship? Who really loves whom?

Who Owns the Psyche/Body?

A lady to whom I was related in the present life, but who is deceased for some years now, came on the astral side to discuss the matter of sexual loyalty between human beings. She is of the opinion that it is near impossible for anyone to be sexually loyal to another person, as that is defined in the physical world by people who tout religion and morality.

I questioned her for evidence of this. When she was alive on the physical side, she was one of the persons who staunchly believed in religion, and in its use to keep human beings in a moral conduct.

I said this to her.

"What you are saying now makes no sense, when it is taken in reference to your ideas of morality when you used the last body. Formerly, you believed in one man with one woman who were married before sexual familiarity. You took a vow to never part until death from your lawfully married spouse. Now you suggest something else. Please elaborate."

She replied with this.

"The problem is reincarnation, as well as the existence of the astral world. When I was the last body which died, I did not research reincarnation. The big mistake then was the lack of focus on the dream world existence. I felt before that the dream world was of no consequence. Now I know that it is meaningful. After being deprived of physical access, one is left with the dream world. That is my experience of the hereafter so far.

"I was religious and followed the system of faith which I was conditioned to, since the birth of my physical body. I had dreams and minimized those experiences. I dismissed them. That was the mistake.

"In dreams, I had sexual encounters with men besides my husband. Even though it never happened on the physical side, it happened in dreams. I did not rate it as factual as the physical experience. There were times, when it seemed that a dream experience was simultaneously a physical one. I experienced two occurrences simultaneously, that of dream love-making with another man, and that of a physical love-making.

"In such experiences during a dream, there was no physical evidence of any love act with any other man but still to me, it felt that my physical self experienced a love act. When considered now, that seems to be a state of disloyalty. But I had little or no control over those events. Those were overpowering incidences.

"How is morality to be defined. Was my husband experiencing sexual encounters with other women?

"There is another type of experience which puts to question the entire situation of morality, which is when one has an experience of being in the feelings of another person, who is in a sexual act with someone else, to whom one is sexually attracted.

"This did not happen frequently but it did occur. I can remember that there was a man who was married to a relative of mine., He used to flirt with women but no one considered it to be offensive. He was a jovial person. He would enliven a group of people.

"Once I felt that I was in a dreamy state, where I became the body of his wife, who was my relation. She was there as well. It was as if both of us were the same body. This happened in their bed in the dead of night. They began to make love. I indulged just the same. It was so real as to be physical. What do you make of that? How is morality regarded in that?"

My response was this.

"It is perplexing. During the life of the physical body, a person should be aware of, and should note his/her actions which are psychic. That behavior has value. It should be checked and rechecked. Once the physical system is lost, one will be left with psychic incidences only.

"As for morality. When considered as only a physical reference, it is over-rated as you concluded once you died to physical existence, and became only a psychic self."

Yogi Sleeping in My Psyche

One of my yoga teachers who is deceased, began living in my psyche some time now. I found him sleeping in the chest area of my subtle body. His head lay to the left of the chest. His subtle body was as small as that of an embryo which was curled in its mother's body. The body was in a fetal position as he laid there. When I first saw him, I also felt that he was in a deep healthy sleep.

Later the same day, my eyes shifted to look at someone. Then I realized that it did so because he wanted to see that person. He was in the left corner of my pupil and looked out to see. Did I permit him?

No consent was given. For that matter I do not recall discussing with him that he could lodge in the psyche. However, it is a fact that in the subtle body, related persons may take residence with or without permission.

Just as one may not deny an ancestor from using the body, one cannot refuse certain people permission to reside in one's psyche. The body is a joint enterprise with the prominent observer in the body, as only one of the persons who have rights to use it.

On the day when I realized that this yogi resided in my psyche, it was some four hours after when he said this.

"I am here hiding from some persons who want to converse with me. They cannot find me, if I am in here. When they track my vibration, they will be unable to locate me. I need to rest for a time. There are things to consider. As for my being here, it will not interrupt anything for you. Whatever you routinely do, you can continue. If someone finds my astral place, that person can come to you. You can give instructions on my behalf. In the meantime, I review and test some *samadhi* practices. If I need to see a physical item, I will use your eyes. Overlook that. Conduct yourself as you normally would."

Two Mystics / One Body

I ate ice-cream which had a rich coating of cream and bee pollen, served with it. I realized that there was another tongue which enjoyed it. Someone else was in my body, using my tongue to eat from the same bowl which I used. I realized this when my head turned to see a lady. I had no interest in doing so. My interest energy remained not looking at the person. Another interest energy of someone else who inhabited my psyche, split off to see the lady.

In a split second, I saw the other seer. I saw him. He was a man who began a spiritual society but who is now deceased. I said to him.

"How is it that you eat using my body? Why do you crave these sweet foods?"

He said this.

"It is nothing. Since I was an infant in the last body, I got used to eating rich gourmet food preparations. Later when I was a guru and I became wealthy, I was honored with delicious sanctified foods. It was a habit. We are friends. Do not take it to heart. And besides, as you often said, 'Who owns the body?'

"Really, whose body, is it?"

After this conversation, we continued eating from the same bowl until the delicious food was finished. I decided not to confront him again about this.

Celibacy in Yoga

I was at a meeting of ten or so persons on the astral side. They discussed the principle of celibacy in the yogic, philosophical, and devotional groups which begun in India. There were specific topics.

- How can a family man practice celibacy?
- How is celibacy defined for a sannyasi who took a vow never to be sexually expressive?
- Can anyone become liberated if that person is not celibate?

Needless to say, there was confusion in the astral meeting. No one could give a definition of celibacy which included subtle breaches of the discipline. When asked for clear statements about celibacy, no one provided any. Their specific lineages did not render clarity on the matter.

Some years ago, I asked a recently licensed sannyasi, if he was given a special technique for maintaining a celibate condition of his body. He flatly said no. And this was a person in a leading devotional group from India.

In the meeting, when requested I gave these opinions.

The leading exponent of celibacy for the Advaita Vedantists is Shankara. He is the one who is responsible for the sannyasis order in both the devotional and non-devotional groups from India. Shankara was so extreme in the matter, that when he challenged the leading pandit in India to a debate about Indian philosophy and conclusions, he stipulated that if he won the philosophical contest, the opponent should abandon family life, and follow as a wife-less disciple of Shankara.

However, there is a question from Shankara's behavior where his first round of arguments with Mandana Mishra were interrupted at Shankara's request. Shankara was unable to answer questions about sexual love. Thus, he could not be proclaimed as knowing everything about everything. To deal with this, Shankara asked for an intermission to prepare himself for such questions.

It is written that he left the debating arena and went where a prince just died. He mystically possessed the king's body and aroused it to a living condition. Then he went and lived as that king who had several wives. Shankara then indulged fully in sexual love. Sometime after, he dispossessed himself from that prince's body. He returned to the arena and perfectly answered the questions, thus winning the debate.

There is a text, the *Amaru Shatakam* which is attributed to Shankara. It is all about sexual love *(kama sutra),* but it is said that Shankara composed it after he made love to the numerous wives of the prince.

This brings to fore the matter of celibacy, as to if it is defined as having no sexual expression, nor carnal experience, in the physical body only, or in the physical and subtle bodies. What is the definition?

In the astral discussion, I mentioned this other incidence.

I knew a sannyasis from a devotional sect who used to daydream and dream about having sexual experiences. He discussed this with me privately because he wanted to better understand the sexual urge. Once he told me that a woman, who was his disciple, carried a child for him, while her husband, who was also his disciple, was convinced that the child was his (the husband's). He would smile when he told me this, confidentially.

Once I questioned him.

"Who is the factual father of the child, you or your disciple?"

This was his reply, "I am the father in the deeper sense because the lady loves me deeply. To protect my sannyasi celibate profile, myself and the lady agreed to let her husband feel, that he is the father."

Then I said this.

"My inquiry is about the person who had sexual entry with her to produce the infant. How did you maneuver yourself to have a sexual act with her. You are watched day and night by junior bachelors, who are your assistants."

He replied like this.

"O that is a simple matter. I did not have sex with her physically only psychically. Our love was heavenly. The pleasure of it was pure bliss. Her husband can take credit physically but I am the one she loves. How can my assistants know about this. They have no psychic perception."

I replied like this,

"This material existence has several layers. What sannyasi are you if you consciously breach the vows? What about your self-honesty? How do you negotiate that?"

He did not reply.

To the astral group in the meeting, I also stated this.

How is it possible to license someone as a sannyasi, if he was a family man or had sexual expression, even masturbation, before taking the sannyasis vow.

It seems to me that once there is sexual experience in the form of sex with a female or male, either on the physical or astral sides of existence, and if there is masturbation or any self-stimulation, that person cannot be a sannyasis in fact. The subtle body which is the body which carries the subtle impressions of one's acts, will have the sexual tendency aroused in it, for the period of life of the physical body.

What I declare is that sannyasi vows should not be taken by anyone who in the present body, has sexual experience. In cases where a boy has no sexual expression and has also no masturbation tendency, his physical body is celibate. It is without sexual experience. As for his subtle body, one must assume that it had sexual experience in other lives, in other physical bodies, but there is no memory or mental impression of that in this life.

Since it is near impossible for a human being to be outfitted like that as a fetus, where it has no sexual potential, where for instance, he would be like a five-year-old boy for even the adult stage of the body, then the entire talk about celibacy is pretentious.

Sannyasi or celibacy license as it is used in the lineages from India, is for status and gaining automatic respect from the public, and from others who are officials in the respective religious and philosophical institutions. It is flawed. My view is that it should be abolish.

The persons who are leaders, founders, and officials of the lineages and who hold ceremonies to certify their advanced disciples as sannyasis, should desist from this certification. In the past, so many of these leading priests, yogis, founders, and licensed followers, breached the vows, if not physically, then psychically, if not so, then by masturbation.

Any type of sexual arousal of any sort towards a female or male, or even when no other person is present, is a breach of celibacy. The miscalculation occurs because we falsely attribute total sex control to human beings. That is not possible, unless one is born with a body that has no sexual potential. As soon as we become self-honest and realize that sexual urge cannot be absolutely controlled by any limited being, we can see that it is unreasonable to expect full celibacy. To certify a limited self to be celibate is a farce.

It is not up to any individual to be fully celibate. No limited being can control Nature in that way. It will not happen. Nature is not concerned with anyone's puny willpower, no more than it is concerned with anyone living physically forever.

The idea about celibacy is idealism which is something that has no place in the realm of Nature. It is better that we negotiate this life with realism, where we recognize, and do the best with what Nature displays.

Observing Social Duties and Reducing Social Interactions

For the purpose of yoga, one should simultaneously reduce social interactions and also observe mandatory social duties. This sounds contradictory but it is required for anyone who is serious about attaining liberation.

If one avoids all social duties, one has to be careful that the lack of involvement does not cause one to become more involved in the present or future. The first thing is to reduce social interaction. This is done by remaining isolated as much as possible, but by doing so, whereby others do not realize that one has reduced the interaction.

The reason for this is that if someone knows that one reduces social involvement, that person may take steps to get one more involved. One should quietly reduce participation.

While doing so, one should selectively complete social obligations, but in such a way as to not cause the interactions to increase. It is not the people who want a yogi to remain hogtied to social interaction. The threat comes from Nature *(prakriti),* which hunts a yogi, because it regards him as a criminal, who should remain in confinement.

One must recognize Nature's authority, and work with it to pay off accounts from past lives. One should not do any deals with Nature to increase those accounts. This means hiding and realizing that Nature has the upper hand. Never mind God. God is there but God is not a threat. The most God can do is to explain how a yogi can act to reduce his account with Nature. But the idea that God will cancel or pay off the account is nonsense. The entity himself/herself must pay off the account, but he should take God's advice in how to do so.

Confusing Astral World

There was an astral encounter with a lady whom I knew some years ago. She wanted me to travel with her and another woman to an astral domain, where she would arrange the existence there to her wishes. She was dead set on having several conveniences in the astral place. She planned accordingly. These were some items which she felt to be necessary for a pleasant life hereafter.

- automobile
- comfortable residence
- refrigerator

- playing children
- other women who were always congenial
- free roaming cows
- fertile land
- pleasant sunlight
- smooth highways
- a husband who never disagrees with her
- effective medical treatment for any disease

At first when we set out in her automobile, it began on a smooth highway. It was herself, another woman, and myself. I was in the back seat of the vehicle. I was there as a capable handyman.

First, we stopped at a medical clinic, where she worked. When she went into the place, she went to her supervisor's area. Her friend and myself sat in a lobby. This is where the situation began to go off-tract.

She came to the lobby and said that her friend and myself should go to a nearby building to be treated medically so that no disease would infect us. We immediately got up to find the clinic she described. There however, in that astral place, there was an intuition which informed us that the clinic may not exist and that if we went to it, we would never find it.

At this point we went back to the vehicle on the highway but the highway was no longer there. Instead, there was a dirt road. The lady came out and told us to sit in the vehicle as we did before. We noticed that the road changed but she acted as if everything was the same. She said that we would go to a place which was populated. There she would get a residence where we would stay.

She drove on the dirt road for a time. Then there was a flooded roadway on one side, so that half the road was flooded and half was dry. I wanted to bring that to her attention but I could not. In that astral place, one can say nothing which is contrary to anyone else.

After driving like this with one side's tires in about ten inches of water, and the other side's tires on dry dirt, we reached the village where her residence was located. The roadway ceased at this point. She stopped and instructed that we should disembark and find the place. It should be noted that there was no engine sound in the car. It was silent with no mechanism for acceleration. It was powered by her willpower.

As soon as we exited the vehicle, there was pleasing light in all directions, soft daylight. There was no sun to be seen. The sun was not present in that dimension. Nevertheless, light was spread in all directions. There were houses on lots, with each on specific premises, such that one knew where one property began and another ended.

Some people had cows but these animals were aware of boundaries and did not enter the property of anyone besides their owners. We entered one house and noticed that there were three children who were left unattended. Even though these were toddlers, they moved about crawling but being aware that they should not leave the room which was assigned to them.

At this place there was an energy which stated that this place was designed to be a hell for some persons who had impractical ideas while living in the physical world. Because their ideas were strongly expressed, and because they did not learn that they were subordinate to Nature, such persons went to such a place after death. At that place some ideas about social arrangements and residential situations were denied. This was to make them understand that Nature is capable of fulfilling only some desires of any entity.

At this place, instead of asphalt surfaces, there were dirt roads. There was no concrete paving. People left their infants at home in psychological confinement, while the parents went elsewhere. There were no nannies or substitute parents with these infants, while the parents were absent for many hours during the day.

Vehicles in that world were dependent on the willpower and creative energy of the owners, such that people who could not imagine a vehicle did not and count not use one.

Yogi meets Hunter with One Arrow

In an astral encounter with someone who is deceased, there was a resentment to be solved but which could not be resolved. In fact, the tension of the circumstance ceased but only to continue again on some other astral or physical occasion.

Since this person is deceased, the only means of resolution was by psychic interaction but since this person was physically focused, that was not possible. Hence there was a postponement of the issue. It was then that I realized that this person with a resentment towards me, was like a hunter who had one arrow with which she was determined to kill a single victim.

If her aim was bad, the victim would hear the arrow and would flee. If her aim was perfect, still then there was the likelihood that the victim would move slightly just before the arrow would pierce its body.

I knew this lady some years ago, when during the teen years, I was attracted to her sexually. At the time, the relationship developed. But as fate would have it, the relationship ceased. Many years went by. This person died and was only a psychic being. Despite the shattering of the relationship early on, she held a resentment toward me, such that now in the deceased state on the astral side, a dissatisfaction is present.

Due to this, my astral body was drawn into an astral place in which this person has a residence, which is similar to one she lived in, during the teen years. When I found myself in that place, I was on a dirt road in the process of going to the psychic copy of the house she physically resided during her last life. I met her on the road, but when there was twenty feet between us, there was a barrier energy which caused our astral forms to stop.

The lady was distraught, sour of face, grievously hurting on the emotional side of her existence. I could not say a word. She turned to go in the opposite direction, but with the hard feelings continuing. It was then that I realized that she was like a hunter with one arrow with which to kill the target. It was due to being possessed by a romantic desire.

Fate gives an opportunity, but it has no intention of perfect fulfillment of the desire. Even which there is fulfillment, it is partial only. Fate has no idea about any limited self's relevance.

If you have one sharp deadly arrow and one tense bow, if you are a marksman, if the victim is within range but it is skittish, what are you to do, if somehow you miss the target? Suppose the victim was struct in the wrong place so that it was not fatally wounded. It left the scene in haste with the arrow stuck in a wound which would heal as soon as the arrow falls away.

You have no other arrow. You are helpless. The opportunity was there but fate conspired with the victim. What to do?

Part 5

Relationship Hoax

Nature provides many relationships which are phony. For the most part, these emotional situations do not endure. It begins at birth, where the child bonds with a parent or guardian. There is no way to avoid this. And yet, even though it must be formatted, there is no proof that it will endure. Was the father or mother, the parent in the last life? Will either parent be the parent in the next life?

A human being spends much time and energy in the formation of a relationship which he or she cannot certify as an eternal situation. And yet it is not sensible to neglect some of these emotional formations. There is no point in acting irresponsibly or inconsiderately. For the time being, a yogi should service obligations even though he/she knows or figures that there is no eternal time support for these relational formations.

As Nature builds this body in the womb of its mother, and then Nature matures this body when it is expelled from the mother's passage, and then Nature again neglects the maintenance of this form, and causes its definite death, so one should assist in the formation of relationships, their maturity and then disintegration. But one should know that these relational constructions are hoaxes.

Is it possible that any of these situations is enduring?

That should be researched in meditation.

I met an old fellow on the astral side. He was deceased for over seventy years. I asked him how it was, living in the astral existence for such a long time. He reflected for some time. He said this.

"Now I have no view about a relationship with a mother, father, wife, or even a friend. Where I am, there is no one else but myself. I know that others are nearby in parallel dimensions but I do not see them. I find myself awake and alone. Then again, I find myself lying down, floating and alone. I have no idea about living with any other person.

"There is a blank space in my psyche which would be filled with relational energy if I were to be a physical person again. I considered this to see how it would be if I was to be an infant, who sucked a mother's breast. How would that blank space for emotional energy be filled with love for a mother, and then change to love for a girlfriend, then to be estranged from that lover, then to fall in love with another woman. Then to have children and to be fond of them. Then to die again. Then to be a child again.

Divine Eye / Shift of Focus

Under the supervision of Yogeshwarananda on the astral side of existence, I currently work on the development and use of the divine eye. I worked on this for fifty years. Recently however Yogeshwarananda and myself worked conjointly to derive a definite and tested method for those who use the Patanjali *ashtanga* yoga process.

In that procedure there are three highest of eight practices. These three as a collective, or sequence of development, are termed as *samyama*, which can be translated to be meditation in the English language. These are *dharana* focus of attention, *dhyana* spontaneous focus and *samadhi* prolonged and spontaneous focus. Besides this *samyama*, there are the five lower processes of which the highest of these is *pratyahar* sensual energy withdrawal. That is a psychological action just as the higher three are, but it is not considered to be meditation by Patanjali. It is preliminary to meditation.

If before meditation, the withdrawal of interest to things outside the psyche, is not achieved, the focus will be sporadic. Hence, before meditating, the yogi should have a radical, but effective method of achieving, the interiorization of interest.

For instance, if a yogi spends thirty minutes sitting to introspect. If twenty-five minutes of that time is spent retracting interest in internal and external distractions, then only five minutes of that session was used for meditation, for *samyama*. This means that one must distinguish meditation from the retracting of interest in external things.

It is best that one, not regard *pratyahar* sensual energy withdrawal as meditation. Follow Patanjali's syllabus and regard *pratyahar* as being preliminary. The classic method of doing *pratyahar* is to use *pranayama* breath infusion to put the psyche in a state of internal focus. Then, when one sits to meditate, *pratyahar* would be achieved because of the breath infusion practice, and one can proceed with *dharana* focus, or with *dhyana* spontaneous focus, or with *samadhi* prolonged spontaneous focus.

Yogeshwarananda is of the opinion that unless the psyche already affords the yogi a supernatural or spiritual portal, he should apply a focus to the frontal part of the subtle head, to the area of the brow chakra or to any other area. That focus should be held steady with no shifting.

If, however, when the focus is applied, there is shifting, where the yogi cannot halt the shifts, then he may apply some method to stabilize the focus. He may use a mantra which is sounded mentally only. He may anchor part of his focus to the naad sound resonance. As soon as he realizes that his focus shifted, he should slowly gather it and refocus it. This may happen repeatedly during a session.

In some sessions, the energy of the mind will be such, that this rarely happens. While at other times, it will happen regularly, even though a struggle will be required with the mind.

Suppose the yogi does breath infusion, then sits to meditate. In meditation he applies a frontal focus to the center of the eyebrows. This focus remains with his attention being on a tiny spot of color or on a small area of scattered color. Then he remains in that focus for only fifteen seconds. He then finds that he shifted downward to the right where his focus dropped about two inches down to the right. He should retrieve the focus and bring it back to the center where it was an originally placed.

In that session of meditation, this should be done repeatedly with the yogi noting what happens on each readjustment. This is the way to work on developing the divine eye. For that, one must hold the steady focus.

Hyper-Reactive Mind

One comes into this world with a hyper-reactive mentality. It operates involuntarily. This is both beneficial and detrimental. In the beginning at the birth of the body, one needs spontaneous internal operations in the body. At that stage one has neither the knowledge or power to operate the body. Its involuntary biological functions which operate automatically are essential for the continuation of life in the body.

And yet, some operations which are conducted are harmful to the self. When one makes an attempt to control the mind, one finds that one is not allowed to direct the mind fully. It cooperates with one's desire some of the time. It conducts mental and emotional activities which were neither initiated nor approved by the self.

In meditation a yogi realizes his/her lack of mind control. The key factor however is the focus of the self. The senses and the monitor of the senses, both operate independent of the self. But these also may on a whim cooperate with the self.

When a sense discovers anything which it may target, there is an expression of an interest in the object. This is for the most part involuntary, where the self has no authority to stop the mind's interest. With rapidity, a sense reaches its target. It collects information. It relays that knowledge to the intellect, which rapidly makes a decision on how the sense should proceed with investigation, as to the value of the target, and as to if it should be exploited.

Once the value is assessed, the intellect gives a command for increased surveillance. In the meantime, it sends a request to the memory chambers for information which relates to the target. This knowledge is given instantly.

The intellect then makes a conclusion, which the mind uses to supervise further investigation, as to how to consume all or part of the target.

In meditation and also when not meditating, a yogi is required to monitor this behavior of the mind, so that it does not pursue every target it encounters. As soon as there is a detection of a target, the self should determine if it should consider the information, which comes in through a particular sense. If the self determines that there should be no pursuit, the self should command the psyche, so that it no longer continues the investigation.

The self should not allow the mind to respond with replies to every thought query which comes into the psyche. Any effort of the mind to regard the incoming information should be squelched.

Any opinions which first are developed by the intellect, should be ignored if not rejected outright by the self. There should be no incoming appeal which is followed by responses, one after the other. This is necessary for mind control, otherwise the self will continue to be a pawn of the intellect and the senses.

Craving the Pinnacle of Youth

Once one arrives in this existence as an infant, the main craving which continues day after day, and moment after moment, is the apex state of the body. It is at that point that one may exploit the best of what this body offers.

Due to this, and during the first stage of the growth of the body, there is a hustle to reach the highpoint of its growth. This craving is so intense and sustaining, that one does not realize when the body reached its peak of growth. Like a man who keeps jogging as he ascends a mountain, one reaches the top and feels the momentum of that as a continuation of growth, as a swelling.

The fact is however that if anyone objectively reviews what happened at the peak of the growth of the body, that person would realize that the peak stage of development, only lasted for less than a moment. At the zenith one was not allowed to enjoy the body fully. It stayed at its peak for only an instant. Beyond that it was downhill with gravity aggressively pulling one through the full maturity stage, and then slowly but surely, conveying one to the elderly years.

Why is everyone clambering after the peak stage of the body? What is so special about that? If at every stage of growth there are special features to experience, either to enjoy or to detest, then it should be, that every stage is precious. Every stage has features which are worth the experience, even those features which were negative, like for instance stages where the body was afflicted with disease.

The adult stage of the body, the early part of it, is the segment of the lifespan which most entities crave. This feature is craved even in the childhood stage, but the urge for experiencing it at that time, is subliminal, where the person cannot understand the need which is felt.

A hurricane which developed over a sea, and which is far from land, cannot engage its winds to spin and uproot vegetation. And yet, it will spin as it moves across the ocean. As soon as it reaches land, it will engage with trees to demolish them.

The spinning force is there when the storm was formed over the ocean but it could not exert itself fully because it did not have objects which could interact with its torquing power.

Another example, a common one, is sex desire. It is present in the psyche from day one, from the moment when the body is birthed into the physical world, but the entity does not realize it until the physical body grows into sexual maturity. That level before the adult stage is also a learning experience, but the sexual urge in its subliminal state causes one to under-appreciate the experiences of youth.

Masturbation is an example of a hurricane which searches for a land mass with trees. As soon as it reaches such a forest, it engages to demolish the trees, there it gets satisfaction from applying its torquing power, because over the ocean it does not feel its effects on anything.

Actually, some hurricanes engage the water of the sea, and are satisfied applying itself in that way. Some other hurricanes form but do not touch the ocean. They remain high in the atmosphere and are satisfied not applying their torque to anything.

Why then is one hurricane satisfied, with no application of itself to ocean waves, while another hurricane is only satisfied by such application, and yet another one will roam the ocean until its contacts a land mass, where it can demolish trees.

In the elderly years, many experiences which are regarded negatively should be positively appreciated, and assessed, as having value just the same. But instead, one usually looks back, and recalls the peak point of sexuality. One ponders the sexually maturity experience.

Design of the Psyche

A yogi should come to terms with the design of the psyche. There should be a detailed thorough study of it. The first consideration is that the yogi did not create his psyche.

Think of it?

If you were offered the opportunity to change what you did not like in the psyche, what change would that be?

To answer this, someone may simply refuse the offer and instead apply for the creatorGod or creatorForce to eliminate it. Since one discovered oneself to be a psyche which was already designed, and which had only limited facilities for redesign, one should do the best, to change whatever can be changed in it. One should suspend parts of its operation if that is possible. One should encourage usage of the parts which one thinks are positive for the self.

In my research of the operation of the psyche which I am, my conclusion is that there are parts which cannot be adjusted. But there are parts which can be disabled temporarily. Some parts can be controlled for a moment of time but not for a long period.

Some achievements of advanced yogis, cannot be realized by lesser ascetics. One can appreciate what the senior ones achieved, but one must be satisfied with that, and do one's best to alter, or suspend, whatever one has the power to adjust.

There are many sensual dangers. For instance, color is one such attribute or sensual pursuit. But that does not mean that one can change the psyche's attitude for craving contact with color. One may, however, keep the psyche in an environment in which it is not molested by colors, which cause it to crave certain forms, which are highlighted in specific colors.

It is more than a matter of color resistance or form resistance. It is also a matter of transiting to an environment, in which the colors carry only positive connotations, and are without hidden responsibilities and obligations.

For the time being one should study the design of the psyche, but in the long term, it is a matter of moving to another existential situation, which has only positive implications.

Yoga Samadhi Limit

Yogeshwarananda gave information about *samadhi* duration times. It is crucial that a yogi aspire for, recognize and experience *samadhi* states. *Samadhi* is the highest of the eight segments of yoga practice.

Not attaining *samadhi* is the bane of a serious yogi. That served to end the career of many yogis, who heard descriptions of *samadhi*, practiced methods, and yet did not attain it, or attained it momentarily, and did not recognize it.

Yogeshwarananda declared this.

"There are many myths about *samadhi*. The fact is, however, that from this end of existence, from where one is as an *atma* limited coreSelf, one cannot dictate to existence as to how long *samadhi* will last, and as to if one will even have the ability to recognize it if it occurs. Know for sure, that samadhi will occur mostly as an involuntary state. It will happen to some yogis but they may not recognize it. Or they may not control the duration of it, whether it be for a moment or for a minute or longer.

"After the death of the physical body, one cannot control the duration of samadhi. Ask this question of yourself, 'How did I control my sleeping and waking hours when I was a newborn infant?'

"That question is absurd for the very reason that the observing self was not positioned existentially to exercise control. Think of liberation. Many yogis aspire for that, but when asked to define it, hardly anyone can give a sensible description. They do not know what it is, and certainly even if they can assure their fanatical disciples about it, they cannot guarantee that they will attain what they consider it to be.

"*Samadhi?* What is it?"

Single Focus Meditation

Lahiri Mahashaya appeared in my subtle head on September 9, 2023. He said that the linchpin of *samyama* meditation is the application of consistent focus to a single objective.

If the person is a Shaivite, Vaishnava, Buddhist, Vedantists or whatever, it does not matter in this practice. The point is to hold steady mental focus within the mind. One must practice to measure how long one can hold a focus. One common focus could be naad sound resonance. Focus on that either as inner sound in a general area or as the central focus or node of inner sound.

Alternately, if it is a light in the mind space, for instance in the center of the head in the frontal lobe, that too is permissible. Can the yogi hold the focus? For how long can he apply without shifting or being shifted to something else? That is the challenge, the focus.

Purified Abdomen Plexus

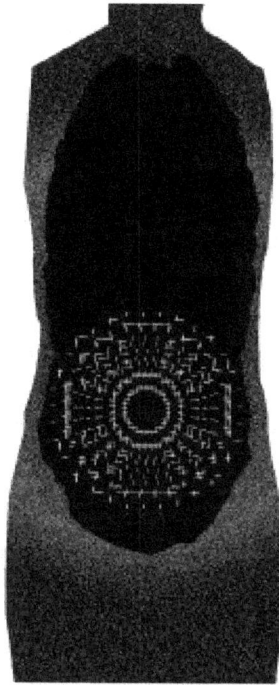

subtle body
purified abdomen conglomerate
joint plexus

This diagram shows the purified abdomen conglomerate joint plexus in the subtle body. This happens after there is curbing of the physical intestinal track using *pranayama* breath infusion and tight regulation of diet and time of eating, with efficient digestion and excretion.

Instead of having a parallel subtle body abdomen which has intestines, colon, and rectum, a plexus appears instead. Except by doing *hatha* yoga purificatory means with *pranayama* breath infusion, there is no radical method of achieving this. With that, it is required to cease certain other habits which I list.

- curb time of eating
- curb from eating peppers, spices, and sugar
- curb sexual secretions

- curb dietary products which are not conducive to efficient nutrient absorption and prompt evacuation
- check passage of food from mouth to anus on a daily basis
- do stomach churning exercises twice per day
- do two daily sessions of pranayama breath infusion, during which fresh air in the blood stream is pushed into the higher and lower intestines
- attack the sexual complex to uproot its expressive influence

Sexual fluid expression is a form of bleeding. One has to come to terms with that, using some method which curtails it step by step. Consider a vat (water storage) which has several spigots. To conserve the liquid, one should shut the spigots. However, if even after doing that, one finds that the liquid is not conserved and that some spigots leak, one should fix those valves to stop the drainage. Each yogi must deal with the issue himself/herself.

The subtle body is affected by the dietary and excretory process of the physical form. Hence those yogis who are careless, will in time regret it. The belief that one is not the body, and hence one does not have to regard its condition, is for foolish yogis. Being something different from the physical system, does not in any way, remove the body's influence.

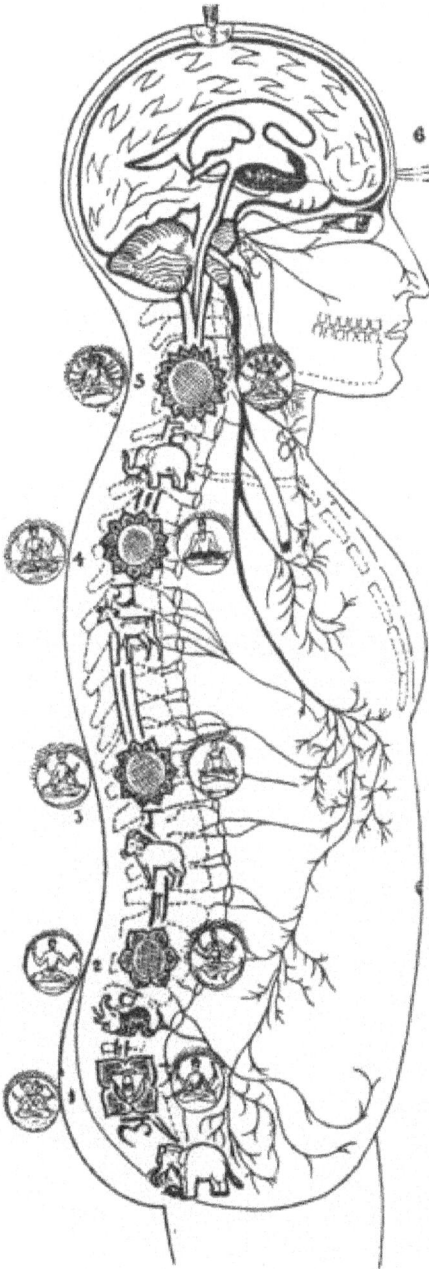

SYMBOLICAL

Six Chakras of Yoga with Petals and Deity — — Symbols — —

1. The Earth Chakra is of Yellow color, has four Petals, a Beast, Two Deities and Kundalini.

2. The Water Chakra is White, has Six Petals, a Beast and Two Deities.

4. The Air Chakra is Black, has Twelve Petals, a Beast and Two Deities.

5. The Ether Chakra is like Sea Water, has Sixteen Petals, a Beast and Two Deities.

6. The Mental Chakra has Two Petals and a Deity.

Sahasrara is Above All and is called, the One Thousand Petalled Lotus.

This is Rishi Singh Gherwal's diagram of the chakras. I give it here for the record because he is one of the lineage teachers of the inSelf Yoga ™ process. I learnt the process from several teachers. This is due to the fact that it is a complicated system. Each teacher may be the master of only a part of it. I attended several teachers. Under pressure of time, I did manage so far to itemize and describe the various complexities involved in mastering each state.

As for Rishi Singh Gherwal, I did not meet his last physical body. I did however wander about and searched for the yogi, early on from 1969. I began searching after I met Arthur Beverford who was Rishi's disciple. This was in the Philippines where Arthur Beverford taught Japanese Martial Arts at the main gym on Clark Air Base.

It was from Authur Beverford, without my requesting, that I got a set of Rishi's books. I went through these but found that there was not much information about the mystic process of yoga. However, that is the traditional way of Indian yogis, where certain processes are not divulged in books.

Beverford did introduce me to third eye focus. He also showed *anuloma-viloma pranayama* and some *hatha* yoga practices, like swallowing a long cloth and then gradually pulling it out through the mouth. He taught how to use a *neti* pot to inhale water through the nostrils.

Beverford later requested me to find a farm where he could establish a spiritual community. He had the idea to do that. When he returned to the USA, he was in Ohai-Ventura area of California, but there was an advanced student of Rishi who lived in Santa Barbara. Beverford mentioned this place because he got the set of Rishi's books from there.

As far as Rishi's books are concerned. I checked them around 1973 when I got them from Beverford. At the time I travelled with Freeman Farr. We made two trips by automobile, from New York City to Los Angeles. We used a VW van and got money by stopping here and there to do construction jobs.

Rishi Singh wrote a set of books called, *Great Masters of the Himalayas*. According to Beverford, Paramhansa Yogananda stole the format of those books and produced a similar book called *Autobiography of a Yogi*. When Yogananda passed on, his disciples tried to establish that the body was in a state of incorruptibility, where it would remain undecayed for some time.

Beverford said that Rishi visited the body soon after Yogananda's demise and reported that the body was not in that state. This was based on the pranic condition of the body.

Later on, when I got in touch with Rishi astrally, he told me that Yogananda's physical body was not in the pranic energy state which qualified it as being in a state where its decay could be delayed.

However, for the record, I should state that initially, after I got the set of Rishi's books from Beverford, and read those, I tried to reach Rishi but failed to do so. This was an astral effort because his physical body was already deceased.

I combed through the astral domains but found no trace. Later when I met him after about thirty years or so, he told me that because of my sexual involvement, he was out of reach. He could not afford to make communication which may result in his taking an embryo.

Of Rishi's books which I received from Beverford, his *Yoga Vashishtha or Heaven Found* was carefully read by me, but the one of most interest was his translation of the small portion of the *Mahabharata* about Markandeya adventures in Krishna's supernatural bodies.

This book is out of print. It was a booklet. I no longer have the copy which Beverford gave me. However, later, under the influence of Rishi Singh, I translated and explained the story about Markandeya and published it, titled, *Krishna Cosmic Body (Markandeya Samasya English)*. Sometime after publishing that book, Rishi inspired me to translate and comment on the *Anu Gita*. The title for that is *Anu Gita Explained*.

He made his biggest contribution to my translation work by suggesting that I translate the *Hatha Yoga Pradipika*. That was published as *Kundalini Hatha Yoga Pradipika*. In a sense even though my name is listed as the author, it is the fact that much of the book was astrally ghost written by him. There were Sanskrit combination words which I could not break apart for translation. But after struggling for a time, suddenly he would appear and give the breaks and meanings. This saved my face for doing that book. When I could not describe a certain technical process, he provided detailed information on the astral side and save the day.

Rishi Singh is in isolation in an astral dimension, where he continues *samadhi* practice. He cannot be reached by anyone unless he expressly wants to communicate.

I have not seen him for some time. He is anti-social. Supposedly, Rishi Singh's wife was an advanced yogini. I did not meet this person but for some reason, Beverford told me of an incidence in Santa Barbara. During a meditation session which Rishi conducted, Beverford tried to mentally contact Rishi's wife who sat behind him with other students.

It was a session in which there was to be silence and inner focus. Suddenly, the yogini slapped Beverford from the behind. It was a subtle body action only, as there was no physical movement. No one else besides Beverford and the yogini heard or were aware of the event. Beverford grinned when he told me about this in Ventura, California.

I was asked by a few persons about a method for reaching Rishi Singh. I do not know of any method. I tried to reach him by combing through many astral domains, and tracking other yogis who knew him. I could not reach him. After some years, over about 30 years after Beverford gave me Rishi's books, the Rishi appeared to me on the astral side but he did not initially teach anything. It was his request for me to write the three books mentioned. I have no method for anyone, even myself, to contacted him.

The more important information is that while in his astral presence, I was unable to ask questions. This implies that his astral conditions is such that even if one met him, one would find that one cannot verbalize any questions to him.

Desire as Rebirth Cause

I had an astral encounter with a lady who is now deceased, and whom I met and associated with in the 1970s. Physically I have not seen this person since 1979. On the astral side, I meet her infrequently since she passed from her physical body some six years ago (2019).

When someone passes, even though one had little contact prior on the physical plane, one may have dreams involving that person. I did a garden related chore, when she arrived on the astral side.

She said this.

"We should be together. We should be involved in a garden just as we were when I met you so many years ago. I will wait for your full transfer to the psychic plane. Then we can take new bodies so that we can meet in the teen years, fall in love, and then be married and engage in a flourishing garden. I know you have a knack for growing edibles and flowering plants."

I did not reply because I could not, under the circumstance, give my view of the request. However, my view is that it is unreasonable to expect that a yogi would take another body based on someone's desire, even a loved one. Of course, such an invitation includes sexual promise. But even then, is it worth it?

One may even get a body in an area where the other person would get one, and then the fate may change where one's parents leave that area and one has no chance of meeting and then marrying the said person.

But what should a yogi do? Should the proposal be rejected? What does it mean to love somebody?

Slit Sky Entry

There are events in meditation which are abstract to the yogi, where he/she does not recognize the perception. If one has a high experience and cannot identify it as such, there is the likelihood that one will dismiss it as being meaningless.

In the diagram which follows, this was an experience, where when meditating in the darkness of the mind, which is represented as jet black, there occurred an opening to another sky. The opening had a slit irregular shape. The sky on the other side of it, had a greyish color.

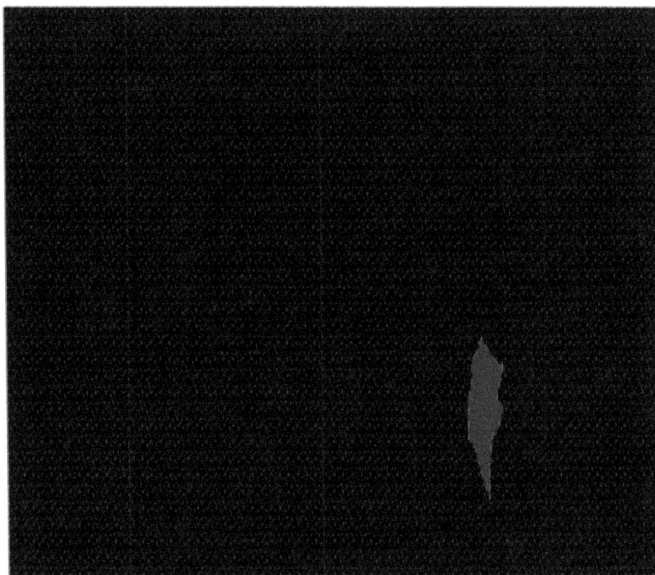

Such experiences are involuntary, occurring on their own. When they happen, the yogi may only see the opening for a number of seconds. He/She should recognize them as entries or slits into another environment.

Self Adhesives

The formulation and willful enforcement of the socialPerson, either of a morally inclined person or a criminally minded self, causes the fault whereby the self cannot sort itself from its psychic adjuncts.

What is the importance of this?

How will anyone live, even a good person, if he/she does not act in a moral way?

The person will live, undoubtedly, at least until his/her physical body is disabled by fate. In the meantime, however, the solution is to live with loose enforcement of the socialPerson. This self is the subtle body container interspaced in the physical system. While that happens, the core should sort itself from its adjuncts and remain somewhat detached from them. This accessory equipment, though necessary, should not be fused with the core, otherwise their influences cannot be resisted. What difference is there, if the core is bullied by its adjuncts?

Yogi Bhajan

This is the original photo of Yogi Bhajan which was used when he began teaching kundalini yoga in the USA. I first saw this outside a curio shop in Kansas City, Missouri in 1971.

As fate would have it, I returned to the USA from the Philippines, and was stationed awaiting discharge at an Air Force Base near Kansas City. I was desperate to find an advanced yogi for learning the kundalini arousal process.

I saw this photo with information about a place in Kansas City where classes were given. I went there but I was told that the yogi was absent. Classes were given by his student.

I could not attend those classes because I did not have transportation to travel regularly from the Base. I was informed that there was an ashram in Denver. This was convenient because I planned to go to Denver as soon as the discharge papers were processed.

Use the photo to reach the yogi.

Yogi's Elderly Years

There is this idea that a human being should beat the odds either using modern medicine or ancient methods. People sincerely ignore the impending death of the body, while looking towards the promise of eternal life for the physical self.

So far there is no physical evidence that accommodates the craving for eternal physical life. Nature relentlessly insures that there is no such possibility. Yet the idea continues unabated through the centuries.

Taken collectively, humanity now considers living somewhere else in the universe. This is because of the threat for the end of life on earth, not just human life but all live. If the sun bakes the planet, no life form even the most rudimentary ones, will be accommodated.

Since humanity cannot create a planet, there is the idea that perhaps there is some habitation somewhere in the universe, to which a set of humans may migrate. If these could reproduce there, that would guarantee the continuation of the human species.

The craving for physical life is endless. It is there on the psychic side as well, where when someone only has a psychic self, he, or she, feels unfulfilled because of not having physical access.

In the early life of a body, the responsibility for its health and wellbeing is with the parents. Unless they are all-knowing people, they make mistakes. This means that when one becomes the guardian of himself/herself, one will find that something is amiss in the body, something that the parents neglected.

Then one may scramble and with the help of science, one may do things to the body in the hope of repairing what was damaged in it. In the meantime, Nature continues its assault, such that some of her attacks are hidden. Many faults in the body cannot be realized even by the scientific community, what to speak of the average person. One commits actions which later result in misery and in permanent damage to certain parts of the body.

How should one resolve this?

How to ignore the quest for eternal physical life?

Sitting to meditate

When sitting to meditate, an easy posture should be used. When practicing posture yoga *(asana),* easy and difficult forms may be practiced. I advise that one should not mix meditation yoga with posture yoga. Do posture yoga first. Then do meditation yoga.

Or do posture yoga, then do *pranayama* breath infusion, then do meditation yoga. Or do a combination of posture yoga and *pranayama* breath infusion, then sit in an easy, a very easy, posture to do meditation.

If you utilize a difficult posture while doing meditation, it is likely that your attention will be split, between tolerating the pains of the posture, and focusing on the meditation method. This attention split is undesirable.

One way to consider it, is that posture yoga, *asana*, is mostly for the benefit of the physical body, while breath infusion is for both the physical and subtle bodies, and meditation yoga is for the subtle body specifically.

To master postures, do posture yoga. To infuse energy into the physical and subtle bodies, do *pranayama* breath infusion yoga. To target one's psychology, do meditation yoga but use an easy posture.

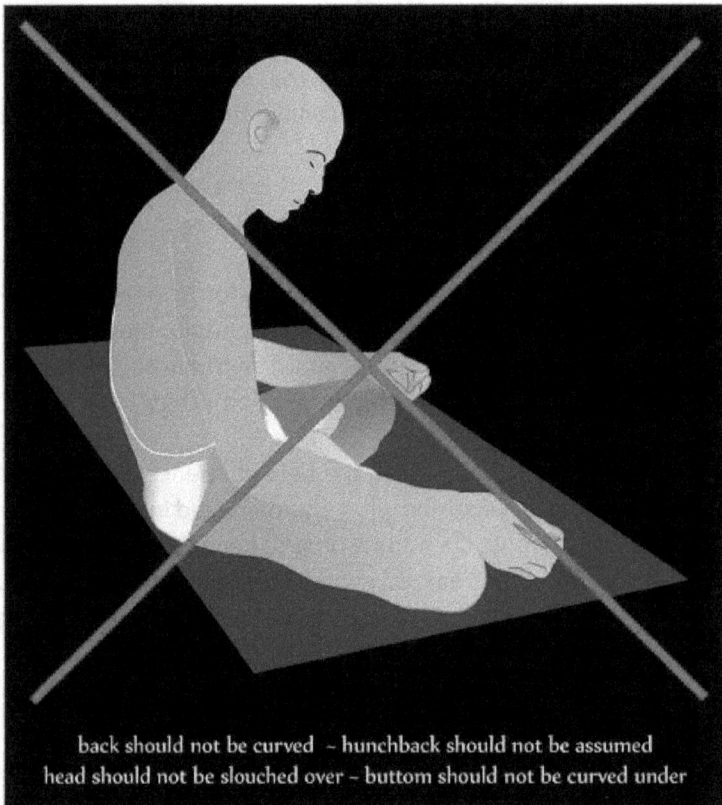

back should not be curved ~ hunchback should not be assumed
head should not be slouched over ~ buttom should not be curved under

The natural deterioration of the body implies that even with an ardent practice of yoga postures, still there will be conditions which the postures cannot improve and will not affect. One has to live with this. There are changes in diet and actions which aid in easing various pains in the body. But when all is said, and when whatever should be done is instituted, one will be left with certain conditions which simply do not improve.

One example is the suction of used blood upwards from the feet and legs of the body. If for instance the check valves in the veins of the legs work with inefficiency, no amount of yoga will change the behavior of leaky valves. These valves will progressively deteriorate.

In a plumbing system, valves are easily replaced. In the body, the surgery for this is complicated and is beset with further risks. It is interesting how a yogi assumes a mood of resignation when he/she realizes that Nature has the upper hand. It was preset to be out of his favor all along, even in the youth of the body, when those valves and other parts worked in an optimum way.

I suggest that to help the body to transport used blood from the feet and legs, the yogi should do a foot-up and hands-up posture in a relaxed way, for at least twenty (20) minutes once per day. A chair should be used for elevating the feet and legs.

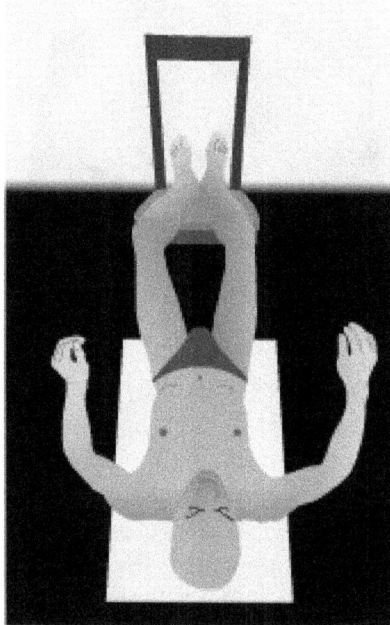

This posture allows polluted used blood to flow back to the lungs for extraction of carbon dioxide and other unwanted gases. This compensates for the leaky valves, which are experienced as pain and fatigue in the feet and legs. It may be observed as swollen feet and legs.

To meditate while doing this, one may use a blindfold which will keep light from entering the head through the skull. In that way one would benefit in a dual way for the twenty minutes.

If there is extra time, one may do the dead man's pose for at least ten minutes. During that time, the subtle body may astral project. One may enter trance states which are beneficial.

Third Eye Focus Legendary

It may be that the person who did the most to popularize the third eye and its glories was Sri Paramhansa Yogananda. Regardless of whether one likes him or not, and he is deceased, one should give him credit for whatever he achieved. His book, *Autobiography of a Yogi,* is legendary.

Interestingly, the guru of one of my gurus, claimed that Yogananda stole the format of *Great Masters of Himalayas* (by Rishi Singh Gherwal), to create *Autobiography of a Yogi*. It should be told that in that book Yogananda did mention the assistance he got from W. Evans-Wentz.

There is a video which I saw where Yogananda from a sitting position, lay his bloated obese body on a surface, rolled his eyes up and apparently went into meditation, into what he termed to be the blissful Infinite.

That idea about rolling the eyes up into the head to get into a blissful condition with union with the Infinite, is misleading in my view.

While I was in the Philippines in 1970, I heard about focusing upward from Arthur Beverford. He explained that Rishi Singh Gherwal divulged a method to him when Beverford was in Santa Barbara years prior when Beverford was in the USA.

This was the instruction.

- Do *asana* postures
- Do alternate breathing
- Sit comfortably with spine straight
- Put a bit of minted oil (embrocation) on the tip of the right middle finger
- Rub this on the center of the eyebrows
- With eyes closed, meditate on that spot.

This was to be done for at least thirty minutes

Beverford did not give a mantra with this.

After doing this for some months, I found that the rubbing of the embrocation, which was peppermint and camphor oil mainly, was not felt between the eyebrows. It did not help to apply it. The attention ignored it. The cooling feel from the embrocation disappeared quickly.

Regarding holding the attention at the center of the eyebrows, that was a struggle. In some sessions it was easy. In others, despite much mental effort, the mind's attentive focus drifted.

The practice of alternate breathing did not work, except now and again. The main reason was that the count in each stroke did not hold always. Thus, each complete stroke could not be maintained because of losing track of each count. Once I got access to an isolated basement. There I applied a tremendous inner mental pressure, and did it successfully but the positive results of that did not last for a long time, only for some minutes before the mind resumed its normal thought operations.

The alternate breathing consisted of an inhale from one side, say the left side, for a certain count, and arresting of the breath inhaled for a certain count. Then an exhale from the other nostril for a certain count. Then ceasing breathing for a certain count.

Then one does the reverse. Then one switches again. This continues for a time, with full concentration within. This should be done with the eyes closed but it may be done with eyes open, provided there is inner focus to keep the counts. The ratio of the counts is given by the teacher, who may change the ratio as the student progresses.

The problem with this process is to maintain the count. As soon as the count is fractured for some reason, the sequence must begin again. That is frustrating.

The other important feature is that when there is an inhale, the breath energy which is absorbed into the lungs should be mentally directed with great care to the base of the spine. Some teachers give it as the corresponding or opposing side of the base. This would mean that some yogis inhale through say the left nostril and guide the breath down to the left side of the base of the spine while others inhale through the left and guide it down to the right of the base.

But other yogis guide it down to the center of the base chakra. This frees the yogi from having to exert much concentration to direct the infuse energy to the left or right of the base.

There is a question about the result of this practice. There should be an accumulated charge of energy, which should after some practice, cause a sparkling energy to arise. This is the kundalini. If this happens the student should consult a yogi about the next achievement in the practice.

This concerns the awakening of kundalini from the base chakra *muladhar*. The value of awakening of kundalini is that eventually, it rises through the spine and enters the brain, where it causes astral light to sparkle at the center of the head, between the eyebrows and at the crown chakra which is at the top of the head.

That result will cause experiences of other levels of existence. Portals will open in the mind to higher levels.

If, however one does not energize the kundalini, one's meditation will rarely cause one to enter higher levels of consciousness. This means that senior yogis who give only meditation between the eyebrows, divulge incomplete methods, from which the results intended will rarely be experienced.

Beverford did divulge a method of seeing the third eye *ajna* chakra. This consist of pressing the closed eyes with the fingers. This will cause one to see light in the center of the forehead, at the place where the third eye is located.

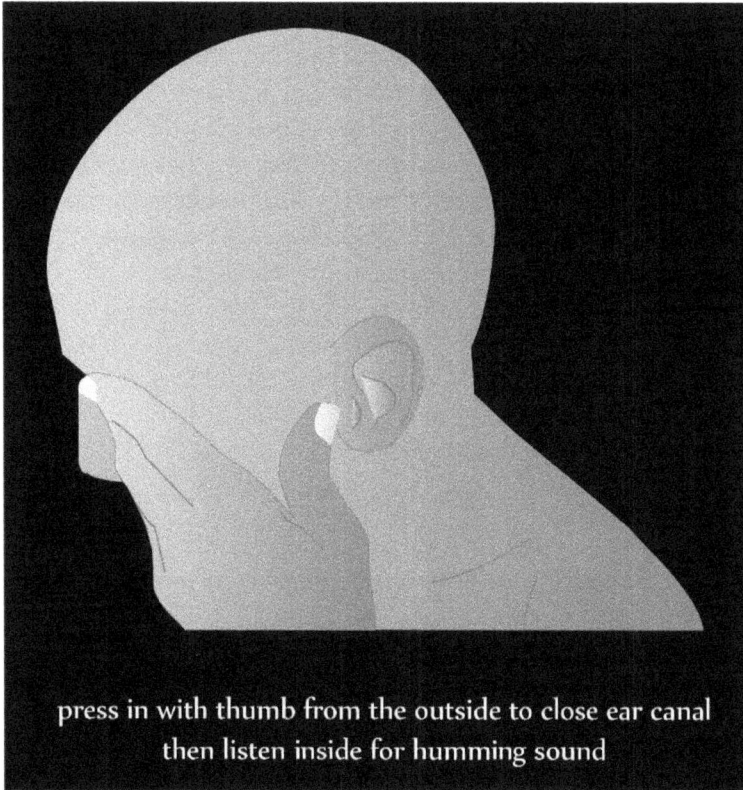

press in with thumb from the outside to close ear canal
then listen inside for humming sound

On some days, this may not happen when one presses the fingers against the closed eyelids but it should happen now and again. This gives one confidence that the third eye chakra does exist at that place.

A more efficient method for this is to do *kapalabhati/bhastrika* rapid breathing while pressing the fingers and focusing in the center of the lights which one sees. This causes infusion of energy into the brow chakra. This results in a bright donut-shaped light which may increase in brilliance, changing colors as the infusion intensifies.

Confidential Yoga

Yoga concerns the entire psyche not just the parts of the body which are approved for discussion by the moral precepts of any society. Yoga is personal in the sense that each yogi/yogini is responsible to do self research to investigate the coreSelf and its relationship to the psychic adjuncts, which it is related to, and which it cannot shed because these are attached to the self by a power which is different from and greater than the core.

What can the core do?

It can regulate some aspects of its relationship to the adjuncts. To discover the means for this, meditation is required. This diagram below is the *mukhasana* posture, the cow face pose. It is vital for females in their bid to understand the purpose and operation of the breasts which are organs which find their best expression as milk ducts for infants. Besides this there is a pleasure feeling which emanates. There is also an interaction between the breast and the genitals. There is a biological clock which causes the breast to develop and exude milk in reference to the delivery of an infant from the female sexual apparatus.

To understand how this operates, a yogini should study the subtle body to know its distribution circuits and its suction of hormonal aspects in the physical and subtle bodies.

Note the diagram of the physical body in contrast to the second image which is of the subtle body.

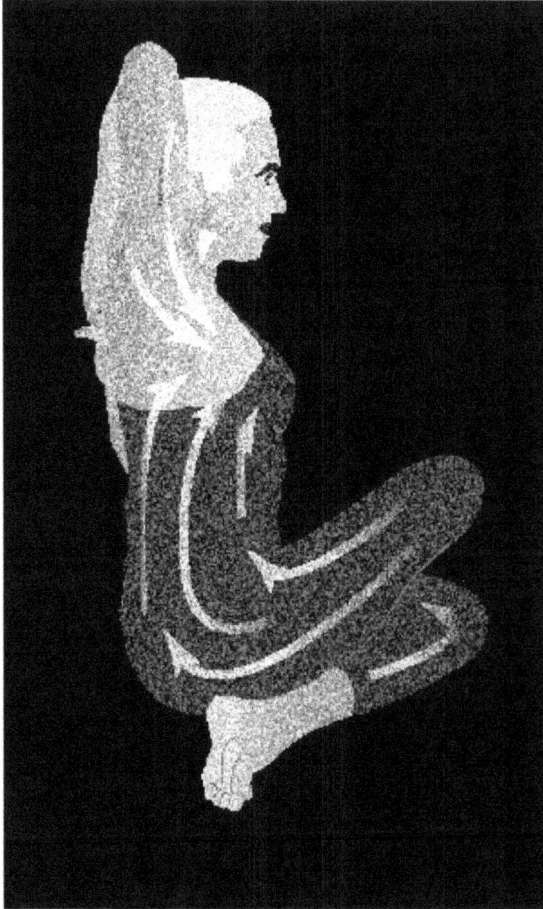

Meditating on Yoga Postures

It is advised in both the *Bhagavad Gita* and the *Yoga Sutras* that one should sit to meditate while using an easy posture. There is a standard which is that people try to meditate in the lotus posture, *padmasana*. This happened because of seeing many statues and images of famous yogis sitting in that pose.

Initially when I began to practice yoga, I did not have a physical teacher. I began intuitively to assume postures. Some months after while I was in Trinidad in 1966, I saw a yoga book in a store in Port of Spain. I looked through this book with interest.

Later after I got some instruction from Arthur Beverford, I became determined to assume many postures. This was in the Philippines in 1970. Some postures were difficult. The *padmasana* lotus pose was impossible at that time. This was due to the stiffness of the thighs, legs and feet. I did not have a muscular frame, and still my muscles, whatever little there was of it, was resistant to the poses.

Once I forced myself in lotus pose and remained seated in it for about fifteen minutes. To avoid being seen by others who were not familiar with such poses, I locked myself in a closet. It was very painful to get into the pose, to remain in it and to take the legs and feet out of it. I decided to invent some poses which would relax the muscles and tendons in my feet, legs, and thighs.

That is not meditation. It is a part of the *asana* part of yoga. One can do poses but one should not assign that as yoga. It is only part of the *asana* part. If one sits to meditate and is forced to focus on the pains of a posture, that is not meditation. It is however part of the practice of *asana* which is the third in the list of eight aspects which form the process of yoga.

One can do difficult *asana* poses and meditate on the effects of those positions. If this is done, that is considered to be a type of meditation. It is not the pose itself which is meditation in this case. It is the focusing investigation which one does which is the meditation portion.

For instance, in the pose shown below, the yogi sits on his legs and heels but with his toes spread to each side, instead of being under the body. That particular pose is a variation of the *vajrasana* thunderbolt posture.

In that pose, the toes flare to each side. The buttocks press on the heels. In that pose, the yogi can meditate to investigate the energy distribution during the use of that position. That would be a meditation on that pose. In one of the diagrams, the energy flow in the subtle body, which happens during that pose, is shown.

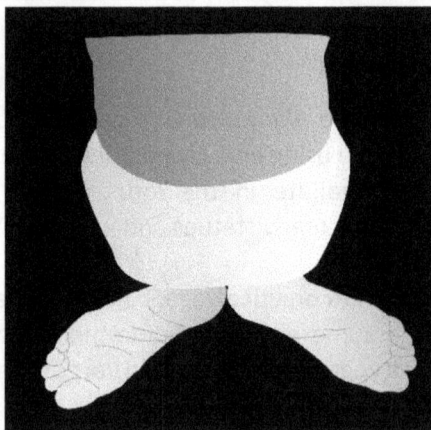

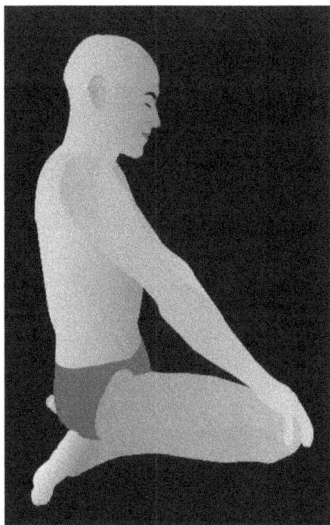

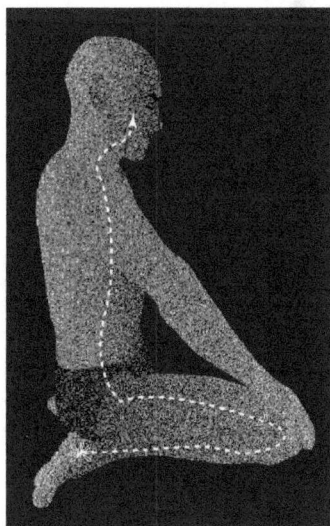

Lurching Throat Posture

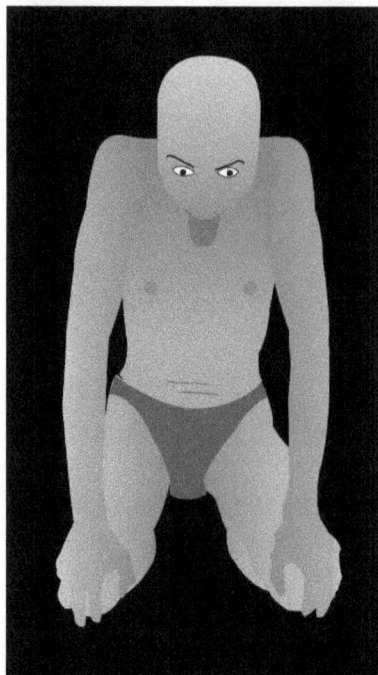

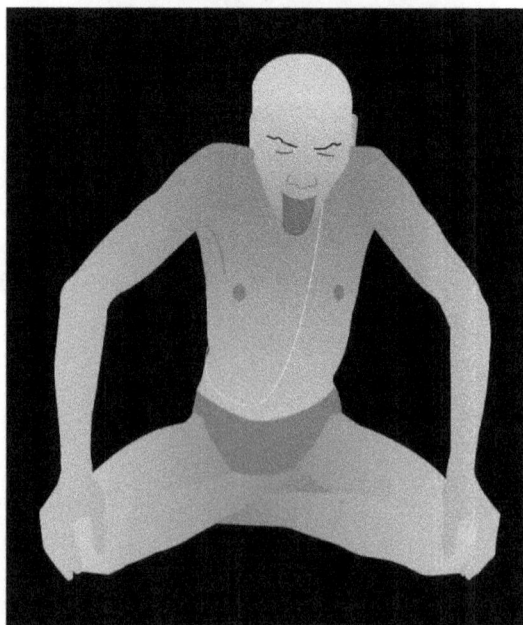

This is the lion pose, *singhasana*. There are as many poses as they are body configurations in the various species of life. These include species which are extinct and those which are yet to be produced by Nature.

Besides any set of primary poses, there are variations depending on whether these are assumed from a sitting or standing position. There is no set number of poses which limit an individual. In fact, each person should study the effects of posture in his body, and adapt poses, and even be inspired uniquely to assume poses, which he did or did not learn from a teacher.

According to the obstructions which certain poses can remove in the physical and subtle bodies, the yogi should regularly assume poses. He should test their value and check to be sure that they assist in the objective of having a healthy physical body and an energy infused subtle one.

The lion-pose tones the throat. It pulls up or lurches everything that is connected to the tongue, even the tubing which connects to the stomach.

Lower Body Locks

As part of the *asana* third portion of yoga, there are muscle compression locks which have mento-emotional energy compression as its psychic counterpart. These locks are used effectively during *pranayama* breath infusion which is the fourth portion of yoga. The containment and compression of subtle energy serves the purpose to cause purification of psychic energy.

There are many locks. Some are discovered in the advanced stage of the practice. Some are introduced as routine movements during particular postures and meditation sessions.

There are three primary locks at the bottom of the trunk. These are.
- anus retraction
- urinary muscle contraction upwards
- sexual apparatus retraction upward and backward simultaneously

Initially these three locks seem to be two locks, where the urinary and sexual locks function as one compression. As a student practices, it becomes evident within the body, that the urinary and sexual retractions are two distinct movements.

However, these locks are usually applied together, even though a student should practice to sort them.

When doing breath infusion, when there is compression and pushing of the infused breath energy downwards through the trunk of the body, the student must apply those three lower locks, so that the infused energy does not dissipate outwards through those areas. There should be a containment and then compression of the energy which comes down the trunk of the body, and which mixes with the anal and sexual complex of energy in the physical and subtle bodies.

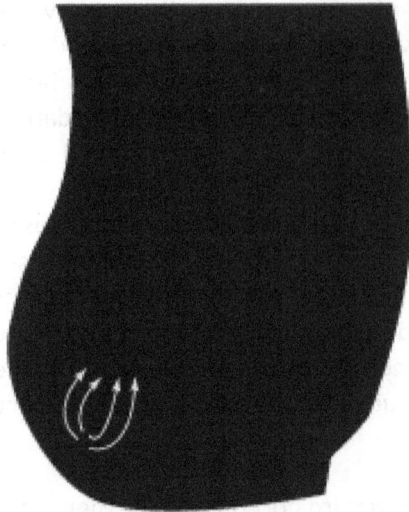

pull-up anal sphincter muscle

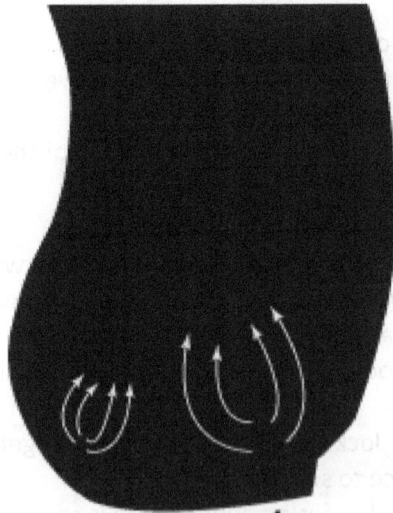

pull-up perineum
and urinary muscle

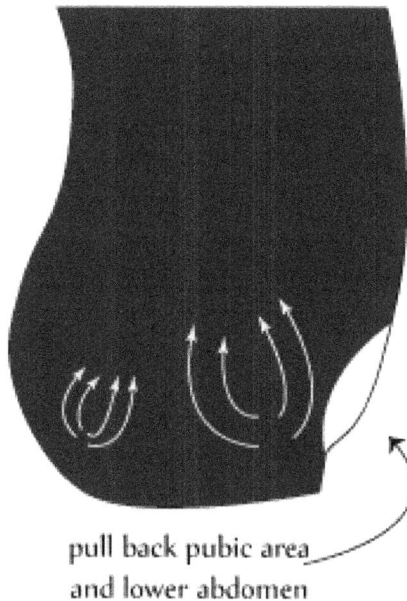

pull back pubic area
and lower abdomen

Subtle Body Ingestion and Digestion

It is natural that one who practices yoga, should use the physical body as the reference. However, as a student progress he/she will advance into a position of thinking that the physical body is not as important as the subtle one. Nevertheless, even after making this adjustment, there will be a residual force for the importance of the physical system.

After all, even if one believes in reincarnation, or even if one has experiences, which verify that one was reborn, and had previous lives, still, the habit of being the physical body, and using it as the basic meter, will remain.

From yogic literature, we heard of ascetics who were exceptional, and who used the psyche as the reference, and minimized the importance, which most persons place on the physical form.

When doing *pranayama* breath infusion, one learns about the lungs. But this education is more about the subtle body. The parallel of the physical lungs are the subtle lungs, except that the physical lungs are located, only in the upper part of the physical chest. On the subtle side, those lungs are spread through the trunk of the subtle body, such that there are no intestines and colon in that psychic format.

Hence when doing *pranayama*, it is suggested that one should take the breath down to the base chakra. How is that possible if the physical lungs do not extend that far down in the body? For that matter the physical lungs are in the upper half of the physical trunk.

Consider if the subtle lungs, the pranic absorption part, spread through the entire length of the subtle trunk.

What then?

There is a foot note for this.

After doing *pranayama* for some time, it happens that one begins to experience this extended subtle lung system. One no longer feels as if the lungs are only in the upper chest.

Lotus Posture Advice

For most people, it is best not to sit in lotus posture to do meditation. If the limbs are quite flexible, if there is no strain or pain when assuming lotus, it can be used during meditation.

If a yogi/yogini is not flexible, he/she, should sit in a comfortable pose for meditation. Unless the meditation objective is to study the situation in the body during difficult postures, aches and pains should not be felt during the session.

One should practice difficult postures but one should not do so during the meditation session. Any distractions during meditation, any pain in the body as a result of difficult postures, any tension from the posture, should be avoided.

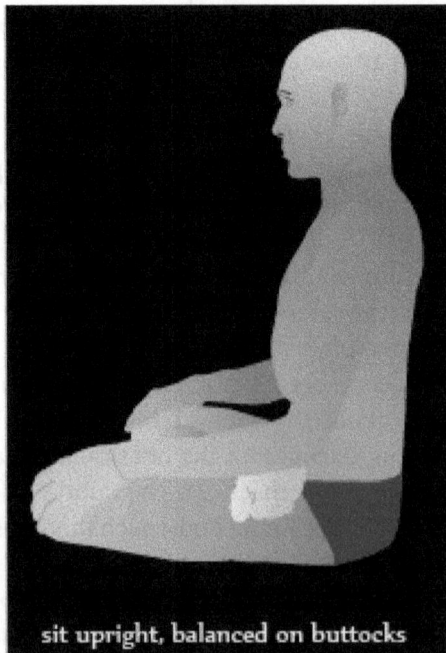

sit upright, balanced on buttocks

Sex as Fire and Smoke

On October 15, 2023, just before retiring for the night, there was a presence in my psyche. That self was Yogeshwarananda. I felt an arousal of energy at the base chakra which was a movement upward and to the front of the body. At first it was a flash of white light. Then it pointed to the sex organ chakra. It assumed an orange and red color like the color of flames from a wood fire. It flashed and blared as it correlated itself to the physical sexual apparatus.

Just then I felt a minor sexual arousal which was like the beginning of a sexual action. Then, that arousal subsided to nothing. The flames disappeared because I did not assign any focus to the sexual area of the body, especially to its psychic or physical operation.

I realized that this was ignited by Yogeshwarananda who was in my psyche at the time. He experimented to study the operation of the base chakra when it is routed through the sex organ apparatus. He looked at how it developed stage by stage, step by step.

Seeing that he conducted research, I did not interfere. However, I wondered because one day prior, I discovered an image which I made some years ago but which was in a stored file. That illustrated what happened to kundalini during Yogesh's experiment.

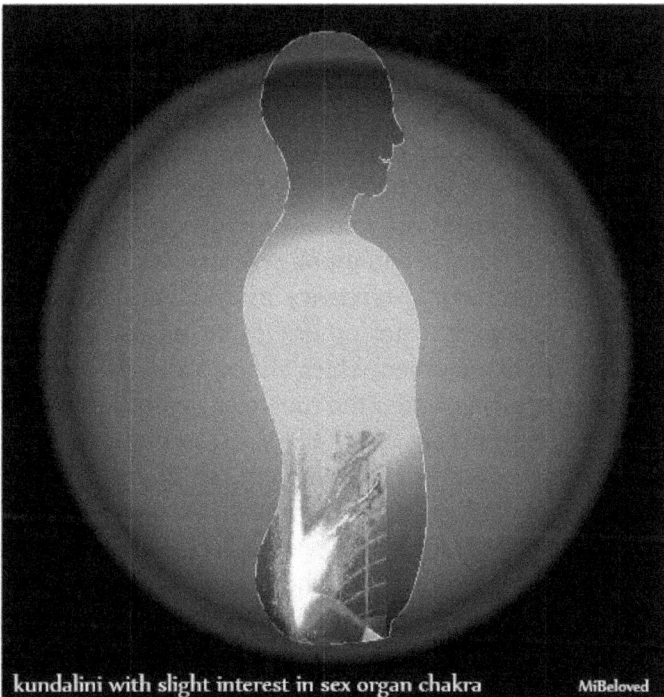

kundalini with slight interest in sex organ chakra   MiBeloved

Psychic Sex Research

An ascetic has a task to do self investigation into the development and dismantling of the physical sex urge. If one begins with the birth of a body, the natural terminal will be its death. But if the research is limited to that, one may not pry into the dismantling of the urge. That would be an incomplete investigation.

Using my body, Yogeshwarananda from the astral side of existence, investigated the operation of the sex impulse. He did this because in his last body, there was no sexual involvement with a female. With no recent experience in that regard, he felt it necessary to study the process. However, with no desire for the enjoying aspect of sex experience, he did not have a strong need to again became a physical being. Thus, he took the opportunity of using my body which is familiar with sexual intercourse, because it was not kept in a celibate condition after the teen years.

In his investigation, there were several stages where he formed conclusions. At one point he said this.

"Sex feelings are activated by the touch sensation. That uses the other senses to gain information and alerts about the availability of the opportunities. To curtail the influence of touch, the coreSelf would have to disregard touch alerts as soon as they are detected. Otherwise, if there is no action to disregard or ignore, there will be an increase of the urge, where the core is coerced to render its attention, which strengthens the urge, and makes it an irresistible force.

"As you know, I tested this idea in your psyche. It works most of the time. I cannot say that it works in every arousal, because the particular coreSelf does not have full autonomy. There are other factors, such as ancestors who need bodies, and there may be other powerful influences, supernatural powers. Still a yogi should squelch this sexual intercourse tendency as soon as the urge is sensed. Actually, this applies to any other type of sensual activity. Sex is only one type. There are others which also serve to disrupt yoga practice, and bury the ascetic under the rubble of so many involvements."

After this, Yogeshwarananda did some research using some memories from my teen years. He observed how when this body was in infancy and until it was fourteen, it did not have a sexual interest, except for a curiosity about the design of the sexual organs. There was no access to nude bodies, except those of animals like dogs, cats, goats, and sheep. The sexual intercourses of these animals had no commanding interest. There was only a slight curiosity if these creatures were seen in coition. The idea of the emotional interplay of the sexual partners was absent.

Suddenly there was sexual maturity. This happened because sexual urge in the infant and teenaged body piled up little by little, as if suddenly from nothing to something. Yogeshwarananda observed how it happened in my body, but he was unable to see it clearly in his previous body, because there was no sexual impetus coming from females to him, when that previous body was in infancy and teen years.

Apparently if a male is isolated from sexual stimuli, the sexual maturity event may not happen as a pronounced urge.

He checked on the mental point of reference which was present in my psyche when puberty occurred. He found that it swelled whenever the senses were confronted with the sexual forms of a female in the environment. If that was absent nothing happened. There was no interest in sexual proximity to anyone.

When such interest developed, it was found that there was no information in the psyche, which indicated the possibility of pregnancy. Even though there were pregnancies in humans and in pet animals who were seen, there was no interpretation of that as being the result of sexual attraction, which was completed to the point of sexual intercourse.

The insight about it was incomplete, nil, where the only thing perceived was the short version, of first getting the body close to the person whom it was attracted to. Once the distance between my body and the other person, (female), was reduced, physical touching and visual contact were made. Then Nature suggested kissing. Then Nature suggested increased closeness of the bodies. Then sexual arousal became impetuous. Then there was indication of Nature for sexual insertion. None of this had with it the understanding of a potential pregnancy. Nothing about the development and then birth of a baby was perceived.

No link was made to the pregnancies of women and of female animals. This means that the memory from past lives when there was sexual intercourse, was unavailable. The self had no access to it in the infant and teen years. Hence, he/she could not make informed decisions. Nature did not intent to provide the history. The only way the individual could learn about it would be from senior humans who explained it. Unfortunately, that is not reliable. Many elder human beings, do not divulge that insight to their infants and teen children. This is due to Nature's installation of a privacy tendency in the psyche.

Marijuana Hereafter

I was pulled into an astral dimension last night, during which I was with an uncle who is deceased. At first one of his sons was sent to call me. Then that son left me in another astral region where I was located. His father asked him to bring me to the place where they stayed in South America. It was in a ghetto village which dimensionally, was adjacent to this physical world.

When I arrived at that place, the son who called me was present with the uncle, and his other son. The one who called me had left a trace energy for me to follow to that location.

The old uncle was partially crippled. They sat on a wooden floor of old boards, smoking marijuana. The astral bodies of the two sons were of the age of about twelve and ten years of age. My uncle was proud that he was with his sons, as if they were a family group which drank liquor together. Except that in their case, it was marijuana.

The astral place had no asphalt roads. There were only dirt tracks. There were no automobiles, nor modern items. After a short bit, after my uncle was satisfied that I saw him with his sons, smoking pot, he wanted to tour me through the place. He got up and began to walk to another place. The situation was shabby. It was similar to how some indigenous people live in the jungle of the Amazon in South America.

The place had a long table made of rough lumber. On the table there were pots and pans made out of enameled tin. A lady was near a wood fire. She used non fashionable clothing as if it was over four hundred years ago.

After this my uncle mentioned his wife, saying that he had not seen her for a time. She sent a letter which one of her sisters conveyed to him. After that conversation, I left that astral place.

There was nothing that I could say or do. In that psychic location, visitors are not allowed to express approval or disapproval, but only to act as neutral witnesses to what happens there. That is an astral world which accommodates people who are addicted to marijuana.

After the uncle left, I was switched to a parallel place where one of his sons wanted me to talk to a man, who was a marijuana supplier. This person had a cell phone but it was a dusty looking device. As soon as I was aware that he had it, I felt one in my pocket. My uncle's son also felt one. Mine had a map which they needed. The supplier took my phone and punched some of the keys. He said he has to set something in it.

Soon after he returned the phone, but it had a psychic signal which he secretly installed into it. This was a signal for me to begin getting marijuana from that supplier.

I left that place with my uncle's son, but did not tell him that the phone was tampered. He wanted to go to another place where there were shops selling various items. For some reason, I immediately found myself in possession of a low power motorcycle, which he borrowed. With it he left and went to another place. I wanted to tell him what happened with the phone being tampered, but he was in a hurry to go somewhere else.

A question arises as to why I went to that place. The reason is the relationship with the uncle. These social relationships could lead to getting shifted to an undesirable place hereafter. These factors should be carefully monitored.

Retardative Influence Irresistible

In *Bhagavad Gita*, Lord Krishna divulged that there are three primary influences in the physical existence. He lists them as clarifying, enthusing and retardative energies. These constantly assault a living being to push that person in one direction or the other.

Each of these influences are present in the psyche of an individual. They can be observed. To some extent they can be monitored. For the most part, they are overpowering.

A yogi should self-study to know when one, or a combination of these influences, cause the self to act in a productive or nonproductive manner. He should also study how he is overpowered by a single, or combination of these. For instance, when the physical body is tired, one is overpowered by the retardative force. That causes drowsiness which converts into sleep. To a limited extent, that influence can be thwarted but mostly it must be accepted.

Under certain conditions, when the self is aware of the predominance of the retardative mood, that self cannot adjust it. He/She must endure it. In some situations when a self becomes aware of that lowest of the influences, that person may shift the psyche to be under the clarifying force, so that it can act in the interest of the self.

For instance, during sleep, one may awaken in a drowsy condition, and become aware that the bladder should be emptied, that one should arise and urinate. However, the retardative influence may be so strong, that even though one is aware of the body's situation, one cannot arouse the body. One fails to direct it to move to a latrine. The result of this lack of enthusiasm to urinate, is that the bladder becomes inflated, as urine may keep flowing into it.

This would be an admittance that the self was overpowered by the retardative force, and was unable to accept the enthusing power, which operates the body, to move it to a place where the urine could be discharged.

This happens even to persons who advertise themselves as liberated beings, as spiritually advanced persons. Even they fall under the influence of that retardative mood.

Astral San Francisco

I was in a predominantly black area of San Francisco during the night of October 31, 2023. At first, I was with a friend who is deceased some years now. I sat on a street corner in the Haight Ashbury area of the city. My deceased friend came there to meet me. However, he could not recognize anything. Due to long use of cocaine while he abused in his previous physical body, his subtle body functions to go to familiar places, but it could not perceive anyone, and did not respond sensibly in conversations.

The astral side of San Francisco was an exact copy of the physical locations. After my friend, who has a white body, failed to recognize me, I was transferred instantly to a street corner, which was used by predominately black residents of the city. I stood in a queue at a fast foods shop. There was nothing on the menu that I could eat because there were no vegetarian meals. The lady who served the customers looked at me and mentally communicated that she wanted me for a partner. I was transferred across the street, where there was a large stone building which was a theatre. It was massive. Nearby there was a subway rail station. I was supposed to use that transit to get to the heart of the city.

When I attempted to cross the street to buy a subway ticket, I became aware of a long queue of people. It had about three hundred people in it. I decided to find another way to get to the center of the city. Just them a man approached and told me that I could use the subway if I waited a bit. He mentally commented that soon a train would arrive which would convey passengers.

This happened within moments. Then I went into the subway entrance. As soon as I was to step on the base level, I was shifted to the center of the city. In that place there are ideas of trains but there are no trains. One used the idea of a train and that itself was the means of transport.

When I got to the central part of the city, the houses were neatly arranged. There was not one person on the street. There were no automobiles. One got the feeling that the people were in a state of suspended animation. There was no noise. The place was silent.

Yoga Practice / Insufficient Time

It happens that a yogi makes a commitment to his yoga teacher, or to himself, to complete the practice session daily, once, or twice per day. However, as time would have it, this yogi is not the supreme controller and cannot meet that commitment every single day.

When it happens, that circumstances deny one the time to complete the practice, one may have some little time, or have half the time, where one must decide if one should attempt to practice, or if one should leave aside that session completely, abandoning one's commitment for the time being.

There are many reasons for not having sufficient time for practice. These causes include the following.

- over-sleeping
- malaise resulting from laziness
- physical tiredness due to over-exertion
- over-eating
- tiredness due to sexual expression
- discouragement due to absorption of retardative energy from non-yogis

These aspects affect the energy in the psyche. These can cause a yogi not to rise to practice, where he/she is overcome with a mood which depresses the impulses for practice.

If a practice session of *asana* postures, *pranayama* breath infusion, *pratyahar* interiorization, and *samyama* meditation, requires forty (40) minutes of time for completion, and if one only has twenty (20) minutes for it, one should do the breath infusion session to the fullest and use the remaining time for interiorization and meditation. If there is no time left, the interiorization and meditation should be cancelled for that session.

By completing the *pranayama* breath infusion, the subtle body will be fully charged with fresh energy which should be the basic achievement. This is important in the quest to get the subtle body to be relieved of the tendency to get energy from eating physical food. It has that tendency, which should be removed from it, before one is evicted from the physical system at death.

One basic achievement is to get the subtle body to forego, to wash out, its need for subtle energy from physical food. That has to happen if one is to realistically not be compelled to take another physical body.

Relationship Issue

For the atheists it is easy because for them, at this moment of being a physical body, there is no God to account to, and no heaven hereafter to qualify for. For the theist it is a confusion which they currently avoid.

What is the issue? It is the factor of relationship, as to what comparative age one will be, when one gets to heaven, and as to where others will fit in the relationship display, in the beatific and magnificently conceived place.

- Who will the mother?
- Who will be the father?
- Who will be the son?
- Who will be the daughter?
- Who will be the husband?

- Who will be the wife?
- Will there be grandparents?
- Will any such relationship be perpetual?
- Will there be interchanges where for a certain period, one is a father or mother, and then for another time, one may be a daughter or son?
- Will the person who is the mother in this life, be the mother in heaven as well?
- Will one grow up to be an adult there?
- Will one remain as a child forever, as an obedient infant of the same parents one had on earth?
- At what age will one be as that dear child of those elders?

Tendency or Application of Tendency

For inSelf Yoga™, the matter is tendency not its application. And yet for a beginner the application of tendency is important. It is the clue that leads the yogi to discover, and then reform or eliminate the tendency.

The application of tendency has no handle on it, whereby one can come to grips with it. For that one must discover and handle the tendency directly, regardless of if, it is in use, or is in dormancy. However, because tendency is extreme subtle, and is in many cases so subjective to a self as it impossible to sort or recognize, one should begin this quest by focusing on its application.

When one hones to the application, one can over time researching in many meditation sessions, discover the tendency root. Then one can hold it, and make the effort to reform, or eliminated it.

Some students cannot be assisted in this regard. They are so fused with a tendency that they cannot objectivity themselves in reference to it. In fact, if the yoga teacher makes the effort to show them how to sort themselves from the tendency, they become annoyed. They resist vehemently.

Each yogi/yogini should endeavor to get to the root of a tendency. If necessary, focus first on recognizing the application of the tendency. Then patiently over time with self honesty, focus on the tendency itself.

Focusing on ceasing an unwanted application of tendency is an improvement, but it is a superficial fix. One must sort the tendency, and sink into the psyche to locate and reform the self's use of it.

Astral Hot Planet

On the night of December 6, 2023, I was in an astral dimension on an earth-like planet, where there was no sea nor mountains. The surface was liquid rock, which seethed and fumed. Even though the temperature on the surface was intolerable, the body used in that dimension did not burn. It was a body which was a head only. All persons on that planet were heads alone. All heads faced upward, away from the planet. Each stared into the sky.

The atmosphere above could not be seen. There were chemical clouds of vapor passing over head. These were so thick that nothing in the sky could be seen. I tried to speak of it to some persons who were near to me, but the idea of speech was the only thing I could do. Speech itself was not possible.

At one point, a part of the planet's surface crusted. It dried into being hard rock. Just them there was stuttering and vibrating like in an earthquake. The situation was unstable. Someone nearby said, "Move, move, do you not see? Do you not hear? It is an earthquake. We will be swallowed. Do something. Let us save ourselves."

As that person said this, everyone who heard him realized that they were helpless, and would have to endure whatever happened. Sometime after, I was shifted from that astral place. It rendered some idea about how planets cool down after forming into large roundish objects in space.

Life Copy Issue

There is much literature about reincarnation, as to its relevance. There is so much fascination about it. However, a greater mystery for humankind is the life copy issue. It is something that is before every living individual, but something which is repeatedly ignored. It confronts every creature, and yet it is not reviewed. It is free for the taking, and yet it is rejected outright.

The life copy issue is the fact that every life form which is produced is coded to perform in a certain way. This does not mean predestination. Rather it means destination, that whatever there is, a certain course is copied within it, for performance.

From the birth of the body, at its eviction from the mother's form, it is coded to perform in a certain way, in response to what occurs in the environment. We have not heard of a single fetus which directed, or caused its removal from its mother's womb.

Stated precisely, not one single fetus had control over its birth. None maneuvered from being inside the mother to being outside with its own air consumption. The coding or ordered principle which caused its birth, is an unknown power. Not one form appeared as an adult which did not develop so through growth.

In some cases, that order principle failed to deliver as in the case where a surgeon cuts the body of the mother and removes the fetus. But that does not change the fact that the fetus itself did no deliver itself.

After birth, the scene remains the same, where the ordered principle, a biological process, continues to grow and mature the body, making it act in one way or the other, according to the growth process.

During this growth sequence there is a stage where there is a call for companionship. That may or may not result in sexual union with someone of the opposite sex. That in turn may result in a pregnancy. How much of that is controlled by the two entities who indulged?

Even if one is given information about the formation of a pregnancy, still the process is not controlled by oneself. Yes, one may engage sexually with intention to beget or one may engage with no idea that there may be a pregnancy. But either way, one does not absolutely control the process. The development of the fetus is a nature process, an ordered development which one may or may not observe. If one observes it, much of the process will be hidden from oneself. Even if one uses scientific instruments which extends one's knowledge, still, the ordered process has many hidden actions which are so covert, that one cannot perceive them.

The realization is that one is a coded reality which was confronted by other segments of other coded realities. To a certain extent, one must perform as a motive, function, or driving force. One is reduced to that. One is a minor phase in a function of Nature.

Part 6

Hazards of Guru Power

Guru Power is real but it comes with hazards, the foremost which is the flow of energy from followers into the psyche of the guru and the flow of power from the guru into the followers.

A guru cannot all by himself/herself run a mission, and represent a lineage, or create a new one. He/She must take help from others. In doing so there is a two-way flow from the follower to the guru and from the guru to the follower. This is the hazard.

I met a departed person who was a guru in the immediate past life but who was ruined before he was deprived of his physical body. There were legal complexities and accusation which were sensational and severe.

After drifting here to there in the astral world which is parallel to our physical situation, he now stays at Yogeshwarananda's astral ashram which is nearby. His subtle body is sick. It is swollen. It lacks vital energy.

He appealed to me that I should transfer to his psyche, any excess energy which accumulates during breath infusion pranayama practice. This is similar to a blood transfusion, where someone with a high blood count, agrees to give blood to someone who is anemic.

I have no idea how long I will do this. However, because in his past life, I learned some breath infusion methods from him, I am obligated to help this person.

There is also another issue which he requested help with, which was to remove some energy, which was transferred from his subtle body to a disciple of his, who became empowered by that energy, but who later resented him, and still has the energy, and uses it.

His idea is that I should remove the energy from that person, and keep it in my psyche for the time being, until someone appears who should have that empowerment from him. This also means that in the meantime, I would function with that energy, as an agent for its distribution.

The guru role or being empowered as a guru for an astral or physical lineage is a risky skill. It is best that one avoids it. There is no guarantee that one will only gain good from such a role. It has risks.

Triangle Portal

A portal which is a two-way or three-way facility in the subtle head, may be discovered suddenly when doing meditation after surcharging the subtle head using breath infusion *bhastrika* or *kapalabhati* process. Examining this diagram.

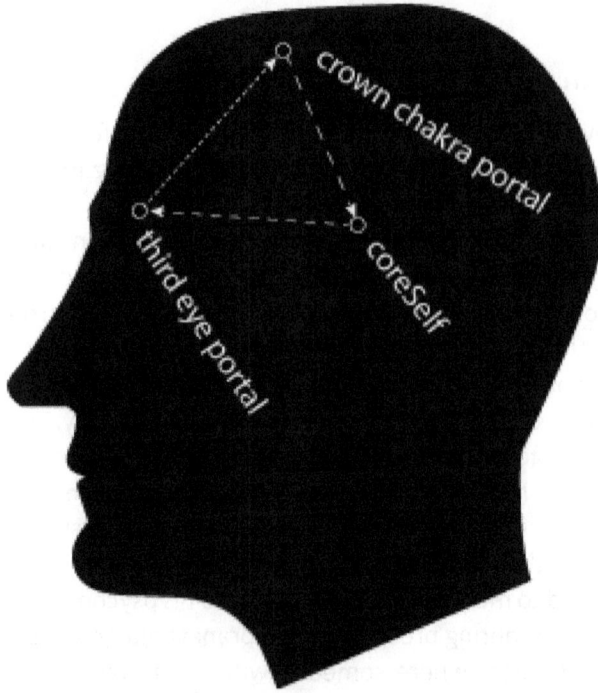

There is a passage horizontally from the coreSelf to the third eye portal. This is easy to detect. There is a passage which may be slightly curved. That is from the third eye portal to the crown chakra complex.

If it reaches the crown chakra and lodges there, there may be another portal which completes the loop. That is from the crown chakra to the coreSelf. A yogi may activate these passages which began at the coreSelf and loops back to it. There may be a continuous flow of communication between these three factors.

End of the Road

The evolutionary journey through various species of life is one achievement. It is full of curiosities and surprises. In it is hidden the master plan which is repeated in various ways, as a journey through a maze, which has familiar and unfamiliar passages. Getting out is not part of it, except to escape to safety which means reaching a state of incorruptibility, a state of no decay, a condition in which there is no threat of a violent or painful condition.

Each coreSelf is challenged to complete the course where there is an ever-promise of vitality and maximum monitorship. But that happens for a moment, if it even happens in one dip. Then the powers and opportunities are confiscated, suddenly or gradually. Then again there is birth or re-emergence. The cycle of actions begins afresh.

A pack of cards which are shuffled, then served to a player, gives him the hope that he will be served the winning hand over and over. Of course, it does not happen in that way but his mind tells him that there is a promise, where he will be served the winning hand.

But will he?

The idiot!

He still does not understand that even if he is given the win, still he will lose. He will be reduced. He will be frustrated.

If he is not disappointed, if he plays for the sake of playing, because he must, because it is set in that way, still then no matter his detachment, he will be on the losing end, again and again.

What is the alternative?

Play the game friend, because you must, because it is so arranged, because destiny has the upper hand!

Play the game. You are a cog of little if any significance. Do not begrudge the absolute which you are not.

You resent being a function of time?

But that is an overestimation.

You may be a function of a function of a function, diminutively!

It is acceptable to be a near-nothing.

Necessary Isolation in Yoga

For ideal yoga practice, a major ingredient is isolation. Without that a yogi will find that he/she becomes involved in associations, which utilize time, and which cause the focus of the self to be linked to non-yogic affairs.

There are many people who learn something about yoga, especially about meditation. Most of these individuals are not interested in the hard end of the practice, which has psychic isolation as a requirement. These superficial yogis do harm to the sincere ones, when attempts are made to draw a sincere ascetic, into relationships which are not yogic.

Even if a yogi is advanced in practice, even if he/she is commissioned to teach others, still such association, with students who are loaded with non-yogic relationships, is harmful to the yogi.

By all means every yogi should curtail non-yogic association. This will protect one and all. We must have the insight to see that every person using a material body, carries a package of desire and relational energies which is harmful to yoga. It stifles practice.

A yogi should carefully manage his desires and relationships. The students should do so as well. Bringing every friend or relative to the teacher is harmful. It is risky for the teacher. Instead, those energies should be curtailed and compressed in the nature of the student by the student.

As far as possible, desires and need energies in the psyche should be contained, examined, compressed, or eliminated. People should dig into their psyches, root up unfavorable motivations and tendencies, and make the effort to suppress or eliminate those unwanted psychic features.

Except for an advanced yogi, who is in relative isolation, every entity carries a package of non-yogic, yogically-corrosive energy. Hence the students of yoga should observe relationships, and keep them quarantined and restricted. Otherwise, their pollution will spread to other yogis and even to the advanced teacher.

Every simpleton yogi is a bag of pollution. Unless the bag is kept isolated and is discovered, analyzed, cataloged, further packaged, and securely treated, the polluted contents will spread to others, even to a teacher. Every yogi, the advanced and the simpleton, should be on guard to keep polluted associations curtailed or eliminated.

End of Desire

Just as the waves on an ocean have no termination, desire has no ending. As soon as a wave collapses, some other force arises either from the absorption of the wave's energy or from resistance to it. Meeting someone else involves the generation of desire energies. But with that is the absorption or crash of other desire forces, which were already moving to expend or upend energy.

Even a slight contact with someone, may cause a tidal swell in a desire clash between one and some other. It may arise immediately. It may be delayed where it swells immediately, or remains unfulfilled for the time being. In either case, a yogi should gage the potential outcome. Then he/she may see a way to adjust or cancel, if that is possible.

Sometimes in the ocean, one wave meets another head-on. Each expends a full or partial force to cancel or reinforce the other. Such it is that when two persons meet, their collective desire force may clash, or a portion of that collective, may entangle with a portion from the other person. Both clash for a particular outcome. It has as factors, the time and circumstance.

Some waves meet so as to reinforce each other. Then, as a combined energy, they ride as one challenge to whatever is in their vicinity. Eventually however after meeting a greater power, they expend. Some fizz due to losing supportive structure. A compound desire which is from this and that persons, cannot continue without a supportive base. The base must move with the expression. Otherwise, the expression will be imperiled. It may lose its footing altogether. What would it be if a human being suddenly found himself/herself with no earth under its feet? The collapse would be frightening.

Each person comes into being with desires. Some are current. Some were expended. Some reside in dormancy. Each has a particular force, and will arise with or without the appropriate support. For two people in a partnership, their individual desires may clash positively or negatively. If the partnership is splintered, the desires may recede, may go into dormancy, may disappear. And yet, those desires will arise again. After a calm night, sometimes, the ocean produces turmoil again.

Rush here!

Rush there!

Variation is the constant.

One wave in the Atlantic desires to be near another in the Pacific.

How will they shift the time and the place?

Thoughts in Meditation

There are many mental and emotional events which occur when one sits to meditate. It depends on the mind content, the activation of subconscious energy, and the massive, or infantile power of the meditator.

Those who practice proficiently, who have some mastery over the mind, may banish any mental or emotional disturbance in a split second. They bring the mind to order rapidly. Others, the novices, even after years, may struggle to control what is unwanted in the mind, with the mind getting the best of their attention, day after day.

Respect!

- Does the mind have respect for the observing self, the witnessing faculty?
- Who or what is that witness?
- What is its function?
- What is its authority?
- Where do the emotions fit in?

Some meditation methods dictate that all thoughts which arise in the mind should be ignored or brushed aside. This idea is based on the declared premise that the thoughts are ephemeral, useless, a humbug; that they are of no consequence. They are figments and have no value.

It is declared that one should be a witness to thoughts which come and go. One should be a silent non-reactive observer, like a sun in a solar system which witnesses but does not react with or respond to the planets, asteroids, and meteors which flash around it.

What do I recommend?

There is value in attending to thoughts which arise in meditation. That value should be accessed during some meditations even though in some others, it should be ignored, or left aside for the time being.

This is because mere brushing a thought aside, does not necessarily remove the thought from the psyche, even though it may cause the thought to be dormant, or to be suppressed for a time.

One may observe thoughts as they come, one after the other, keeping them in an orderly queue, instead of allowing them to flash by at a rapid speed at their own rate. One may throttle them at a slow speed, examining one after the other for their source force, to determine how they were formulated, and how they derived the power to flash into the mind, as to how they derive the power to command the mind to display them, as to if they originated from someone else, and then penetrated the psyche, like a bullet which entered a body and lodged in it.

This examination if done precisely and with great care, as compared to ignoring the energy, may cause the permanent removal of that thought energy from the psyche. It may even cause the mind to develop an automatic deletion of similar energies which would, in the future arise in the mind.

Here are some skills which one may fail to develop, if one always only ignores the thoughts and urges, which arise in the mind.

- identification of persons who somehow has the power to penetrate the psyche
- identification of specific sensual addictions which are innate to the self
- identification of subconscious cravings which normally operate covertly in the psyche
- identification of thought pattern behaviors which are self-destructive energies
- being able to throttle the speed at which the mind displays thoughts
- having the ability to sort which thoughts have great value, and which are trivial
- understanding the relationship between the memory and the thought production mechanism (the intellect)
- sorting the observer-witness from the thought-producing adjunct in the mind
- getting clarity to know how the thoughts are mentally generated, illustrated, and displayed

Hence in inSelf Yoga™, it is recommended that one should confront thoughts during some meditations.

When should one not do this?

This should not be done when specifically, one is in a high control state, where somehow one has very little thought packages or no such packages. Then one should proceed with the advanced meditation method or state, where no thoughts occur, or where there are very few thoughts being generated.

Death Transfer

The preparation for death is simply the honest assessment of where one is likely to be hereafter. In fact, part of this is the consideration that one may cease to exist as the psychological being one knows oneself to be.

But why bring this into consideration?

On the first day of the year 2024, I spoke to a deceased friend mentally. Our discussion had to do with desire, which we agreed is the driving force behind what happens in this existence. By desire, we do not mean whatever is wanted mentally or emotionally, and which takes a rational format, but that which is wanted and which is driven by urges which assert themselves despite one's assertion of, or resistance to them.

In any direction one turns the face, one is confronted by desire or by a lack of that with a corresponding delay or gap, which only last for as long as providence would allow that. Then again one is engaged with desire.

Those who say that they are desireless are either being dishonest, or just do not understand what this existence is made of. There is a misunderstanding whereby someone who ceases to desire, feels that he/she may control the emergence, display, and formulation of desire.

This physical existence as well as the astral counterpart to it, comprises desire, just as a yarn comprises of threads which are woven as it.

Seeing desire in every direction I turn, knowing that this body winds down to its termination, I look to the astral existence. I befriend many people who exist there. There is no point in expanding association with physical people. In a short time, the perception of those folks in so far as they are physical, will cease. In contrast to that is the subtle people whose forms will be more pronounced after the death of my physical utility.

Recently within the past three years, I practiced switching to the subtle side. For instance, instead of teaching kundalini yoga and Patanjali meditation to physical people, I shifted to teach subtle people, even though some students still have physical bodies.

Do those subtle people with physical bodies, recall what they are taught in the dream state?

This question presupposes that I care about this. The fact is that I do not. People are taught on the physical side upon request. Many of these persons do not continue the practice. The astral side has some failure as well.

More and more, as the physical system ages, a yogi should shift to the subtle level, the psychic existence. This should be such that the switch over which will be enforced by Nature at its convenience, would happen without surprises. Already a person switches every night, or every time there is the major session of sleep, within twenty-four hours. Why not develop more awareness of this, and use it to get some footing for the final transfer?

There is a need for community. That should be switched to the psychic side. There is a need for a heavenly environment. Why not seek that from the psychic level? One should practice to abandon the physical reference.

Divine Eye Elementary Development

Meditation on the *ajna* brow chakra is the most popular proposal for assuming use of the divine eye. This method is mentioned even in the *Bhagavad Gita*.

प्रयाणकाले मनसाचलेन

भक्त्या युक्तो योगबलेन चैव ।

भ्रुवोर्मध्ये प्राणमावेश्य सम्यक्

स तं परं पुरुषमुपैति दिव्यम् ॥८.१०॥

prayāṇakāle manasācalena
bhaktyā yukto yogabalena caiva
bhruvormadhye prāṇam āveśya samyak
sa taṁ paraṁ puruṣamupaiti divyam (8.10)

prayāṇakāle — at the time of death; manasācalena = manasā — by the mind + acalena- by unwavering; bhaktyā — with devotion; yukto = yuktaḥ — connected; yogabalena — with psychological power developed through yoga practice; caiva = ca — and + eva — indeed; bhruvor = bhruvoḥ — of the two eyebrows; madhye — in the middle; prāṇam — energizing breath; āveśya- having caused to enter; samyak — precisely; sa = saḥ — he; tam - this; param — supreme; puruṣam- person; upaiti — he goes; divyam — divine

...and that meditator who even at the time of death, with an unwavering mind, being connected devotedly, with psychological power developed through yoga practice, and having caused the energizing breath to enter between the eyebrows with precision, goes to the Divine Supreme Person. (Bhagavad Gita 8.10)

However, when questioned about its development, finding a yogi who was successful in that tradition, is hard to locate. Why?

The reason is that there are a series of sensual deprivations and mental restrictions which must be practiced before one can achieve complete *pratyahar*, which is withdrawal of sensual interest from the physical and lower astral dimensions. If one does not practice *pranayama* breath infusion, it is a daunting task to achieve full settled *pratyahar*, where during meditation, at least, the sensual interest does not proceed in its normal way which is to aggressively acquire external fulfillments.

What I advise is that a yogi should fully master internal retraction of the senses, so that the interest no longer has the compelling urge to course out of the psyche, with intentions to grab fulfillments, from what is outside the physical or subtle body. The normal condition of the energy when one sits to meditate, should be that it is settled, and does not flow outward, even if no effort is made to compel it to be restrained.

There are several practices which may be done, after the sensual energy assumes a relaxed condition by remaining still, and not clambering to go out. Each yogi should find, or should be taught, a method which is effective.

Here I present an advice, I was given by a Lord Shiva deity. He directed that I use the short focus. This means that one should move from full withdrawal into an extending short focus, from across the gap from the coreSelf to the edge of the psyche. This is about the distance of two inches in the mental space in the forehead. What happens is that one finds the self to be in a subtle darkness, which is like being outdoors in a forest on a dark moon night, where outlines of objects are barely seen. This will be in the mental space between the coreSelf, and the edge of the psyche. It will not have any perception outside the psyche, or anywhere else. One should quietly remain there observing what is revealed.

There should be no anxiety nor sense of boredom, nor hankering for clarity. One should quietly remain in that dark mental space. One should wait there.

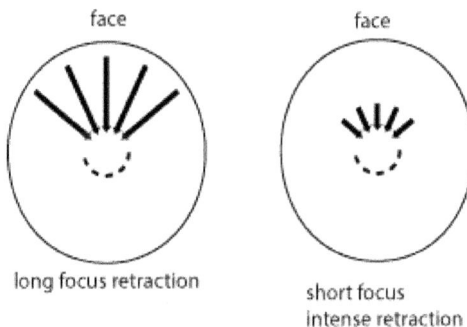

long focus retraction

short focus
intense retraction

Relationship Puzzle

If after death of the physical body, one will continue existing, then a new set of challenges will be present. If one will de-exist at that point and enter a sublime or blank energy state, where personality will no longer exist, then one does not have to figure it at this time. In that case, everything will be settled, once and for all, because one will not have to fit into any personality association format.

But if one will find oneself in an environment where personality is a factor, then the experiences in this life, indicate that one will have to fit in, somehow, somewhere. Will one be a perpetual adult, child, or elderly somebody? How will one be appreciated? What will one do? Whom will one serve? Who will serve one in turn?

In this life, at the start, we experienced ourselves as being subordinate to parents and teachers. We had no choice in the matter. Even some of us, who were born with body status as the son or daughter of wealthy or influential people, had to kowtow to parents and teachers on occasion. That is how this started.

Once we reached the adult stage, it was the physical body which was regarded, and not the personality which was expressed through the body. Which stage is preferred? In what place, at what time, and with whom, will one associate hereafter?

Will one be stuck as someone's child forever, never growing to be an adult, with no freedom to centralize oneself in a family or business?

What will be the situation hereafter?

To get clarity regarding psychic experiences as contrasted to imagination actions in the mind, one should practice remaining in the mind space during meditation, with no thoughts, images, or imaginations, taking place.

After repeated practice in the silent non-image-producing mind, one will develop the ability to sort imagination from actual psychic events.

Past Life Inquiry

If one has psychic experiences of past lives, should one publish information about this?

Secondly, why are yogis typically reluctant to reveal their past life activities and corresponding identities?

Response:

It is up to each yogi to reveal to others information or experience of a past life. There is no set rule which applies to each yogi. As great a yogi as Gautam Buddha gave details of his past lives, even lives as an aquatic. Buddha was a yogi who denied, or did not assert, that individuality is real. Still, he spoke of incidences not only of his past life but his past life while living in the past with others, who were or were not his disciples, even one when a disciple of his, who was hostile to Buddha, was antagonistic in more than one past life.

However, one must think it over, before one releases information which was derived from mystic experiences or intuition in a past life. One may be laughed out of the room by others who may disbelieve the information. One runs the risk of being rated as an arrogant fool.

One must be courageous to release such information. One must be tough to stand the ridicule, or even resentment, which may be projected from others, who may read or hear about a past life intuition or vision.

Kundalini Arousal Using Pranayama

Someone inquired if a yogi should have a kundalini arousal during each session of *kapalabhati/bhastrika pranayama* breath infusion practice. The answer is that one should have arousal of kundalini during each session. However, if one fails to do so, one should not be discouraged but should persist with the daily or twice-daily effort.

A practice should be for at least twenty minutes. It could be for even forty-five minutes or one hour. It may be longer. The time spent would depends on how long it takes the yogi to infuse enough fresh air and fresh subtle air, into the physical and subtle bodies.

Even though I stated that there should be a kundalini arousal, that does not mean that kundalini will rise in the same way in each practice. At the beginner's stage, the arousal of kundalini is a sensation, which may or may not rise through the spine, and enter the brain. Kundalini arousal may be compared to the following.

- sexual orgasmic feelings
- bunched intense pleasure feelings in some part of the body and psyche
- flashes of light darting with neutral energy or pleasure feeling
- scattered bliss feelings which can or cannot be identified.

In the beginning it is the sexual orgasmic feelings, which flash through the spine, or burst into the head, which are the regular experience.

As one practices, the various nadi subtle passages for electric energy become cleared of low energy, and allow the flow of fresh energy at all times. Then, because there is no accumulation of negative energy in the passages, the practice will not result in kundalini bursting through blocked passages. This happens with the result that the yogi remains in a higher state of consciousness continuous, even when he does not practice. Then when he practices, he will find that kundalini does not break through any massive blockages.

At that time, there will be a shift in practice, where the yogi will find that the breath, accumulates in bunched areas of the body. This energy will gather in a region. It will compress on itself, then burst or explode, then compress on itself, then burst again. This will be repeated until that area is cleared of dense energy.

As the fire in a log is not seen until the log is burnt, and as the log disintegrates as it burns, so a dense energy in some part of the subtle body, will be ignited by the subtle fire which is infused into the subtle body. When this is compressed, it will increase to a concentration which will cause it to be demolished.

Yes, kundalini should be aroused in each session, but that does not mean that such arousal will be of the same configuration during each session. It depends on the stage of practice, the intensity of compaction, the correct infusion method, and the application of other techniques.

Fall of Sexual Energy

A yogi who is on the astral side only, and who uses my body time and again, was in my body during a meditation session. I worked on the inSelf process for developing the divine eye. Suddenly there was a sound. When I look, I noticed that a cylindrical capsule, which was about one quarter of an inch in diameter and two inches long, rapidly fell through a cylindrical passage. This was located between the navel and the sexual zone of the subtle body. Simultaneously, there was a memory of a sexual encounter I had with a young lady over fifty years ago. I was in that experience again.

I realized that this was caused by that yogi who had somehow erupted a long-lost memory in my psyche, and to such an extent, that even though it was long forgotten, and did not seem to have much significance, I experienced it again.

I looked to the yogi for an explanation.

He said this.

"I found that. I looked for it because I needed to review such experiences to see the details of how these events are enacted. I notice that neither you, nor the female, had control over the sexual urge.

"There was no accompanying understanding or consideration about a possible pregnancy. I found no social and financial support for a sexual act which may have resulted in a pregnancy. Where would you live with that female? How would you manage a family with a child? You had no income. What would have happened?

"As for the sexual experience, you had no control over it. It happened with such rapidity that you could hardly understand what occurred. Did you see the fast-descending cylinder? That was the sexual energy package, the reproductive force, which would become a fetus, if conditions in the female's system were ideal.

"But the female was alarmed, disappointed, and depressed because you did not control the rapidity which cause the orgasmic pleasure to be out of sync with her own. Wherefrom such an idea? She was born recently in about twenty years prior and so was yourself. Neither created the body and its potential. Wherefrom the idea that one can control that reproductive force?"

Focus of Attention / Yogic Investigation

After the completion or near-completion of *pratyahar* sensual energy withdrawal in the *ashtanga* yoga of Patanjali, one feels as if one accomplished *pratyahar* sensual energy withdrawal. However, due to the design of the psyche, this success is shifted because one finds that even then, even after causing the outward going tendency to reverse, still then, one is taunted by what is outside the psyche.

This happens because of hidden and unsubdued memories as well as by fresh incidences with the physical and subtle bodies, which manufacture new impressions which carry a compelling energy.

It is at this point that one realizes that the bid for liberation may just be a fantasy. However, if one was in good spirits, and harbored no resentment against the physical and subtle Nature, one will continue the practice.

Despite knowing that liberation may never happen in the complete sense, and that it may only occur sporadically, one will still keep the endeavor for success. Others who suspect or who realize that liberation is hardly likely, that it is uncertain, will resign from yoga practice. They will be satisfied and relieved actually, to resume their relationship with Nature. Such people will either adopt a righteous lifestyle or will be outright criminals in the creation.

Once the sensual energy withdrawal is attained, it is highlighted by noticing that in meditation, there is no effort of the self-energy to go out of the psyche. This is similar to a train depot, where usually some trains enter it, and some depart from it. There is much activity, except on major holidays, when the trains remain still and in place in the depot. There are no sounds of engines, no squeaks of brakes, no workmen adjusting and checking machinery.

Pratyahar the fifth stage of yoga, comes to proficiency, when in the mind space, the yogi notices that he does not have to exert a retraction pulling force, to keep his energies from coursing out of the psyche. The energies stay retracted in meditation. They lack interest in going outside the psyche. They are reluctant to pursue anything.

It is then that another challenge surfaces, where the yogi must study his focus of attention, not as one cohesive impetus but as two; one being the focus of attention, and the other being the focus on *being the focus of attention*.

This focus on being the focus, is bewildering. It is a dangerous impetus which a yogi should never underestimate, as to its power, subtlety, and surreptitiousness. This tendency will not permit a complete *pratyahar* practice. It will allow a partial one, with the yogi becoming arrogant, and not knowing that it affects him. It waits patiently in the dark corners of the mind. It springs into action when the yogi is relaxed, and does not understand that he is under a subtle influence.

Instead of focusing one's attention, a part of the psyche focuses secretly on not doing that, but on focusing on being the center of everyone's attention. One becomes passive but with an active objective, which is the movement of the active attention of others. One remains stationary with a power to capture the moving attention of other entities.

Yoga Teaching Focus

On Feb 16, 2024, Babaji spoke this instruction.

"Cease the physical teaching. Develop the studentship situation on the astral side of life. Close the physical access. Assign those duties to others."

Astral Migration

Are you ready to move to a destination which you are uncertain of?

How many moments, minutes, hours, days, or years would it be before your property will be confiscated, your physical person will die, and you will find yourself evicted from physical history?

Who will greet you in the other country, an astral place?

What property and documents will you have?

Which residence will you be assigned?

Will you have a mother?

What about a father?

What about grandparents?

What about an adoption agency to supervise your impoverished situation, and award someone as your qualified guardian?

The astral migration?

How will it be?

Currently, in considering my situation of using a seventy-plus physical body, there is only one priority which is to pack my bags, put together my important documents, secure the proper transportation, and plan to voluntarily relinquish my physical assets, along with some of my psychological property. I should close many relationships, scrap many connections, lose interest in many subjects, and come to an agreement with myself to be deprived of many endearing memories.

Yoga Institution Flaw

On February 22, 2024, on the astral side, a deceased yoga teacher appeared. This person, Swami Muktananda Paramahamsa, was deprived of his physical body some forty years ago. When he was physically present, he claimed to teach siddha yoga. However, as fate would have it, he was accused of sexual exploitation.

What he said to me was this:

"There should be no institution formed around a yoga teacher. Anyone who is somewhat successful as a yogi, is encouraged by students and admirers to establish an institution, and to standardize the teaching process. This is a trap however. To do that one comes under the influence of others who feel that the institution is like a fort, which is a secured citadel, which is infallible and flawless.

"The truth is however that in the past, most of the institutions which were establish by accomplished yogins, came to ruin. At some point they develop so much dysfunctionality that they fall apart. Gradually they fade from history. Then what is left, is a bad name, or a shadow idea of what it was supposed to be.

"The real danger however, is that once an accomplished yogi becomes the center of attention for the institution he founded, that guru no longer has sufficient time to accept and process his personal fate. In fact, his fated circumstances multiply, because the institution acts as a magnet to attract many fated energies, which otherwise would come to him at a slower pace.

"He becomes the target of many persons to whom he has obligations from previous lives. Due to the intensity, and rapidity of the approach of persons from past life, he finds that there is not sufficient time for his personal yoga practice. He relaxes that and engages in institution building, and in responding to the demands which surface, because his name became famous, and others were attracted to him. These others make demands, which are due to past life obligations which he left aside in previous bodies.

"He finds that he cannot manage this energy. Mishaps occurs. He may refuse to service many past life relationships and obligations. That produces resentments, which in turn causes caustic acts, which affect him and the institution.

"The solution?

"The correction is that one should not begin an institution. One should accept students and allows them to proceed with their social obligations, with application of yoga methods in their lifestyles, gradually over time. But one should not surround oneself with an institution, and with many people clambering to communicate with and serve oneself.

"Have students whom one can instruct individually, but do not have many. Do not establish an organization, and manufacture a doctrine of the yoga process. Do not use students to convert and attract others. If one does this, the rapidity with which Nature will hurl obligations from past life to oneself, will be such that one will be ruined, due to the lack of ability to monitor, and service satisfactorily such obligations.

"Any increase in the number of students or disciples, inflates the risk of one becoming entangled in awkward situations, which arise because of sexual attraction, financial collection, attention distribution, and many other features of relationship. The point is that one will be unable to manage the rapid increase in emotional energy, which is from those disciples.

"Here is an example. If one has six (6) students, that means six complications of destiny, where unsolved features of relationships will be presented by Nature for those six interactions. Now if those six students converted and attracted six other students each, that would mean that one exponentially increased the following from six to forty-two (42). There will be a rapid jump of the mental, and emotional energy from past lives. These will bud quickly. The teacher may not efficiently manage every situation. The time taken to deal with these psychological situations, will cancel time for his/her personal practice. And besides, Nature may not service each of the relationships in its past life format. That will result in inefficient servicing of the obligations. Some disciples will be dissatisfied and resentful.

"Suppose for instance that in a past life, the teacher had a sexual relationship with one of the converts. He may not be powerful enough to cancel that energy. In that case he will proceed as encouraged by subconscious forces. That will be intuitively felt by some other students who may approve or disapprove. This, in either case of approval or disapproval, will affect the overall situation.

"Now further, if the forty-two disciples, converted another six people each, then now there will be two hundred and ninety-four (294) disciples. How will the guru manage this? Even if he sorts the more advanced students and use them as teachers under his supervision, still there will be mismanagement, because that is how Nature functions. It wants complications and entanglements. It wants frustration and bickering. There will more compounded relationships, where some of this will be ideal. Some will cause complications, which the teacher cannot manage.

"The key issue is that the time for his individual practice will be reduced. The feeling that the teacher is so advanced that he does not need to practice is bunkum. We read in the *Srimad Bhagavatam,* that even though it aggravated his numerous wives, Lord Krishna arose early to meditate. If God feels the necessity, then what to speak of a guru?

"The whole idea of creating an institution and increasing the number of followers is the plan of a mad man. I did it. I was crazy for doing so."

Romantic Love in Yoga Practice

What does yoga have to do with sexual love?

Introspection in yoga, could help to break down the composite emotional energy which is usually experienced as a love feeling. That is a composite or combination energy. On occasion, however, this much-desired energy converts in a jiffy to being a disliking and rejection force.

Is it like milk, where if it is not kept at a certain temperature, it converts into something sour? If this love is the sweetest feeling in the world, how is it that it may change into hard feelings, resentment, or depression.

There is a practice in yoga which is termed as *pratyahar* (prat-yaah-haar). It is a system of energy and interest retraction, which is difficult to master. Many, who meditate have no idea of it, and still, they present themselves as yogis or yoginis. Patanjali listed *pratyahar* as the fifth stage of yoga, the stage just before the final three stages which may be experienced as one progression into another or one degression from another. *Pratyahar* means sensual energy retraction.

This energy retraction is the withdrawal and pulling of the interest of the self into itself. The example of this is given in the Bhagavad Gita as the retraction of its limbs in the case of a tortoise.

This article is about romantic or sexual love. That too should be retracted. Suppose somebody loves someone else but there is no mutual emotion, no matching responding feelings and actions, what should that love-struck person do?

Before we attempt to prescribe a solution, we need to understand what the romance energy is, as to how it arises in the psyche, as to what it does as an emotional and physical action, and as to what its objective is.

Praying for the Near-Dead or Dead Person

What happens when on the physical side someone tries to impose opposing beliefs on a deceased person?

What does a deceased person feel when there is an attempt to pray for him/her, when their belief is not in accordance with what a physical person projects?

What are the repercussions to the deceased person, or to the concerned physical someone who prays for his/her welfare, but who does so with an opposing belief?

The mental battle which would ensue between two persons of opposing views about death, would continue in the afterlife, just as it would have if one of the persons did not die. The feelings would be the same. The possibility of conversion, or of absolute resistance, would remain the same. Eventually, because of the pressure of time and circumstance, those persons would be relieved.

There is an exception. If the deceased person or the physical survivor needs something from the other person, under the pressure of that need, the needy one may compromise, may yield to the opposing idea.

Because one individual no longer has physical ability to act, that person will have an increase of his/her energy on the psychic side, and may have greater impact if the survivor comes under psychic stress as a result. But those who have psychic resistance, which is due to strong physical focus, will effectively resist, and will not be influenced by the deceased one. Instead, the dead someone will feel that the effort was frustrated.

The leverage of the surviving person, the one with the physical body, is that he or she may be in a position, to sponsor the rebirth of the deceased one. That could be a direct sponsorship as a parent or an indirect sponsorship as someone who influenced another physical person to become a parent.

Then the deceased person will yield to the beliefs of the survivor who sponsored rebirth.

Reincarnation Belief

It is one thing to believe in reincarnation/rebirth. It is a different issue to integrate that information into how we related to each other. Because of the need to enjoy various types of relationship, which are based on the age of the body one uses, one is apt to feel confident that one understands the idea of reincarnation, even though one may not integrate that into every relationship one either likes, or dislikes, with some other person.

There is a big arrogance where once the body becomes an adult, and it begets children, one condescends and relates to the infants, or juveniles, as if they are permanent dependents.

Even after one reached the adult stage, one may be treated in that way by one's parents. If the parents are forever making the effort to pin one down as a child, as someone who is not that experienced, and who needs advice, one may resent this deeply.

But then, as Nature would have it, one repeats this behavior with one's children, and the children on occasion, when it is convenient, encourages one to regard them as forever infants.

However, this is based on not integrating the idea of reincarnation/rebirth. If it is factual that the entity who uses a physical body, is not that form, and is a psychic somebody who animates and uses the physical form, then why, from the onset, from the infancy of one's child, one does not regard that somebody as an adult who was deceased, and who because of the force of Nature, assumed an embryo, and was produced as an infant.

Assuming that this deceased somebody, left an adult form behind in this physical world, his/her adoption of an embryo and its subsequent birth, does not make that person an infant.

What happened?

That adult person was adapted into an infant form. He/She was handicapped. That is an adult but it cannot function as such because of the developmental stage of its new body.

But if one gets an enjoyment or a fulfillment from regarding someone as that person's infant body, then it would be impractical to regard that person as the adult who acted as such in its past bodies.

How would it be to see the adult format of that person, where one sees that it is fitted into (forced into) an infant profile?

The adult package of energy of a deceased person is compressed. Some of it is suspended when that person assumes the process of being an embryo. Yes, that former adult cannot manifest adult features when it appears as an infant. But that is due to nature's ability to compress and even suspend, its adult behavior. And yet, that does not mean that it is in the interest of a parent, to think that its child is a child. It is not that!

One should not continue believing and acting as if the child is a permanent infant. One should introspect to see the tendency to play the role of being a parent.

What is love for an infant or juvenile?

Is it affection based on the minority age of the body.

If one had the psychic power, would one prefer that one's child remain as a child forever? Would that give one the privilege of enjoying that person only in an agreeable way?

But time goes by! It will not permit one to freeze the current social relationships.

Mind Control Practicality

In yoga practice, from the stage of *pratyahar* sensual energy withdrawal, the challenge is mind control. Many begin this by thinking that there can be total control of the mental operations and expressions. For example, one may chant a Sanskrit mantra, or focus on some part of the mind or body, even some form or location outside the body.

There are so many methods which are advocated by teachers. Suppose someone got total mind control. A question arises as to the duration of that hold on the mind.

I suggest the following.

Study the mental operations to know how the mind mechanism functions. There are two methods for this. The most popular one concerns hearing about the mind from an advanced yogi. He/She may or may not have a physical body. In either case, one learns about the operations and parts of the mind, then one goes into the mind, does interiorization, to find if one's mind operates in the way described by the teacher.

The other method is where one does not have a description given by a successful yogi. One is inspired by an invisible person, or energy, to observe the mental operations, with the intention of using the experience to better monitor the mind. The objective is to get the cooperation of the mind.

Once one has a schematic of the operations of the mind, where one understands all or some of its parts, and how they involuntarily interact, one may study how to influence the mind to be cooperative. However, one may find that the mind is designed for less than full submission. Then, the practical objective is to acquire its maximum cooperation.

Part 7

Mechanics of Stress

The mechanics of stress must be known if one is to be successful in yoga practice. Gone were the days when someone went to an isolated place to do yoga. Now is the time to do yoga anywhere anyhow. With the advent of highways and airports, with every bit of land being owned and controlled by people of means and power, there is nowhere to run.

A yogi/yogini must stand the ground in the apartment, condominium, cottage, or wherever, and do the practice amidst the hustle and bustle of modern lifestyle. For this some details about the mechanics of stress must be known. A plan to effectively manage stress must be instituted. There should be no fantasy about removing stress altogether. Only the reduction and management of it, should be the practical objective.

If one finds that one's lifestyle is hostile to yoga practice, one should scale back some desires, so as to reduce the encroachment on yoga. One may have to accept less income if one scales back on employment. It is a matter of striking a balance, and playing the game of give and take.

Wishing stress away, abolishing it by using mantras, or feelgood statements, is not the yogic way unless such methods are scientifically tested by the individual yogi/yogini, where the result of their effectiveness or ineffectiveness are tested within the mind of the individual. One should not indulge in self-dishonesty. One should know that Nature cannot be outsmarted. If one gains financially or socially, due to excessive indulgence in a yoga-hostile lifestyle, one should not expect to advanced in the practice. This practice means deep meditation. It does not mean *asana* postures only. That is only one segment of yoga.

Yoga cannot be about wishful thinking, nor about wanting to prove that the universe is responsive to the will of the individual, who uses a body which will not survive for two hundred years.

One must test to know what one does which is hostile to yoga, and which cannot be wished away by mental creativity. Then one must curtail the behavior, if not eliminate it completely. Do not expect to be focused only on physical wellbeing, and to advance with psychic wellbeing all the same.

Existential Dissatisfaction

From day one, from the time of being aware of being an embryo, there is this pressing repetitive need to have Nature confirm to one's self image, and for it to adjust itself, as this idea alters according to the time, and circumstance.

There are times when one feels satisfied with what Nature presents as oneself, but these periods of contentment do not last. What happens is that Nature alters from moment to moment, such that what it presented to oneself as oneself at one time, does not endure. One eventually understands, that circumstance is altered. The body changes both inside and its exterior appearance. Hence, it is a question of acceptance as the changes are made.

This is challenging. It produces a struggle against nature to make it confirm to what one feels is the ideal situation, as the bodily form and its internal feelings. Before sexual maturity, there is the quest for that. Then at maturity there is the position of wanting to remain with the optimum youthfulness. When one realizes that Nature did not support it, and only degraded it over time, there is the effort to suppresses the development of an aged body. This pesters one from moment to moment.

Liberation is not Likely

Why is liberation or salvation not likely? There are two main reasons. Salvation in this usage means the award of liberation by a deity. Liberation means the achievement of liberation by self-effort mostly.

Either of these is unlikely because there are two factors which constantly work against anyone who wishes for liberation. In either case, if salvation may be awarded or if liberation may be achieved, the likelihood of it is questionable. And yet, every person should aspire. Any drowning somebody will try to surface for air. In fact, the last breath is related to the final failed effort to gain a footing on land.

The desire is to subsist in a healthy condition. It is more than mere survival. It is survival with health and vigor.

The desire for liberation must be converted into a massive effort, to be free from the threat of death and disease. If the effort is successfully made by the person, it is considered to be liberation. If the effort is expended by a deity it is considered to be salvation. In either case there are two impediments which prevent success.

- feeling that one should be amply rewarded by others for one's beneficial acts
- being attracted to Nature's current and future circumstances which will reward one as its sees fit.

These two forces, the inner one and the environmental factor, frequently override the need for salvation or liberation. Subsequently, one acts in a way to reduce the effort for liberation or salvation.

One is pulled to the future to meet the amply rewards from others, whom one assisted previously. One is eager to be in those favorable circumstances. One is also supported by a buoyancy force of nature which conveys one to future circumstances, where one could be amply rewarded for cooperating with Nature's schemes.

This attraction to the future is a powerful force, such that it causes one to minimize the need for liberation or salvation. One postpones the urgency. One instinctively avoids its consideration.

Virginity and Reincarnation

The value of virginity varies from culture to culture, ethnicity to ethnicity and religiosity to religiosity. Mostly the stress about it, is referenced to the females in human species. The only reason why it has such pronouncement for females, must be the factor of fetal development which could result from pregnancies. As nature would have it, a male in the human species has no means of developing an embryo. It is only the females whose bodies are the focus for pregnancies. And there lies the levy, where moral attitudes become focused on female sexual access, such that if a female has the first penetration, and does not for one reason or the other, remain espoused to the male which penetrated, a set of moral stipulations are applied to fence the female in, to the moral standards of the particular family and society.

When reincarnation is considered, the entire situation must be recalculated. If it is a fact that each person takes many births, then unless one can prove that in each birth, one is married or sexually linked to the same person, over and over again, then the idea of virginity would apply only to the physical body assumed and not the astral form. That astral form would not be a virgin because in its past life using some other body from some other family, it would not be celibate prior to its assumption of a new physical form as someone else's infant.

There is also the possibility of having sexual intercourse with someone other than the married or partnered person even during the current lifespan, and doing so in dreams either consciously or subconsciously,

If in dreams, the subtle body is liberal in sexual intercourse, if it is beyond one's control in sexuality in previous lives, and in the afterlife period between lives, then the whole idea about sexual purity has value only in a limited way.

For example. Suppose a female indulged sexually during the teen years. Is it only her physical body which was involved? Or was it both the subtle and physical forms which were simultaneously indulged?

Since her subtle form indulged in many other lifetimes, it cannot be considered to be original, as a form which did not have sexual participation. It is not a virgin. In fact, it is a used sexual form. Hence the first sexual indulgence of the physical body is not the first involvement of the subtle form.

The only new factor is the physical form which was created by the sexual act of the parents. The inner self of the physical body is the subtle form, the instance of feelings and psychology. But that is not created in the parents' bodies. That is something which transited from the dying physical body which the person had previously, and which may or may not have indulged sexually in some other lifetime.

The proposal about virginity and its high value only holds up if one can prove that there is only one lifetime, and there is no reincarnation or transmigration. In that case, the person is a new physical body with a new psychology, having no subtle form.

Rebirth Package

If we consider that the psyche is a container of a person's psychological energies, it follows that when one no longer functions as the physical body, the likelihood is that the psychological traits one has, will be forced to leave the physical world, while the subtle aspects of self, involuntarily shift to a psychic plane of existence.

At face value, and if one is excited and happy about the idea of reincarnation, this sounds like a reasonable proposal. But is it?

Yes, he was my friend. He was a good guy. He had one or two bad habits. He was a drug addict. Where is he now? Where are his bad features? Did he leave them behind with the physical body, he so dearly knew himself to be?

The package of himself as a transmigrating somebody which left the physical history, does it have the same desirable and undesirable traits?

Who sheds the unwanted aspects of personality when the body dies?

The rebirth package? What is in it? What tendencies continues to the astral territory hereafter, only to be reconfigured in the new infant form all over again?

Fear of Death

The fear of death is confused with the fear of pain, which is a reality from day one. That applies to anyone who begins physical perception as an embryo. As a physical body, as a new one, a baby, there is no fear of death because there is no memory of that event. The anticipation of threats has to do with pain, not with death.

It concerns unfavorable contact through the skin. This includes the sense of hearing which uses the skin, or an eardrum, for interpreting vibrations. Any movement which yields sensation has the potential for pain. That presupposes the possibility of pain, which may be interpreted as the precursor of death.

There is also the fear of becoming unconscious where one anticipated that this may result in death, or in resumption of awareness in a damaged body. In a new body, one gets the idea that unconsciousness is temporary. There is this instinct that one finds which causes one to become unconscious, but which again releases one as a conscious factor.

But that leads to considering if one may at some time, become unconscious, and then never reawaken again. This leads to another type of fear of death. That is due to existential uncertainty.

Penance of Shiva

One penance of God Shiva was in regards to making the proper use of the reproductive tendency, where it would not lead to degradation which happens due to its pleasure potency. In the first place the sexual pleasure potency is misinterpreted as a source of enjoyment, while in fact it is a fuel for the generation of reproductive fluids and their operations, which result not in pleasure but in responsibility.

I was shown by the God Shiva that in one penance, he clearly figured that the confusion where one interprets reproductive operations as sexual pleasure, occurs because of not understanding that every urge is not to be fulfilled. There is a message force which comes with every urge, and which motivates one to fulfill the said needs. However, there is another energy which tells one that every space is not to be filled.

Somehow one does not perceive the blank space as being purposeful. One assumes eagerness to satisfy. That leads to frustration which converts into hostile emotions. This puts one at a distance from clarity. It hardens one's focus on the wrong conclusion, which is where one feels, that as a central event, one's desire or urge should be serviced.

The fact is that frustration, or blankness, is itself a type of fulfillment which should be appreciated. The interpretation that frustration should be absent, and should be replaced with events which cause contentment, results from a lack of clarity and a misreading of destiny

Yogi Self-Release

A yogi should, step by step, take actions, both physical and psychic, to remove himself/herself from involvement in the history of the world. The idea that one can do some good to this world, or that one can rescue someone from the misery of this place, is for the most part a worthless proposition. It is a bad investment. In fact, it is impractical for the most part. It makes absolutely no sense.

Even if one were to be the greatest most influential person on the planet, still one cannot exert that power forever. At some point it will diminish to nothing. The world will continue in its own way. One will lose grasp on history. One's influence will fade.

As certain shapes of leaves are generated from a tree, season after season, so the people in the world will persist with their destructive and constructive habits, year after year. One's ideas will be ignored. One was produced in this existence as part of it, even as a unique part, which is all the more proof that this process of nature will continue. One's indulgence in it, will definitely be forfeited.

One was here. One did what one could. One realized that one had little or no impact. One got prepared to be transited from this place. One was prevented from participation here. This reality continues as it always did.

Fetus Memory Blank

Much of what happened during the formation, continuation, and then end of a body, is filled in the memory record as blank. This is like listening to a memory storage device, where certain parts of the recording did not happen, because the equipment failed to hold the information, during phases of the recording.

This does not mean that there was no other recording of those blank portions. In fact, there may be recordings done by other devices, and there may be recordings on the device used, but in a way which cannot be accessed coherently by the person listening, simply because his mind's interpreting apparatus could not convert a particular type of recording, because the mind did not have the conversion ability, to make that type of recording into a sensible sound.

This is about

- Fetus Memory Blank

There are phases of a life where the recording does not occur in the apparatus of the psyche. This means that the person cannot use this information to his benefit nor to his detriment. It is simply not available. In the fetal stage much of the incidences which occurred cannot be accessed. This holds true as well for the sperm development and its uterus journey. Its expulsion from the body of the father is lost as well. Even some phases of its elderly years are blank. This is mostly due to brain malfunction, where the recording circuits become damaged, and no clear imprints are made.

The fetus memory blank incidences are known either to the body of the father or mother, but the infant itself has no access to it. Subsequently he/she cannot use it to understand those states of physical presence. And that is a major source of ignorance, which causes the person to pity others who are in that stage, or to ridicule such persons, as if the observing other person did not endure that state.

If someone could remember the sperm life and the fetus formation, this would inspire someone to think seriously about liberation. Otherwise in the quest for understanding the self, this missing information deprives the self of important impetus to know what it endured. Hence it lacks the impetus for liberation, and will not make the full effort for it. In this way Nature successfully keeps that personSelf in its grip, for recycling through the birth and death parade.

World of the Long Dresses

On April 5, 2024, my subtle body was transferred to an astral place where every female has one child, and where each woman wears a long flowing dress so that none of her feet, legs or thighs were shown. These garments have floral designs.

I sat in a room with other males. Some females arrived and passed quickly. They shifted near a wall and sat against it. Suddenly one female shifted and approached me. As she did so my astral body stood up so that she was eye to eye facing me. This happened spontaneously without deliberate thinking.

This person who shifted was someone I knew but had not see in that realm for a long gap in time, for thousands of years. Then I realized that in that realm, there is no sexual activity with sexual organs. There is sexual exchange but it is done through the eyes. The faces of the persons there contained relationship exchange energy. By looking into the eyes there is complete transfer of such energy between two persons.

There is an impulse to speak but it is not expressed verbally. Instead, when the impulse occurs, the energy is transferred to the other person instantly and completely, where the urge is fully expressed.

In the faces of the persons, there is floral arrangements like deeply embedded tattoos. This carries the personal energy which is transmitted rapidly when necessary. When this female approached, she left her child where she first sat. I noticed that just after that child, who was in a basket, disappeared.

Once the energy was exchanged, the woman too disappeared, and so did I, from that *world of the long dresses*.

Spiritualist Uncomfortable Hereafter

A person who built a religious institution, and who was a sannyasi guru in his past life, spoke to me today, April 10, 2024. He said this.

"I am dissatisfied with my life on the astral side. It is not as expected. After death I did not attain the spiritual world described and assured by my guru. None of that happened. Once I got free from the last physical body which was sick and damaged for many years just before it died, it was one astral scene after the other.

"It is interesting that my guru rarely, if ever, discussed that any of his followers would be on the astral side. For him it was physical existence and then total spiritual existence with our deity. But for me, that did not happen.

"Now, to the contrary, I find myself wishing to be a physical child. I feel a high value in desire for physical existence, as if it is the place where one would achieve accomplishments. I again long to be physical, to enter the history of the world, to play a part in it.

"The spiritual world advertised by our guru may be there somewhere but I did not attain it. The only evidence I have is that of the physical side, where I no longer have a direct part to play, and this astral side which is shifty and inconstant.

"What to do about it? Even to take the next physical body is an enigma? What is the process for that? In what way should one act to be a woman's infant again?"

Mental Register Hampers Meditation

The mental register of scenes seen, as well as sounds heard, and feelings felt, may hamper the meditative part of yoga practice.

Images flash in the mind, on the basis of what is or was seen. Sounds are repeated in the mind after they are heard. Feelings are reproduced in the mind after they are felt, either inside the psyche, or on the rim of it, which is represented by the skin in the physical body.

If a visual, aural, or tactile occurrence makes a deep register in the mind, that will affect yoga, but more likely it will be a disruptive effect, and not a supportive one. It will be such that it will hamper the selected meditative focus, and divert the attention of the yogi to the remembered idea.

There is an instruction by Patanjali in his *Yoga Sutras*. It has to do with the power to instantly stop the *chittavritti*, which are the creations and indulgences of the intellect, the lifeForce and the memories. If this instruction is not enforced, the meditation will be of a weak focus which will not give the result intended.

However, there are some instances, where a yogi can give a command in the mind for it to cease the unwanted behavior. But still he will find that some indulgences cannot be curtailed or even reduced. They seem to have a power which is greater than the yogi's command.

This is because of the original register of impressions. A strong register will resist the order of the yogi, such that when he desires to stop it from replaying in the mind, he cannot do so. Its register is stronger than his intention to cease it, from playing before him in the mental space.

Yogeshwarananda instructed that a yogi should be careful, not to allow impressions to carry a strong register. He is of the opinion that for those who want to penetrate to *chit akash* sky of consciousness, or to use the divine eye, the instances with a strong register, will cause their failure to develop divine perception.

Under-Arm Kundalini

There are kundalini zones here and there in the subtle body. Some correspond to areas in the physical form. Some do not. When doing breath infusion, one will, from time to time, realize these areas. This happens when the infused breath energy penetrates and collects in these areas with a shining light, colorful, or compressed feelings energy, on the psychic side of life. Much of this has a physical feeling which runs parallel to the subtle bliss aspect which occurs.

During breath infusion, a yogi should pause to focus on these areas for study of their higher energy saturation. This gives confidence about the practice of *pranayama* and inner focus *(dharana/dhyana/samadhi)*.

On the morning of April 19, 2024, while doing breath infusion, there was a burst of kundalini silverish bliss energy under the arms and in the side of the chest which corresponded to it. This shimmered for a time. I ceased rapid breathing, held the locks, focused on the area, and became absorbed in the study of this energy.

There was this instruction.
Focus on this.
Remember this.
Describe this.
Be absorbed in this.
Do not forget this.

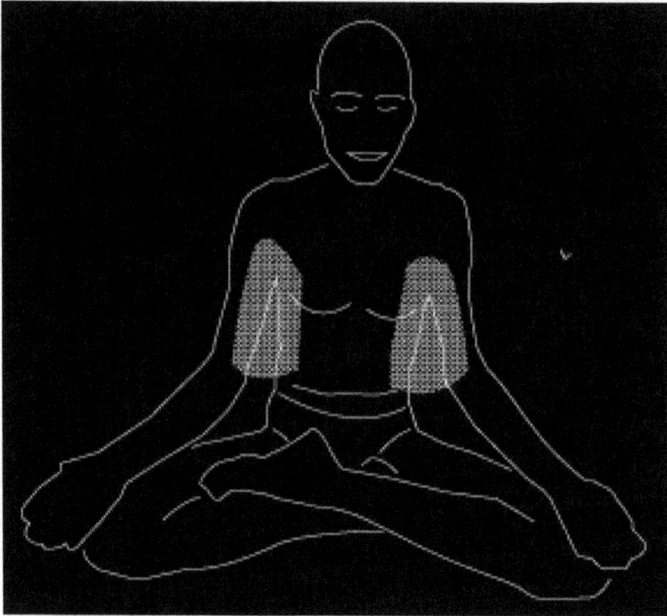

Fulfillment or Frustration ~ Yogic Viewpoint

Is there a difference between a human's fulfillment needs and that of a vegetation. For instance, when a mango drops from its parent-plant, does the seed of it, feel a need to be sprouted. It falls. The pulp is eaten by an animal. The seed remains on the soil. When there is rain, that seed sprouts. A root emerges and penetrates the soil.

It needs wet soil to flourish. Suppose there is no rain for months. What happens to it?

It becomes frustrated. It regrets its place. It wishes for an ideal circumstance where it could grow as intended. However, rains do not form. It shrivels. It dies.

On the night of April 25, 2024, I had an encounter with some persons with whom I associated in the teen years some fifty-plus years ago. Based on desires to meet persons whom they knew in their teen years, these persons caused my astral body to be with theirs.

One individual was sure to ask for a private discussion. She said.

"I never got married. I never found the man of my heart. Life for me was unfulfilling because I longed for that man of my heart. I am sure he exists somewhere but I never met him. What was your history? Did life service your romantic needs?"

I replied with this.

"Even for those whom life seems to service, even they are frustrated in one aspect or the other. In every case there are hidden pains, disappointments, and frustrations. It is as if fulfillment, partial fulfillment, and frustration are of equal standing. These are experiences. In that sense they have equal register as events occurring. There is the dry season, the excessive rains, and the ample weather. Each satisfies or frustrates some creature."

After I said that, she turned away. Just prior to that she considered if there was any chance that I may be the man of her heart. In her mind, she concluded that I was not.

Swami Hereafter

I was with a departed Swami on the night of April 25, 2024. He established an ashram territory, just as he did to a physical place when he used his last body. At first in a large dormitory *(dharmashal)* there was a ceremony in which he was honored with Sanskrit prayers. In a ceremony, some disciples bowed to his feet.

Soon after that ceremony, I was transferred as per his wish to a large astral hall. Some artists and building contractors were present. We entered a room which had a large table with shallow trays. This was an architectural department. The swami took a vase and poured water from it into a square tray. He constructed a miniature landscape, which was the blue print of what was to be built at that place.

The swami was intent on doing this because on the physical side in his last body, his effort to complete a similar place was frustrated. In his psyche there was an energy which dictated to him that this development would be the perfection of his life. He had nothing else on his mind. He felt that the achievement would be his perfection.

He wanted to impress me about the importance of the astral place. I was to be fascinated and was to join his sect. That is how he felt. I looked on with detachment. I rated how the events in one's life in a physical body, feeds over to the life hereafter.

Bhagavad Gita Methods of Spiritual Practice

देवमेवापरे यज्ञं

योगिनः पर्युपासते ।

ब्रह्माग्नावपरे यज्ञं

यज्ञेनैवोपजुह्वति ॥४.२५॥

daivamevāpare yajñaṁ
yoginaḥ paryupāsate

brahmāgnāvapare yajñaṁ
yajñenaivopajuhvati (4.25)

daivam — to a supernatural authority; evāpare = eva — indeed + apare — some; yajñaṁ — austerity and religious ceremony; yoginaḥ — yogis; paryupāsate — practise; brahmāgnāv = brahmāgnau — in the fiery brilliance of spiritual existence; apare — others; yajñaṁ — austerity and religious ceremony; yajñenaivopajuhvati = yajñena — by austerity and religious ceremony; eva — indeed + upajuhvati — they offer

Some yogis perform austerity and religious ceremony in relation to a supernatural authority. Others offer austerity and religious ceremony as the sacrifice into the fiery brilliance of spiritual existence. (Bhagavad Gita 4.25)

- Deity appears and gives a process.
- Yogi focuses on spiritual energy and ushers his disciplinary force and ritual needs to that spiritual zone.

श्रोत्रादीनीन्द्रियाण्यन्ये

संयमाग्निषु जुह्वति ।

शब्दादीन्विषयानन्ये

इन्द्रियाग्निषु जुह्वति ॥४.२६॥

śrotrādīnīndriyāṇyanye
saṁyamāgniṣu juhvati
śabdādīnviṣayānanye
indriyāgniṣu juhvati (4.26)

śrotrādīnīndriyāṇy = śrotrādīnīndriyāṇi = śrotra — hearing + ādīni — and related aspects + indriyāṇi — senses; anye — others; saṁyamāgniṣu = saṁyama — restraint + agniṣu — in the fiery power; juhvati — they offer; śabdādīn = śabda — sound + ādīn — and so on; viṣayān — sensual pursuits; anye — others; indriyāgniṣu — in the fiery energy of sensuality; juhvati — they offer

Other yogis offer hearing and other sensual powers into the fiery power of restraint. Some offer sound and other sensual pursuits into the fiery sensual power. (Bhagavad Gita 4.26)

- Collecting and withdrawing hearing, touching, seeing, tasting, and smelling - *pratyahar* inSelf Yoga™.

- Lack of response to sense objects, which are sound, surface (skin), color (form), flavor, odor. The yogi roots out the tendency to enjoy that. This is a *pratyahar* process.

सर्वाणीन्द्रियकर्माणि

प्राणकर्माणि चापरे ।

आत्मसंयमयोगाग्नौ

जुह्वति ज्ञानदीपिते ॥४.२७॥

sarvāṇīndriyakarmāṇi
prāṇakarmāṇi cāpare
ātmasaṁyamayogāgnau
juhvati jñānadīpite (4.27)

sarvāṇīndriyakarmāṇi = sarvāṇi — all + indriyakarmāṇi — sensual actions; prāṇakarmāṇi = prāṇa — breath function + karmāṇi — activities; cāpare = ca — and + apare — some; ātmasaṁyamayogāgnau = ātmasaṁyama — self-restraint + yogāgnau — in fiery yoga austerities; juhvati — they offer; jñānadīpite = jñāna — experience + dīpite — illuminated

Some ascetics subject the sensual actions and the breath function to self-restraint by fiery yoga austerities, which are illuminated by experience. (Bhagavad Gita 4.27)

- Kundalini sensual action and breath function restraint in the psyche. This is contained and compressed for total inner absorption. It includes *atmasamyama* yoga.

द्रव्ययज्ञास्तपोयज्ञा

योगयज्ञास्तथापरे ।

स्वाध्यायज्ञानयज्ञाश्च

यतयः संशितव्रताः ॥४.२८॥

dravyayajñāstapoyajñā
yogayajñāstathāpare
svādhyāyajñānayajñāśca
yatayaḥ saṁśitavratāḥ (4.28)

dravyayajñās = dravya — property + yajñās — austerity and religious ceremony; tapoyajñā = tapo (tapaḥ) — self denial + yajñā — austerity and religious ceremony; yogayajñās = yoga —eight-part yoga process + yajñāḥ — austerity and religious ceremony; tathāpare = tathā — as well as + apare — some others; svādhyāyajñānayajñāśca = svādhyāya — study of the Veda + jñāna — knowledge + yajñāḥ — austerity and religious ceremony + ca — and; yatayaḥ — ascetics; saṁśitavratāḥ = saṁśita — strict + vratāḥ — vows

Persons whose austerity and religious ceremony involve the control of material possession, those whose austerity and religious life involve some self-denial, as well as some others whose penance and religious procedure is the eight-part yoga discipline, and those whose austerity and religious ceremony is the study of the Veda and the acquirement of knowledge, all these are regarded as ascetics with strict vows. (Bhagavad Gita 4.28)

- control of property *(dravya)* by sensual deprivation
- self-denial for psyche self-discipline *(tapo)*
- yogayajna itself as a process – complete *ashtanga* yoga
- study of Vedas, *svadhyaya*, with absorption of knowledge

अपाने जुह्वति प्राणं

प्राणेऽपानं तथापरे ।

प्राणापानगती रुद्ध्वा

प्राणायामपरायणाः ॥ ४.२९ ॥

apāne juhvati prāṇaṁ
prāṇe'pānaṁ tathāpare
prāṇāpānagatī ruddhvā
prāṇāyāmaparāyaṇāḥ (4.29)

apāne — in exhalation; juhvati — they offer; prāṇam — inhalation; prāṇe — in inhalation; 'pānam = apānaṁ — in exhalation; tathāpare = tathā — similarly + apare — others; prāṇāpāna gatī = prāṇa — energizing air + apāna — de-energizing air + gatī — channel; ruddhvā — restraining; prāṇāyāmaparāyaṇāḥ = prāṇa — inhaling + āyāma — regulate + parāyaṇāḥ — intent

Some offer inhalation into the exhalation channels; similarly, others offer the exhalation into the inhalation channels, thus being determined to restrain the channels of the energizing and de-energizing airs. (Bhagavad Gita 4.29)

- *bhastrika pranayama* breath infusion physical and subtle air focus

अपरे नियताहाराः

प्राणान्प्राणेषु जुह्वति ।

सर्वेऽप्येते यज्ञविदो

यज्ञक्षपितकल्मषाः ॥४.३०॥

apare niyatāhārāḥ
prāṇānprāṇeṣu juhvati
sarve'pyete yajñavido
yajñakṣapitakalmaṣāḥ (4.30)

apare — others; niyatāhārāḥ — persons restrained in diet; prāṇān — fresh air; prāṇeṣu — into the previous inhalations; juhvati — impel; sarve — all; 'pyete (apyete) = apy (api) — also + ete — these; yajñavido = yajñavidaḥ — those who know the value of an act of sacrifice; yajñakṣapitakalmaṣāḥ = yajña — austerity and religious ceremony + kṣapita — destroyed, removed + kalmaṣāḥ — impurities

Others who were restrained in diet, impel fresh air into the previously inhaled air. All these ascetics whose impurities were removed by austerity and religious ceremony understand the value of an act of sacrifice. (Bhagavad Gita 4.30)

- *bhastrika* breath infusion with diet control which is due to subtle body directly relying on air *(prana),* rather than on energy from physical eating

यज्ञशिष्टामृतभुजो

यान्ति ब्रह्म सनातनम्।

नायं लोकोऽस्त्ययज्ञस्य

कुतोऽन्यः कुरुसत्तम ॥४.३१॥

yajñaśiṣṭāmṛtabhujo
yānti brahma sanātanam
nāyaṁ loko'styayajñasya
kuto'nyaḥ kurusattama (4.31)

yajñaśiṣṭāmṛtabhujo = yajñaśiṣṭāmṛtabhujaḥ = yajñaśiṣṭa — the physical result of a sacrifice + amṛta — the psychological enjoyment + bhujaḥ —

enjoying; yānti — they go; brahma — to the spiritual region; sanātanam — primeval; nāyam = na — not + ayam — this; loko = lokah — world; 'sty = asty (asti) — is (properly utilized); ayajñasya — of a person who performs no austerity or religious ceremony; kuto = kutah — how can it be? 'nyah = anyah — other; kurusattama — best of the Kurus

Those who enjoy the physical and psychological results of a sacrifice, go to the primeval spiritual region. This world is not properly utilized by those who do not perform austerity or religious ceremony. How then can the other world be, O best of the Kurus? (Bhagavad Gita 4.31)

- psychic testing to see if one is being transferred to higher realms during the life of the physical body.

Vision *Pratyahar* – Elementary Practice

This is done preferably in a dark place with a blindfold. If possible, the top of the head and the eyes must be covered with a dark fabric. Every distraction should be avoided. The skull is such that sunlight penetrates it. Therefore, if possible, the skill should be covered with a dark fabric.

Pratyahar is a vast practice which takes many years, if not lifetimes, to master. Usually, methods given by teachers are either partial processes or bits and pieces of the required effort. This instruction concerns only the vision tendency which a coreSelf has. In that respect it is only an elementary stage of the practice.

The mistake yogis make in doing *pratyahar, dharana, dhyana*, and *samadhi* is that they feel they can master it in no time. They are not prepared to spend years doing any practice, which is just part of a discipline and not all of it. This attitude causes many students to be mediocre.

The psyche of the *atma* coreSelf is designed for expression mostly. This is because this existence is about procuring sensual fulfillment. It is a go, get and consume apparatus, but it is a psychic something. The *atma* coreSelf did not put his psyche together. He/She just realized himself/herself as a being with the psyche. At the spur of the moment, he/she operated the psyche. But it did so haphazardly because it was not pretrained. Imagine what it would be like, if you awaken to find yourself to be the only person in an aircraft. There are no instructions. There is no pilot on board. No stewardess. No one but yourself,

You realize that you are in danger because the aircraft may crash. In fact, it will crash. That is unavoidable. The fuel tank cannot be refilled in flight. You have to figure how to land the machine. You must find a runway. "First things first," you think.

You decided that it is best to slow the aircraft. At its highest speed, it has the least gas efficiency. You need time. The only way to increase that is to cause the aircraft to fly at a slower speed. If that is done, you can search for the manual. You can use the radio to broadcast and reach an aviator.

Undoubtedly the plane will crash because the probability of your finding a runway, and learning how to use the controls, is not in your favor.

Anxiety! Why?

Because we are not in control. We discovered ourselves as bodies, fragile perishable things, with a mind and with little explanation about how we came to be.

With this understanding an attempt is made to slow the aircraft, find a runway, have a clear instruction from the manual on how to land the plane. Will it be a failure?

That does not matter. The important thing is to make the effort.

First you need a blindfold. There is no point in looking out a window because there are dark clouds in every direction. These will not permit your vision to be of any use.

Get the blindfold installed on your head and face. Since you cannot see because of the clouds of dark energy, it is best to close down the seeing facility.

Install the blindfold. Sit down comfortably. Close the door to the pilot's cabin. There are many lights there which will distract you. Be in the middle of the aircraft. With the eyes closed identify the impulse for seeing. That impulse is in your head somewhere. Find it. Pull it back to the center of the head, the center of the energy in the mental space.

If you find that this energy resists your desire to retract it, do not be alarmed. Keep a pressure to draw it to center. If you hear a whistling sound in the back of the aircraft. Note it. There is a name for this whistling sound. It is called naad. Be aware of it. Keep your activity energy pulling back the optic force which usually runs through the eyeballs. Pull this energy back to the center.

Do that practice until you feel that the optic energy no longer courses outwards, to see anything outside of the body.

That is the elementary vision *pratyahar*. How long will it take? This could take for as much time as it would for the aircraft to use all stored fuel. Or it may happen in a short time. Practicing this on and on, day after day, until the plane crashes, or until you master this, and can continue to the next stage.

Astral Day

Last night I was with a friend in an astral day place. We were on the astral side of Guyana, in a place where there are no automobiles, nor electric power, nor mechanization.

He wanted me to be with him and some of his friends in their astral village. They lived in a spacious country side where there was no violence or alcohol consumption. The women of the place were in a parallel dimension. The men stayed in one dimension and the women in a nearby realm.

There was no concept of sexual intercourse. There were no pregnancies. The youngest child was about seven years old. Some people had large farms where they grew paddy for rice consumption. There were no paved roads, nothing made of concrete. Everything was with mud or clay of a light brown color.

At one point the friend, and myself, were with about fifty people, in and around a sports field. The elderly men encouraged the teenaged ones to play a game. When this was over, we were transferred to a small place which was a beverage shop. They called this place, the cake shop. It was hosted by the only female in that dimension. She was a woman of about thirty years of age. She was attired in a dress that was down to her ankle.

About six of us sat at a table. My friend produced a book. It appeared in his hand when he wanted it to be there. He began to speak as he read from it.

This book was the *Srimad Bhagavatam*. He told some stories from that book. Another person in the group was knowledgeable about the stories. He made a few comments but these were transmitted mentally into the minds of everyone there. There was an attempt to speak in that place but no speech was made. Before there could be speech, the information was instantly transferred into the mind of someone, so that there was no need to repeat it by speech. The impulse to speak was felt and that was all.

This impulse is one of the reasons why people in that dimension may again become physical beings or may keep transmigrating as physical beings if they are currently using a physical body and also has an astral one.

After this my friend wanted me to be involved in getting a temple built. I told him that I knew someone who built temples previously, who would willingly do it for him. I tried to find that builder but he could not be located in that astral place.

In that zone, one cannot locate anyone who does not have a direct connection with someone who is permanently resident there. There was no possibility to reach that builder. After this I resumed physical existence here and wrote about this experience.

Quest for a Body

After being deceased from this side of existence, someone may find a compelling need to again be a physical being. This may happen even to persons who were determined not to become a body again. The determination to remain aloof from taking another body may be cancelled by the urge for physicality. If that happens, the desire to exist without physical hassles will be ineffective.

Once when I was simultaneously aware of the physical and the psychic sides of existence, a man who was deceased sometime now, appeared to my right. Simultaneously, a deceased lady whom I knew appeared to my left.

The man wanted to be near the woman but she resisted his advances. I realized that the lady came to do meditation practice at Yogeshwarananda's ashram. The man knew that she came there. He waited to greet her at the place. Seeing him and not wanting to communicate, the lady came to where my subtle body did breath infusion.

It was then that she appeared to my left. The man, who I knew as well, came to my right. Suddenly he changed and was a year-old infant. He moved himself to her body by her breasts. There was no maternal energy exuding from her bosom. He was near it but there was no energy there to encourage him to be her child.

Getting no maternal response from her subtle form, he fell away and appeared again as an adult male to my right. I continued doing breath infusion and gave some instruction to the lady. I then flashed a question to the man, asking him mentally why he harassed the woman, and pressed himself in an infant form near her breasts.

This is what he said.

"I could not help myself. I saw her at the astral ashram and was attracted. I wanted her to be my mother. When I assumed the baby form, that happened spontaneously. I did not plan it. It happened in a flash. I hope she forgave me."

After he said that, he faded from the place. I was there with the lady. We discussed some of the techniques for breath infusion in the subtle body. Then she wanted me to examine her breast. I did so by looking at them using astral perception. There was no maternal energy. She then said this.

"I have no interest to assist that man. There is no feeling for him to be my child. The breasts are present but they do not have the same urges as when I had a physical body."

Intentions Recorded – *Samskaras*

It has legendary reputation as being subliminal energy in the mind, which motivates someone to act, on the basis of events long past in the current or previous life. They are called *samskaras*, subtle impressions, with active powers.

Someone is tagged for the activities done in his/her existence through time. This is regardless of if there is coherent recall. The stored event-memory has with it the intention of the grasper, and the growth potential of the receptor. This includes the rejection potential of the event.

I will give an example.

Once some fifty-five years ago, I climbed a stairway and stood on a platform on the second story of a building. A young lady I knew was on the platform. I did not go there to see her. Instead, I went to meet a friend who was related to her.

There was cordial exchange in the form of greetings but that was all. But it was not so for the time energy which recorded a proposed development, where when I met this person in the psychic existence recently, on May 6, 2024, this person wanted to develop and consume the relationship.

There was no relationship so long ago, but then from another angle there was energy for a future relationship. What happened was that this person appeared in a desireable sexually-mature body. She arrived on the platform and then descended the stair, showing her developed form.

Her view of self was that she was attractive at this stage of body growth, as compared to when she was seen fifty-five years ago. Somehow, she tried to bring my opinion forward, from when it happened so long ago, to what she wanted in my appearance, which was sexually suited to her mature body, which she astrally produced.

This all happened because of samskara, or recorded intention of two people, with one being more forceful and impulsive than the other. What was I to do with her offer of a sexually mature form? Was I to cause my astral body to mutate into a matching sexually mature format with which she could enjoy and assume companionship?

Yogi Color Interest

Even for advanced yogis, the quest for color is something to contend with. I was in a conversation with a lady on the physical side, when I noticed that a vision-scan beam was being rotated in my right eye. I realized that one of my yoga teachers, who is deceased but who is currently on the astral side of existence, was present in my psyche, in the head of the subtle body. He beamed a vision ray to turn my right eye so that it would focus on the arm of the lady.

It searched for her arm. When it identified the color, it pulled that energy through the focusing ray. I inquired.

"How is it friend that you moved one eye to focus on skin color?"

He replied.

"There was this need to see that specific color. It was similar to when a person is thirsty and feels the need for water. Here it was a thirst for a color which comes from the reproductive energy, as distinguished from the sexual pleasure energy.

"It was not a pleasure need. It was the color of the energy to reproduce. That is a distinct energy. It cannot be controlled in every respect. Sometimes it arises. Then, one has to fulfill it. Otherwise, it recurs frequently and upsets the peace of mind."

Chit Akash Calling

A full break into *chit akash* sky of consciousness is for the most part, impossible. This is due to the present mental atmosphere, where one is surrounded and bombarded with psychic energy which prevents reach into full transcendence.

There would be reaches into the sky of consciousness, which are fragmented, and spur of the moment, but these happen involuntarily. When a yogi tries to control this, he fails at the attempt. It happens and then it instantly disappears. Any attempt to cause it to happen, or to make it stay in perception, results in the access being terminated, either gradually or abruptly.

I spoke to Yogeshwarananda. He said that the methods of penetration into *chit akash*, are not methods for doing so, but methods of putting the psyche in a condition in which, the psyche will penetrate into the *chit akash*, or the energy of the *chit akash* will itself penetrate the aura of the coreSelf. He said this.

"A yogi's task is to prepare the psyche for inviting *chit akash* to penetrate. By brute force one cannot penetrate it. Yes, there is history of yogis who forcibly by will power penetrated it, but that is exceptional. One should instead prepare the psyche for entry to the *chit akash*, or for penetration of the *chit akash* into one's psyche.

"There are two ways for this. The first and the one which a yogi has evidence of and confidence in, is that of his vision energy piercing through the cloud of dense subtle energy which surrounds the coreSelf. From within the psyche, the yogi feels a vision access opening to an open sky or to a silver-white energy sky. This feels like an outward going movement into a dot-star-point or an opaque cloud of energy, parting and giving access to another sky.

"The other method is when from within the psyche, there appears to be a tiny star in the distance, either straight up ahead, or to the right or left of center. This may be a slash of light. Or the yogi may see a cosmic torch light which hits or penetrates the psyche with blinding brilliance of a sun-like or moon-like effulgence. This has a bliss aspect to it.

"A yogi may experience none of this. He may experience some of this periodically during meditation or even when he does no practice. After achieving full mental and emotional *pratyahar* in meditation, he finds that his coreSelf energy does not course out of the psyche. It remains in the limits of the edge of the psyche and has no interest in going outwards. This practice becomes firm by doing it again and again, so that a time comes when the energy of the core loses interest in going outwards. It remains still like someone who is totally relaxed and has no impulse to move here or there.

"In that state of full *pratyahar*, the yogi should wait for naad resonance hearing. When he is absorbed in that, he should call for *chit akash* to penetrate his silent, non-moving psyche. There may be some doubt that this call will result in a shift to *chit akash*. The yogi should resist this doubt feature.

"*Chit akash* energy is outside the opaque psychic energy which blocks the *chit akash* contact. From within that opaque energy, the yogi should call *chit akash*. This call is merely a mental desire energy which invites *chit akash* to enter. Initially this open-ness of the yogi will result in penetration in minute amounts. Later this will increase."

Old Age for Yogis

Old age can be beneficial for yogis, if only, they could use it to better understand the profile of youth and adulthood. Old Age is when the youthfulness of the body is lost. Its looks of vibrancy and energy, no longer show. People dismiss it as being handicapped and unwanted in many respects.

This also means that the social pressure which is applied to the body during its youthful and young adult stages, is lifted where there are less demands made for social participation. For instance, even though the very same essential coreSelf resides in an elderly body, as it did when that body was in its youthful years, people do not expect that body to be as interested in sexual acts as it did previously.

This causes a relaxation of the pressure for sexual performance. People do not expect that an elderly body should have sex, beget children, take a strenuous employment, and do many other things.

The benefit of using an elderly body shows, because the self using that form, the same self which used it when it was young, is not expected to act vigorously as it did previously. That self can now observe others, and study the social equations. An elderly yogi can gage himself/herself to consider how during the young body, he/she rated circumstances and events in one way, which was accurate or inaccurate. Elderly folk can see how the psyche adjusted over time, from the youthful condition to that of the elderly one.

The social benefit of old age is its seniority, its rating of experience which a youth lacks. However, if the self misuses the seniority, it is insulted when its mistakes are discovered by others.

The best approach is to forego the seniority. One may use the elderly body as a peephole, to view things which one could not see in the youthful body. One can observe the behavior of younger bodies to learn how a body operates, and how influenced, someone is to the moods and faulty perceptions, which one had when the body was young. It is the observational benefit which one should use in the elderly form.

Some persons do not realize that the viewer who uses the elderly body is not elderly. That is a psychic somebody which is the same as when it used an adolescent form.

There is another advantage to having an elderly body. This is where persons using youthful and young adult forms, rate someone using an elderly body as being an old man or elderly lady. These persons do not realize that the psychic entity using the body has the same capability except that the physical body is unable to express that capability. As a capable driver cannot properly operate a malfunctioning car, so a psychic self cannot commit many functions which an elderly body cannot demonstrate.

On the psychic plane of life, the elderly person is not as handicapped as he/she is on the physical side. Both, the one using the youthful body, and the other one using the elderly one, have the same type of psychic form, and can interact psychically, with no limitation of one or the other physical forms. This should be observed by yogis/yoginis.

Bath for Yogis

In religious ceremonies, prior baths are considered to be mandatory events. The attendees, both the officials and congregation, are expected to bathe before going for the ceremony. This is rated as cleanliness which is a required behavior. A person feels clean and fresh after bathing. Besides that, the body accumulates detestable odors from sweat, urine, and stool. When these are removed, the body feels refreshed, mainly because of removal of the odors, dirt and grease which clog the pores.

Does this mean that a person's irreligious attitude is removed by bathing the body? The answer is that the irreligious attitude is a psychic aspect which is not removed by bath. One person may feel that it is removed, but that is due to a shift in the psyche, where the mind during bathing, moves away from its need to be criminal towards others.

Physical cleanliness, though it is a social convention, and an important one too, is not a psychic feat. Physical cleanliness has its time and place, but one should not be of the view that it results in spiritual shifts.

Bath for yogis concerns the subtle body. It concerns the energy in the subtle body, where that energy should be exchanged for fresh subtle air. This has a physical counterpart, concerning the removal of carbon dioxide and other negative gases which are the byproduct of cell activity in the physical system.

In the subtle body, used subtle air should be removed by doing *pranayama* breath infusion. This action results in a higher grade of energy being used, and more psychic perception for the person concerned.

This is internal bath which is even more important than bath of the physical system. A yogi in isolation has no need to take physical bath regularly. He does not have to be attired for ceremonies. He does not visit others. Hence his physical body does not have to be odorless. He does not have to attend it as tediously as others, who attend religious functions in the home or temple.

Instead, such a yogi should focus on internal cleanliness of the physical body, by removing its pollutions which are gases in the body, which accumulate in the blood stream. He must be keen with the subtle body to keep it surcharged with fresh subtle air, *prana*, so that it operates with the highest grade of that energy.

Index

About the Author

Michael Beloved (Yogi *Madhvāchārya)* took his current body in 1951 in Guyana. In 1965, while living in Trinidad, he instinctively began doing yoga postures and tried to make sense of the supernatural side of life.

Later in 1970, in the Philippines, he approached a Martial Arts Master named Arthur Beverford. He explained to the teacher that he was seeking a yoga instructor. Mr. Beverford identified himself as an advanced disciple of *Śrī* Rishi Singh Gherwal, an Ashtanga Yoga master.

Beverford taught the traditional Ashtanga Yoga with stress on postures, attentive breathing, and brow chakra centering meditation.   In 1972, Michael entered the Denver, Colorado Ashram of *kundalini* yoga Master *Śrī* Harbhajan Singh. There he took instruction in *bhastrika pranayama* and its application to yoga postures. He was supervised mostly by Yogi Bhajan's disciple named Prem Kaur.

In 1979 Michael formally entered the disciplic succession of the Brahmā -Madhava-Gaudiya Sampradaya through *Swāmī* Kirtanananda, who was a prominent sannyasi disciple of the Great Vaishnava Authority *Śrī Swāmī* Bhaktivedanta Prabhupada, the exponent of devotion to Sri Krishna.

However, yoga has a mystic side to it, thus Michael took training and teaching empowerment from several spiritual masters of different aspects of spiritual development. This is consistent with *Śrī* Krishna's advice to Arjuna in the *Bhagavad Gītā*:

Most of the instructions Michael received were given in the astral world. On that side of existence, his most prominent teachers were *Śrī Swāmī* Shivananda of Rishikesh, Yogiraj *Swāmī* Vishnudevananda, *Śrī Bābāji Mahasaya* - the master of the masters of *Kriyā* Yoga, *Śrīla* Yogeshwarananda of Gangotri - the master of the masters of *Rāj* Yoga (spiritual clarity), and Siddha *Swāmī* Nityananda the Brahmā Yoga authority.

The course for kundalini yoga using *pranayama* breath infusion was detailed by Michael in the book *Kundalini Hatha Yoga Pradipika*. This current book was composed from meditation and breath infusion notes which were originally shared in staple bound booklets as Yoga Journals.

Michael's preliminary books relating to this topic are Meditation Pictorial, Meditation Expertise, and Meditation ~ Sense Faculty (co-author). Every technique (kriya) mentioned was tested by him during pranayama breath infusion and samyama deep meditation practice.

This is a result of over forty years of meditation practice with astute subtle observations intending to share the methods and experiences. The information is published freely with no intention of forming an institution or hogtying anyone as a disciple.

Publications

English Series

Bhagavad Gita English
Anu Gita English
Markandeya Samasya English
Yoga Sutras English
Hatha Yoga Pradipika English
Uddhava Gita English

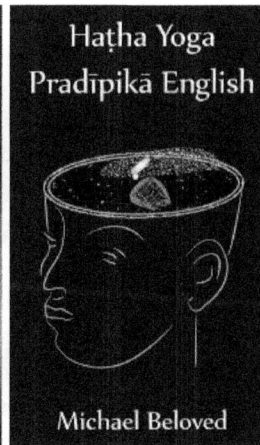

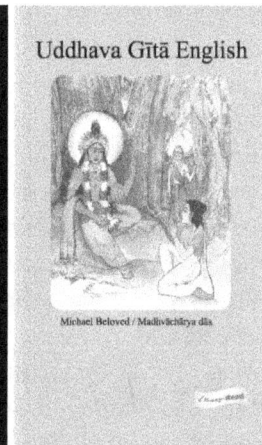

These are in 21st Century English, very precise and exacting. Many Sanskrit words which were considered untranslatable into a Western language, are rendered in precise, expressive, and modern English.

Three of these books are instructions from Krishna. **In Bhagavad Gita English** and **Anu Gita English**, the instructions were for Arjuna. In the **Uddhava Gita English,** it was for Uddhava. Bhagavad Gita and Anu Gita are extracted from the *Mahabharata*. Uddhava Gita was extracted from the 11th Canto of the Srimad Bhagavatam (Bhagavata Purana). One of these books, the **Markandeya Samasya English** is about Krishna, as described by Yogi Markandeya, who survived a cosmic collapse and reached a divine child in whose transcendental body, the collapsed world existed.

Two of this series are the syllabus about yoga practice. The *Yoga Sutras* of Patañjali is elaboration about ashtanga yoga. Hatha Yoga Pradipika English, is the detailed information about *asana* postures, *pranayama* breath-infusion, energy compression, naad sound resonance and advanced meditation. The Sanskrit author is Swatmarama Mahayogin.

My suggestion is that you read **Bhagavad Gita** English, the **Anu Gita English, the Markandeya Samasya English,** the *Yoga Sutras* **English**, the **Hatha Yoga Pradipika** and lastly the **Uddhava Gita English**, which is complicated and detailed.

For each of these books we have at least one commentary, which is published separately. Thus, one's particular interest can be researched further in the commentaries.

The smallest of these commentaries and perhaps the simplest is the one for the Anu Gita. We published its commentary as the Anu Gita Explained. The *Bhagavad Gita* explanations were published in three distinct targeted commentaries. The first is *Bhagavad Gita* Explained, which sheds lights on how people in the time of Krishna and Arjuna regarded the information and applied it. *Bhagavad Gita* is an exposition of the application of yoga practice to cultural activities, which is known in the Sanskrit language as karma yoga.

Interestingly, *Bhagavad Gita* was spoken on a battlefield just before one of the greatest battles in the ancient world. A warrior, Arjuna, lost his wits and had no idea that he could apply his training in yoga to political dealings. Krishna, his charioteer, lectured on the spur of the moment to give Arjuna the skill of using yoga proficiency in cultural dealings including how to deal with corrupt officials on a battlefield.

The second Bhagavad Gita commentary is the Kriya Yoga *Bhagavad Gita*. This clears the air about Krishna's information on the science of kriya yoga, showing that its techniques are clearly described for anyone who takes the time to read *Bhagavad Gita*. Kriya yoga concerns the battlefield which is the psyche of the living being. The internal war and the mental and emotional forces which are hostile to self-realization are dealt with in the kriya yoga practice.

The third commentary is the Brahma Yoga *Bhagavad Gita*. This shows what Krishna had to say outright and what he hinted about which concerns the brahma yoga practice, a mystic process for those who mastered kriya yoga.

There is one commentary for the **Markandeya Samasya English**. The title of that publication is Krishna Cosmic Body.

There are two commentaries to the *Yoga Sutras*. One is the *Yoga Sutras of Patañjali* and the other is the Meditation Expertise. These give detailed explanations of ashtanga Yoga.

The commentary of Hatha Yoga Pradipika is titled Kundalini Hatha Yoga Pradipika.

For the Uddhava Gita, we published the Uddhava Gita Explained. This is a large book and requires concentration and study for integration of the information. Of the books which deal with transcendental topics, my opinion is that the discourse between Krishna and Uddhava has the complete information about the realities in existence. This book is the one which removes massive existential ignorance.

Meditation Series

Meditation Pictorial
Meditation Expertise
CoreSelf Discovery
Meditation Sense Faculty

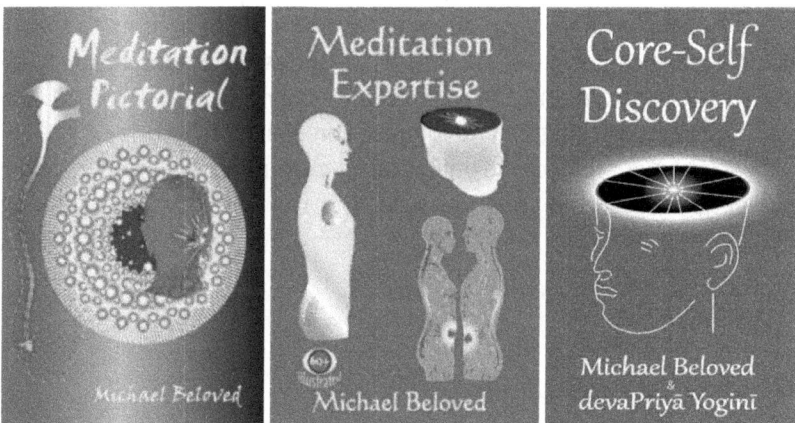

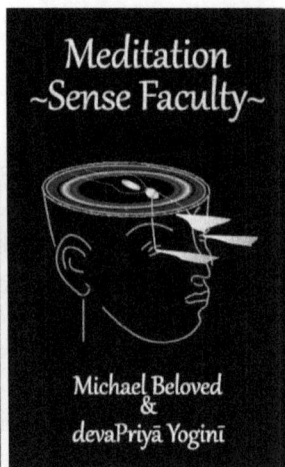

The specialty of these books is the mind diagrams which profusely illustrate what is written. This shows exactly what one has to do mentally to develop and then sustain a meditation practice.

In the **Meditation Pictorial**, one is shown how to develop psychic insight, a feature without which, meditation is imagination and visualization, without mystic experience in fact.

In the **Meditation Expertise**, one is shown how to corral one's practice to bring it in line with the classic syllabus of yoga which Patañjali lays out as the ashtanga yoga eight-staged process.

In **CoreSelf Discovery**, (co-authored with *devaPriya Yogini*) one is taken though the course of *pratyahar* sensual energy withdrawal which is the 5th stage of yoga in the Patañjali ashtanga eight-process complete system of yoga practice. These events lead to the discovery of a coreSelf which is surrounded by psychic organs in the head of the subtle body.

Meditation ~ Sense Faculty (co-authored with *devaPriya Yogini*) is a detailed tutorial with profuse diagrams showing what actions to take in the subtle body to investigate the senses faculties. The meditator must first establish the location and function of the observing self. That self must be screened from the thoughts and ideas which usually hypnotize it.

These books are profusely illustrated with mind diagrams showing the components of psychic consciousness and the inner design of the subtle body.

Explained Series

Bhagavad Gita Explained
Uddhava Gita Explained
Anu Gita Explained

The specialty of these books is that they are free of missionary intentions, cult tactics and philosophical distortion. Instead of using these books to add credence to a philosophy, meditation process, belief, or plea for followers, I spread the information out so that a reader can look through this literature and freely take or leave anything as desired.

When Krishna stressed himself as God, I stated that. When Krishna laid no claims for supremacy, I showed that. The reader is left to form an independent opinion about the validity of the information and the credibility of Krishna.

There is a difference in the discourse with Arjuna in the *Bhagavad Gita* and the one with Uddhava in the Uddhava Gita. In fact, these two books may appear to contradict each other. In the *Bhagavad Gita*, Krishna pressured Arjuna to complete social duties. In the Uddhava Gita, Krishna insisted that Uddhava should abandon the same.

The Anu Gita is not as popular as the *Bhagavad Gita* but it is the conclusion of that text. Anu means what is to follow, what proceeds. In this discourse, an anxious Arjuna request that Krishna should repeat the *Bhagavad Gita* and again show His supernatural and divine forms.

However, Krishna refused to do so and chastised Arjuna for being a disappointment in forgetting what was revealed. Krishna then cited a celestial yogi, a perfected being, who explained the process of transmigration in vivid detail.

Commentaries

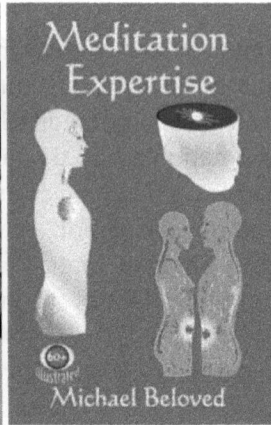

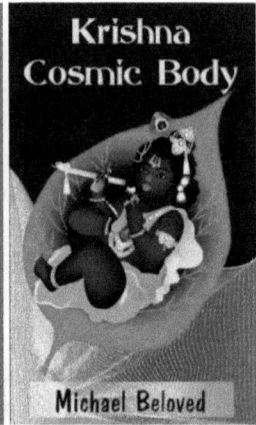

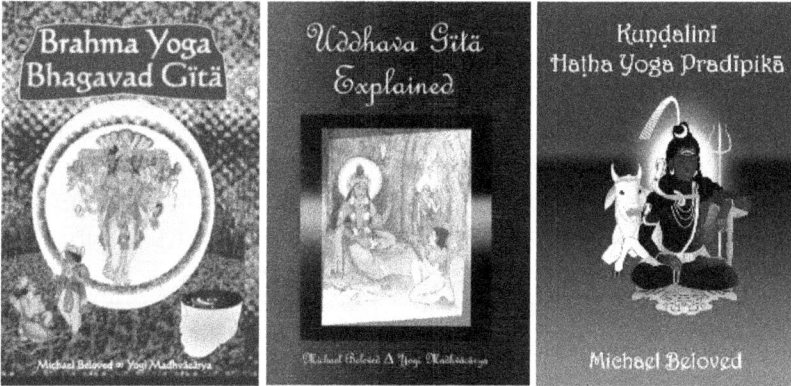

Yoga Sutras of Patañjali is the globally acclaimed text book of yoga. This has detailed expositions of yoga techniques. Many kriya techniques are vividly described in the commentary.

Meditation Expertise is an analysis and application of the *Yoga Sutras*. This book is loaded with illustrations and has detailed explanations of secretive advanced meditation techniques which are called kriyas in the Sanskrit language.

Krishna Cosmic Body is a narrative commentary on the Markandeya Samasya portion of the Aranyaka Parva of the *Mahabharata*. This is the detailed description of the dissolution of the world, as experienced by the great yogin Markandeya who transcended the cosmic deity, Brahma, and reached Brahma's source who is the divine infant, Krishna.

Anu Gita Explained is a detailed explanation of how we endure many material bodies in the course of transmigrating through various life-forms. This is a discourse between Krishna and Arjuna. Arjuna requested of Krishna a display of the Universal Form and a repeat narration of the *Bhagavad Gita* but Krishna declined and explained what a siddha perfected being told the Yadu family about the sequence of existences one endures and the systematic flow of those lives at the convenience of material nature.

Bhagavad Gita **Explained** shows what was said in the Gita without religious overtones and sectarian biases.

Kriya Yoga *Bhagavad Gita* shows the instructions for those who are doing kriya yoga.

Brahma Yoga *Bhagavad Gita* shows the instructions for those who are doing brahma yoga.

Uddhava Gita Explained shows the instructions to Uddhava which are more advanced than the ones given to Arjuna.

Bhagavad Gita is an instruction for applying the expertise of yoga in the cultural field. This is why the process taught to Arjuna is called karma yoga which means karma + yoga or cultural activities done with yogic insight.

Uddhava Gita is an instruction for apply the expertise of yoga to attaining spiritual status. This is why it explains jnana yoga and *bhakti* yoga in detail. Jnana yoga is using mystic skill for knowing the spiritual part of existence. *Bhakti* yoga is for developing affectionate relationships with divine beings.

Karma yoga is for negotiating the social concerns in the material world. It is inferior to *bhakti* yoga which concerns negotiating the social concerns in the spiritual world.

This world has a social environment. The spiritual world has one too.

Currently, Uddhava Gita is the most advanced and informative spiritual book on the planet. There is nothing anywhere which is superior to it or which goes into so much detail as it. It verified that historically Krishna is the most advanced human being to ever have left literary instructions on this planet. Even Patañjali *Yoga Sutras* which I translated and gave an application for in my book, **Meditation Expertise**, does not go as far as the Uddhava Gita.

Some of the information of these two books is identical but while the *Yoga Sutras* are concerned with the personal spiritual emancipation *(kaivalyam)* of the individual spirits, the Uddhava Gita explains that and also explains the situations in the spiritual universes.

Bhagavad Gita is from the *Mahabharata* which is the history of the Pandavas. Arjuna, the student of the Gita, is one of the Pandavas brothers. He was in a social hassle and did not know how to apply yoga expertise to solve it. On the battlefield, Krishna gave him a crash-course on yogic social interactions.

Uddhava Gita is from the *Srimad Bhagavatam (Bhagavata Purana),* which is a history of the incarnations of Krishna. Uddhava was a relative of Krishna. He was concerned about the situation of the deaths of many of his relatives but Krishna diverted Uddhava's attention to the practice of yoga for the purpose of successfully migrating to the spiritual environment.

Kundalini Hatha Yoga Pradipika is the commentary for the Hatha Yoga Pradipika of Swatmarama Mahayogin. This is the detailed process about *asana* posture, *pranayama* breath-infusion, complex compressions of energy, naad sound resonance intonement and advanced meditation practice.

This is the singular book with all the techniques of how to reform and redesign the subtle body, so that it does not have the tendency for physical life forms, and for it to attain the status of a siddha.

These books are based on the author's experiences in meditation, yoga practice and participation in spiritual groups:

Specialty

Spiritual Master
sex you!
Sleep Paralysis
Astral Projection
Masturbation Psychic Details
death You!
Experience You!

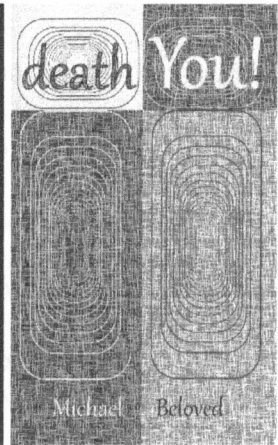

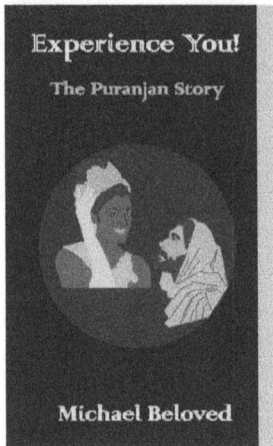

Experience You!

The Puranjan Story

Michael Beloved

In **Spiritual Master**, Michael draws from experience with gurus or with their senior students. His contact with astral gurus is rated. He walks you through the avenue of gurus, showing what you should do, and what you should not do, so as to gain proficiency in whatever area of spirituality the guru has proficiency.

sex you! is a masterpiece about the adventures of an individual spirit's passage through the parents' psyches. The conversion of a departed soul into a sexual urge is described. The transit from the afterlife to residency in the emotions of the parents is detailed. This is about sex and you. Learn about how much of you comprises the romantic energy of one's would-be parents!

Sleep Paralysis clears misconceptions so that one can see what sleep paralysis is and what frightening astral experience occurs while the paralysis is being experienced. This disempowerment has great value in giving you confidence that you can, and do, exist even if one is unable to operate the physical body. The implication is that one can exist apart from, and will survive the loss of the material form.

Astral Projection details experiences Michael had even in childhood, where he assumed incorrectly that everyone was astrally conversant. He discusses the lifeForce psychic mechanism which operates the sleep-wake cycle of the physical form, and which budgets energy into the separated astral form which determines if the individual will have dream recall or no objective awareness during the projections. Astral travel happens on every occasion when the physical body sleeps. What is missing in awareness is the observer status while the astral body is separated.

Masturbation Psychic Details is a surprise presentation which relates what happens on the psychic plane during a masturbation event. This does not tackle moral issues or even addictions but shows the involvement of memory and the sure but hidden subconscious mind which operates many features of the psyche irrespective of the desire or approval of the self-conscious personality.

death You! is about death transit which is the shift to the psychic world with no recourse of a physical presence. Generally human beings service a religion by consigning a dead body to a religious ceremony which promotes the idea of life hereafter in the heaven of a deity. However, the same survivors who sponsor the ceremony usually mourn the physical condition of the person's immobile body.

Experience You! is an allegoric tale from the Srimad Bhagavatam. It was narrated by Narad to King Barhi (Prachinabarhi). Its frames the life of every creature in the physical world, but it is specific for the human species. The tale opens with a wanderer named Puranjan, He was a city tenant but he had no residence. While touring the earth, he got to a place on the southern side of the Himalayan Mountains. There, luckily, he met a beautiful woman who was on the outskirts of her city. They were cordial. They agreed to live together as sweethearts for one hundred years.

inVision Series

Yoga inVision 1
Yoga inVision 2
Yoga inVision 3
Yoga inVision 4
Yoga inVision 5
Yoga inVision 6
Yoga inVision 7
Yoga inVision 8
Yoga inVision 9
Yoga inVision 10
Yoga inVision 11
Yoga inVision 12
Yoga inVision 13
Yoga inVision 14
Yoga inVision 15
Yoga inVision 16
Yoga inVision 17
Yoga inVision 18

Yoga inVision 19
Yoga inVision 20

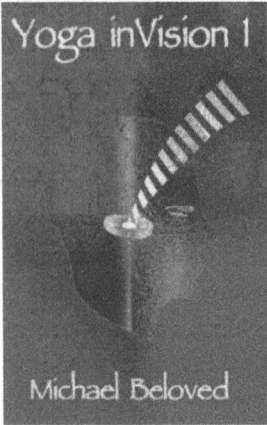
Yoga inVision 1 — Michael Beloved

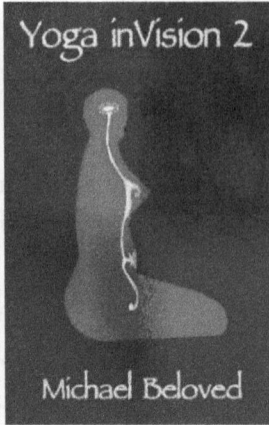
Yoga inVision 2 — Michael Beloved

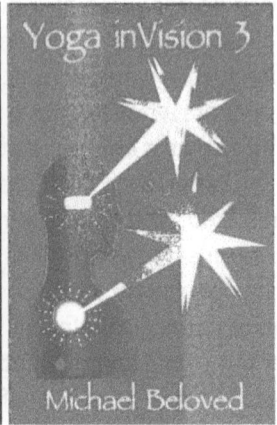
Yoga inVision 3 — Michael Beloved

Yoga inVision 4 — Michael Beloved

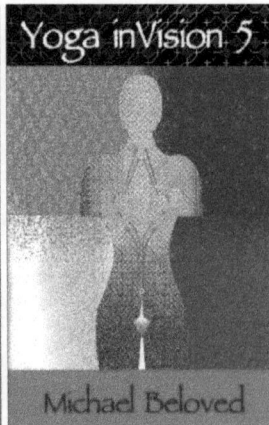
Yoga inVision 5 — Michael Beloved

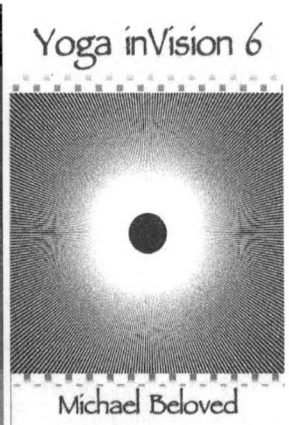
Yoga inVision 6 — Michael Beloved

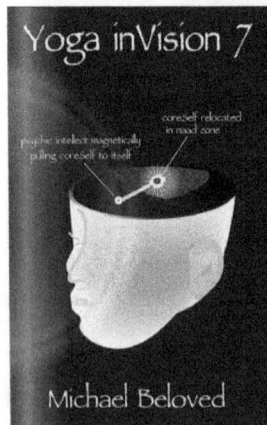
Yoga inVision 7 — Michael Beloved

Yoga inVision 8 — Michael Beloved

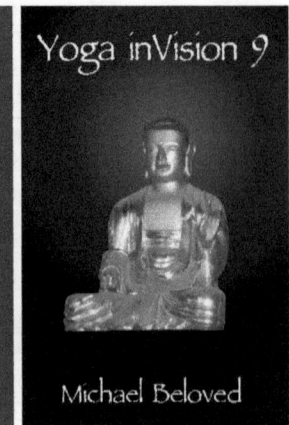
Yoga inVision 9 — Michael Beloved

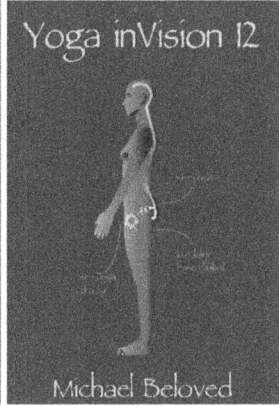

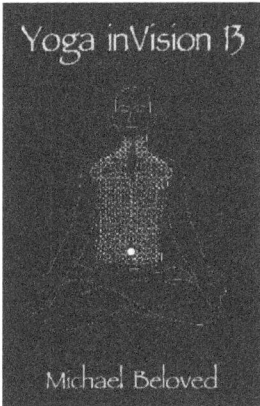

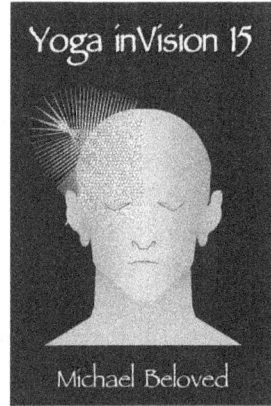

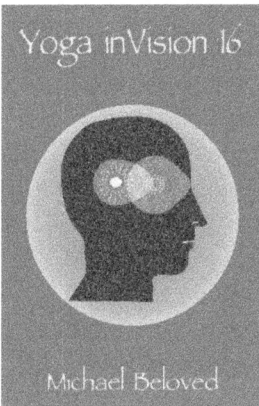

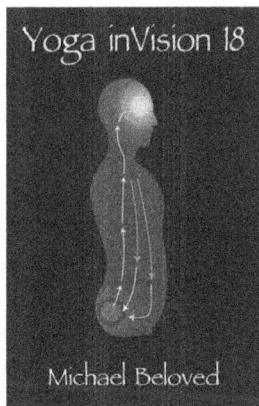

Yoga inVision 1, the first in this series, describes the breath infusion and meditation practices during the years of 1998 and 1999. There are unique, once in a lifetime as well as recurring insights which are elaborated. inFocus during breath infusion and the meditation which follows is an adventure for any yogi. This gives what happened to this particular ascetic.

Yoga inVision 2 reports on the author's experiences from 1999 to 2001. Each day the experience is unique, illustrating the vibrancy of practice. Many rare once-in-a-lifetime perceptions are described.

Yoga inVision 3 reports on the author's experiences from 2001 to 2003.

Yoga inVision 4 reports on the author's experiences from 2006 to 2009.

Yoga inVision 5 reports on the author's experiences from 2006 to 2008.

Yoga inVision 6 reports on the author's experiences in 2010.

Yoga inVision 7 reports on the author's experiences in 2011.

Yoga inVision 8 reports on the author's experiences in 2011.

Yoga inVision 9 reports on the author's experiences in 2012.

Yoga inVision 10 reports on the author's experiences in 2012.

Yoga inVision 11 reports on the author's experiences in 2012.

Yoga inVision 12 reports on the author's experiences in 2012-2013.

Yoga inVision 13 reports on the author's experiences in 2013-2014.

Yoga inVision 14 reports on the author's experiences in 2013-2014.

Yoga inVision 15 reports on the author's experiences in 2014.

Yoga inVision 16 reports on the author's experiences in 2014-2015.

Yoga inVision 17 reports on the author's experiences in 2016-2017.

Yoga inVision 18 reports on the author's experiences in 2017-2019.

Yoga inVision 19 reports on the author's experiences in 2019-2021.

Yoga inVision 20 reports on the author's experiences in 2021-2024.

Online Resources

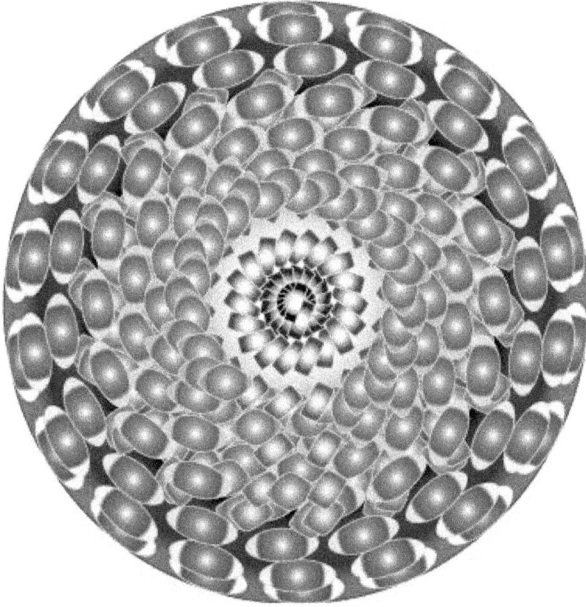

Email: michaelbelovedbooks@gmail.com
                axisnexus@gmail.com

Website: michaelbeloved.com

Forum: inselfyoga.com

Posters: zazzle.com/inself